ABOUT THIS PUBLICATION

FOR SERVICE ASSISTANCE

Customer Service Department
1.704.898.0770

North Carolina General Statues is published by The Muliti-Media Group of Greater Charlotte in Charlotte, North Carolina. Copyright 2015 by the Multi-Media Group of Greater Charlotte. This book or parts thereof may not be reproduced in any form, stored in a retrieval system, or transmitted in any form by any means—electronic, mechanical, photocopy, recording or otherwise—without prior written permission of the publisher, except as provided by United States of America copyright law.

The records required by U.S. Code 2257(a) through (c) and the pertinent regulations 28 C.F.R. Cli. 1, Part 75 with respect to this publication and all materials associated with such records are maintained by The Multi-Media Group of Greater Charlotte, Publisher and available for review by Attorney General.

www.visionbooks.org

Copyright © 2015 by MMGGC
All rights reserved!

TID: 4989448
ISBN (10) digit: 1502305798
ISBN (13) digit: 978-1502305794

123-4-56789-01239-Paperback
123-4-56789-01239-Hardback

First Edition

090520140547

Printed in the United States of America

2015 EDITION

North Carolina Criminal Law And Procedure-Pamphlet # 31

Printed In conjunction with the Administration of the Courts

North Carolina Criminal Law and Procedure
Pamphlet Reference Guide

4

6

9

10

11

13

14

North Carolina Nonprofit Corporation Act.

ARTICLE 1.

General Provisions.

Part 1. Short Title and Reservation of Power.

§ 55A-1-01. Short title.

This Chapter shall be known and may be cited as the "North Carolina Nonprofit Corporation Act". (1993, c. 398, s. 1.)

§ 55A-1-02. Reservation of power to amend or repeal.

The General Assembly has power to amend or repeal all or part of this Chapter at any time and all domestic and foreign corporations subject to this Chapter are governed by the amendment or repeal. (1993, c. 398, s. 1.)

§§ 55A-1-03 through 55A-1-19. Reserved for future codification purposes.

Part 2. Filing Documents.

§ 55A-1-20. Filing requirements.

(a)   A document required or permitted by this Chapter to be filed by the Secretary of State must be filed under Chapter 55D of the General Statutes.

(b)   A document submitted on behalf of a domestic or foreign corporation must be executed:

(1)   By the presiding officer of its board of directors, by its president, or by another of its officers;

(2)   If directors have not been selected or the corporation has not been formed, by an incorporator; or

(3)   If the corporation is in the hands of a receiver, trustee, or other court-appointed fiduciary, by that fiduciary. (1955, c. 1230; 1967, c. 13, s. 2; c. 823, s. 21; 1985 (Reg. Sess., 1986), c. 801, s. 2; 1993, c. 398, s. 1; 1999-369, s. 2.1; 2001-358, s. 7(a); 2001-387, ss. 32, 155, 173, 175(a); 2001-413, s. 6.)

§ 55A-1-21. Forms.

(a)   The Secretary of State may promulgate and furnish on request forms for:

(1)   An application for a certificate of existence;

(2)   A foreign corporation's application for a certificate of authority to conduct affairs in this State;

(3)   A foreign corporation's application for a certificate of withdrawal;

(4)   Designation of Principal Office Address; and

(5)   Corporation's Statement of Change of Principal Office.

If the Secretary of State so requires, use of these forms is mandatory.

(b)   The Secretary of State may promulgate and furnish on request forms for other documents required or permitted to be filed by this Chapter but their use is not mandatory. (1955, c. 1230; 1993, c. 398, s. 1; 1995, c. 539, s. 9.)

§ 55A-1-22. Filing, service, and copying fees.

(a)   The Secretary of State shall collect the following fees when the documents described in this subsection are delivered to the Secretary for filing:

Document	Fee

(1)   Articles of incorporation
$60.00

(2)   Application for reserved name
$10.00

(3)   Notice of transfer of reserved name
$10.00

(4)   Application for registered name
$10.00

(5)   Application for renewal of registered name
$10.00

(6)   Corporation's statement of change of registered agent or registered office or both
$ 5.00

(7)   Agent's statement of change of registered office for each affected corporation $
5.00

(8)   Agent's statement of resignation
No fee

(9)   Designation of registered agent or registered office or both
$ 5.00

(10)   Amendment of articles of incorporation
$25.00

(11)   Restated articles of incorporation without amendment of articles
$10.00

(12)　Restated articles of incorporation with amendment of articles
$25.00

(13)　Articles of merger
$25.00

(14)　Articles of dissolution
$15.00

(15)　Articles of revocation of dissolution
$10.00

(16)　Certificate of administrative dissolution
No fee

(17)　Application for reinstatement following administrative dissolution
$100.00

(18)　Certificate of reinstatement
No fee

(19)　Certificate of judicial dissolution
No fee

(20)　Application for certificate of authority
$125.00

(21)　Application for amended certificate of authority
$25.00

(22)　Application for certificate of withdrawal
$10.00

(23)　Certificate of revocation of authority to conduct affairs
No fee

(24)　Corporation's Statement of Change of Principal Office　　　　$
5.00

(24a)　Designation of Principal Office Address
$　5.00

(25)   Articles of correction
$10.00

(26)   Application for certificate of existence or authorization (paper)
$15.00

(26a)   Application for certificate of existence or authorization (electronic)
$10.00

(27)   Any other document required or permitted to be filed by this Chapter
$10.00

(28)   Repealed by Session Laws 2001-358, s. 7(c), effective January 1, 2002.

(b)   The Secretary of State shall collect a fee of ten dollars ($10.00) each time process is served on the Secretary under this Chapter. The party to a proceeding causing service of process is entitled to recover this fee as costs if the party prevails in the proceeding.

(c)   The Secretary of State shall collect the following fees for copying, comparing, and certifying a copy of any filed document relating to a domestic or foreign corporation:

(1)   One dollar ($1.00) a page for copying or comparing a copy to the original.

(2)   Fifteen dollars ($15.00) for a paper certificate.

(3)   Ten dollars ($10.00) for an electronic certificate.

(1957, c. 1179; 1967, c. 823, s. 24; 1969, c. 875, s. 10; 1975, 2nd Sess., c. 981, s. 2; 1983, c. 713, ss. 39-42; 1991, c. 574, s. 2; 1993, c. 398, s. 1; 1995, c. 539, s. 10; 1997-456, s. 55.3; 1997-475, s. 5.2; 1997-485, s. 11; 2001-358, s. 7(c); 2001-387, ss. 173, 175(a); 2001-413, s. 6; 2002-126, ss. 29A.27, 29A.28.)

§§ 55A-1-22.1 through 55A-1-27: Repealed by Session Laws 2001-358, s. 7(b), effective January 1, 2002.

§ 55A-1-28. Certificate of existence.

(a)   Anyone may apply to the Secretary of State to furnish a certificate of existence for a domestic corporation or a certificate of authorization for a foreign corporation.

(b)   A certificate of existence or authorization sets forth:

(1)   The domestic corporation's corporate name or the foreign corporation's name used in this State;

(2)   That the domestic corporation is duly incorporated under the law of this State, the date of its incorporation, and the period of its duration if less than perpetual; or that the foreign corporation is authorized to conduct affairs in this State;

(3)   That the articles of incorporation of a domestic corporation or the certificate of authority of a foreign corporation has not been suspended for failure to comply with the Revenue Act of this State and that the corporation has not been administratively dissolved for failure to comply with the provisions of this Chapter;

(4)   Repealed by Session Laws c. 539, s. 14.

(5)   That articles of dissolution have not been filed; and

(6)   Other facts of record in the office of the Secretary of State that may be requested by the applicant.

(c)   Subject to any qualification stated in the certificate, a certificate of existence or authorization issued by the Secretary of State may be relied upon as conclusive evidence that the domestic or foreign corporation is in existence or is authorized to conduct affairs in this State. (1955, c. 1230; 1993, c. 398, s. 1; 1995, c. 539, s. 14.)

§ 55A-1-29: Repealed by Session Laws 2001-358, s. 7(b).

Part 3. Secretary of State.

§ 55A-1-30. Powers.

The Secretary of State has the power reasonably necessary to perform the duties required of the Secretary of State by this Chapter. (1955, c. 1230; 1993, c. 398, s. 1.)

§ 55A-1-31. Interrogatories by Secretary of State.

The Secretary of State may propound to any domestic or foreign corporation which the Secretary of State has reason to believe is subject to the provisions of this Chapter, and to any officer or director thereof, any written interrogatories as may be reasonably necessary and proper to enable the Secretary of State to ascertain whether the corporation is subject to the provisions of this Chapter or has complied with all the provisions of this Chapter applicable to it. The interrogatories shall be answered within 30 days after the mailing thereof, or within such additional time as shall be fixed by the Secretary of State, and the answers thereto shall be full and complete and shall be made in writing and under oath. If the interrogatories are directed to an individual, they shall be answered by the individual, and if directed to a corporation, they shall be answered by the presiding officer of the board of directors, the president, or by another officer of the corporation. The Secretary of State shall certify to the Attorney General, for such action as the Attorney General may deem appropriate, all interrogatories and answers thereto which disclose a violation of any of the provisions of this Chapter, requiring or permitting action by the Attorney General. (1955, c. 1230; 1993, c. 398, s. 1.)

§ 55A-1-32. Penalties imposed upon corporations, officers, and directors for failure to answer interrogatories.

(a)　　The knowing failure or refusal of a domestic or foreign corporation to answer truthfully and fully, within the time prescribed in this Chapter, interrogatories propounded by the Secretary of State in accordance with the provisions of this Chapter shall constitute grounds for administrative dissolution under G.S. 55A-14-20 or for revocation under G.S. 55A-15-30, as the case may be.

(b)　　Each officer and director of a domestic or foreign corporation who knowingly fails or refuses, within the time prescribed by this Chapter, to answer truthfully and fully interrogatories propounded to him by the Secretary of State in accordance with the provisions of this Chapter shall be guilty of a Class 1 misdemeanor. (1955, c. 1230; 1993, c. 398, s. 1; 1994, Ex. Sess., c. 14, s. 37.)

§ 55A-1-33. Information disclosed by interrogatories.

Interrogatories propounded by the Secretary of State and the answers thereto shall not be open to public inspection nor shall the Secretary of State disclose any facts or information obtained therefrom except when the Secretary of State's official duty requires disclosure to be made public or when the interrogatories or the answers thereto are required for evidence in any criminal proceeding or in any other action or proceeding by this State. (1993, c. 398, s. 1.)

§§ 55A-1-34 through 55A-1-39. Reserved for future codification purposes.

Part 4. Definitions.

§ 55A-1-40. Chapter definitions.

In this Chapter unless otherwise specifically provided:

(1)　　"Articles of incorporation" include amended and restated articles of incorporation and articles of merger.

(2)   "Board" or "board of directors" means the group of natural persons vested by the corporation with the management of its affairs whether or not the group is designated as directors in the articles of incorporation or bylaws.

(2a)   "Business corporation" or "domestic business corporation" means a corporation as defined in G.S. 55-1-40.

(3)   "Bylaws" means the rules (other than the articles) adopted pursuant to this Chapter for the regulation or management of the affairs of the corporation irrespective of the name or names by which the rules are designated.

(4)   "Charitable or religious corporation" means any corporation that is exempt under section 501(c)(3) of the Internal Revenue Code of 1986 or any successor section, or that is organized exclusively for one or more of the purposes specified in section 501(c)(3) of the Internal Revenue Code of 1986 or any successor section and that upon dissolution shall distribute its assets to a charitable or religious corporation, the United States, a state or an entity that is exempt under section 501(c)(3) of the Internal Revenue Code of 1986 or any successor section.

(4a)   "Conspicuous" means so written that a reasonable person against whom the writing is to operate should have noticed it. For example, printing in italics or boldface or contrasting color, or typing in capitals or underlined, is conspicuous.

(5)   "Corporation" or "domestic corporation" means a nonprofit corporation subject to the provisions of this Chapter, except a foreign corporation.

(6)   "Delegates" means those persons elected or appointed to vote in a representative assembly for the election of a director or directors or on other matters.

(7)   "Deliver" includes mail.

(8)   "Distribution" means a direct or indirect transfer of money or other property or incurrence of indebtedness by a corporation to or for the benefit of its members, directors, or officers, or to or for the benefit of transferees in liquidation under Article 14 of this Chapter (other than creditors).

(8a)   "Domestic limited liability company" has the same meaning as the term "LLC" in G.S. 57D-1-03.

(8b) "Domestic limited partnership" has the same meaning as in G.S. 59-102.

(9) "Effective date of notice" is defined in G.S. 55A-1-41.

(9a) "Electronic" has the same meaning as in G.S. 66-312.

(9b) "Electronic record" has the same meaning as in G.S. 66-312.

(9c) "Electronic signature" has the same meaning as in G.S. 66-312.

(10) "Entity" includes:

a. Any domestic or foreign:

1. Corporation; business corporation; professional corporation;

2. Limited liability company;

3. Profit and nonprofit unincorporated association, chapter or other organizational unit; and

4. Business trust, estate, partnership, trust;

b. Two or more persons having a joint or common economic interest; and

c. The United States, and any state and foreign government.

(10a) "Foreign business corporation" means a foreign corporation as defined in G.S. 55-1-40.

(11) "Foreign corporation" means a corporation (with or without capital stock) organized under a law other than the law of this State for purposes for which a corporation might be organized under this Chapter.

(11a) "Foreign limited liability company" has the same meaning as the term "foreign LLC" in G.S. 57D-1-03.

(11b) "Foreign limited partnership" has the same meaning as in G.S. 59-102.

(12)   "Governmental subdivision" includes authority, county, district, and municipality.

(13)   "Includes" denotes a partial definition.

(14)   "Individual" denotes a natural person legally competent to act and also includes the estate of an incompetent or deceased individual.

(15)   "Means" denotes an exhaustive definition.

(16)   "Member" means a person who is, by the articles of incorporation or bylaws of the corporation, either (i) specifically designated as a member or (ii) included in a category of persons specifically designated as members. A person is not a member solely by reason of having voting rights or other rights associated with membership.

(17)   "Nonprofit corporation" means a corporation intended to have no income or intended to have income none of which is distributable to its members, directors, or officers, except as permitted by Article 13 of this Chapter, and includes all associations without capital stock formed under Subchapter V of Chapter 54 of the General Statutes or under any act or acts replaced thereby.

(18)   "Notice" includes demand and is defined in G.S. 55A-1-41.

(19)   "Person" includes individual and entity.

(20)   "Principal office" means the office (in or out of this State) where the principal offices of a domestic or foreign corporation are located, as most recently designated by the domestic or foreign corporation in its articles of incorporation, a Designation of Principal Office Address form, a Corporation's Statement of Change of Principal Office Address form, or in the case of a foreign corporation, its application for a certificate of authority.

(21)   "Proceeding" includes civil suit and criminal, administrative, and investigatory action.

(22)   "Record date" means the date established under Article 7 of this Chapter on which a corporation determines the identity of its members for the purposes of this Chapter.

(23)   "Secretary" means the corporate officer to whom the board of directors has delegated responsibility under G.S. 55A-8-40(c) for custody of the minutes of the meetings of the board of directors and of the members and for authenticating records of the corporation.

(24)   "State," when referring to a part of the United States, includes a state and commonwealth (and their agencies and governmental subdivisions) and a territory, and insular possession (and their agencies and governmental subdivisions) of the United States.

(24a)   "Unincorporated entity" means a domestic or foreign limited liability company, a domestic or foreign limited partnership, a registered limited liability partnership or foreign limited liability partnership as defined in G.S. 59-32, or any other partnership as defined in G.S. 59-36, whether or not formed under the laws of this State.

(25)   "United States" includes district, authority, bureau, commission, department, and any other agency of the United States.

(26)   "Vote" includes authorization by written ballot and written consent, including electronic ballot and electronic consent. (1955, c. 1230; 1959, c. 1161, s. 4; 1985 (Reg. Sess., 1986), c. 801, s. 1; 1993, c. 398, s. 1; 1995, c. 539, s. 15; 1999-369, s. 2.2; 2001-358, s. 5(b); 2001-387, ss. 33, 34, 35, 173, 175(a); 2001-413, s. 6; 2001-487, s. 62(e); 2008-37, s. 1; 2013-157, s. 4.)

§ 55A-1-41. Notice.

(a)   Notice under this Chapter shall be in writing unless oral notice is authorized in the corporation's articles of incorporation or bylaws and written notice is not specifically required by this Chapter.

(b)   Notice may be communicated in person; by electronic means; or by mail or private carrier. If these forms of personal notice are impracticable as to one or more persons, notice may be communicated to such persons by publishing notice in a newspaper, or by radio, television, or other form of public broadcast communication, in the county where the corporation has its principal place of business in the State, or if it has no principal place of business in the State, the county where it has its registered office.

26

(c)   Written notice by a domestic or foreign corporation to its member is effective when deposited in the United States mail with postage thereon prepaid and correctly addressed to the member's address shown in the corporation's current record of members. To the extent the corporation pursuant to G.S. 55A-1-70 and the member have agreed, notice by a domestic corporation to its member in the form of an electronic record sent by electronic means is effective when it is sent as provided in G.S. 66-325. A member may terminate any such agreement at any time on a prospective basis effective upon written notice of termination to the corporation or upon such later date as may be specified in the notice.

(d)   Written notice to a domestic or foreign corporation (authorized to conduct affairs in this State) may be addressed to its registered agent at its registered office or to the corporation or its secretary at its principal office shown in its articles of incorporation, the Designation of Principal Office Address form, or any Corporation's Statement of Change of Principal Office Address form filed with the Secretary of State.

(e)   Except as provided in subsection (c) of this section, written notice is effective at the earliest of the following:

(1)   When received;

(2)   Five days after its deposit in the United States mail, as evidenced by the postmark or otherwise, if mailed with at least first-class postage thereon prepaid and correctly addressed;

(3)   On the date shown on the return receipt, if sent by registered or certified mail, return receipt requested, and the receipt is signed by or on behalf of the addressee;

(4)   If mailed with less than first-class postage, 30 days after its deposit in the United States mail, as evidenced by the postmark or otherwise, if mailed with postage thereon prepaid and correctly addressed;

(5)   When delivered to the member's address shown in the corporation's current list of members.

In the case of notice in the form of an electronic record sent by electronic means, the time of receipt shall be determined as provided in G.S. 66-325.

(f)   Written notice is correctly addressed to a member of a domestic or foreign corporation if addressed to the member's address shown in the corporation's current list of members. In the case of members who are residents of the same household and who have the same address, the corporation's bylaws may provide that a single notice may be given to such members jointly.

(g)   Oral notice is effective when actually communicated to the person entitled to oral notice.

(h)   If this Chapter prescribes notice requirements for particular circumstances, those requirements govern. If articles of incorporation or bylaws prescribe notice requirements not inconsistent with this section or other provisions of this Chapter, those requirements govern.

(i)   Written notice need not be provided in a separate document and may be included as part of a newsletter, magazine, or other publication regularly sent to members if conspicuously identified as a notice. (1993, c. 398, s. 1; 1995, c. 539, s. 16; 2008-37, s. 2.)

§§ 55A-1-42 through 55A-1-49. Reserved for future codification purposes.

Part 5. Private Foundations.

§ 55A-1-50. Private Foundations.

Except where otherwise determined by a court of competent jurisdiction, a corporation that is a private foundation as defined in section 509(a) of the Internal Revenue Code of 1986:

(1)   Shall distribute such amounts for each taxable year at such time and in such manner as not to subject the corporation to tax under section 4942 of the Code.

(2)   Shall not engage in any act of self-dealing as defined in section 4941(d) of the Code.

(3)   Shall not retain any excess business holdings as defined in section 4943(c) of the Code.

(4)   Shall not make any investments in such manner as to subject the corporation to tax under section 4944 of the Code.

(5)   Shall not make any taxable expenditures as defined in section 4945(d) of the Code.

All references in this section to sections of the Code shall be to sections of the Internal Revenue Code of 1986 as amended from time to time, or to corresponding provisions of subsequent internal revenue laws of the United States. (1955, c. 1230; 1957, c. 783, s. 7; 1969, c. 875, s. 4; 1971, c. 1136, s. 1; 1977, c. 236, s. 1, c. 663; 1979, c. 1027; 1985, c. 505; 1985 (Reg. Sess., 1986), c. 801, ss. 8-14; 1993, c. 398, s. 1.)

§§ 55A-1-51 through 55A-1-59. Reserved for future codification purposes.

Part 6. Judicial Relief.

§ 55A-1-60. Judicial relief.

(a)   If for any reason it is impracticable for any corporation to call or conduct a meeting of its members, delegates, or directors, or otherwise obtain their consent, in the manner prescribed by its articles of incorporation, bylaws, or this Chapter, then upon petition of a director, officer, delegate, member, or the Attorney General, the superior court may order that such a meeting be held or that a written ballot or other method be used for obtaining the vote of members, delegates, or directors, in such a manner as the court finds fair and equitable under the circumstances.

(b)   The court shall, in an order issued pursuant to this section, provide for a method of notice reasonably designed to give actual notice to all such persons who would be entitled to notice of a meeting held pursuant to the articles of incorporation, bylaws, and this Chapter, and notice given in this manner shall be effective whether or not it results in actual notice to all such persons or conforms to the notice requirements that would otherwise apply. Notice shall be given in this manner to all persons determined by the court to be members or directors.

(c)   The order issued pursuant to this section may, to the extent the court finds it reasonably required under the circumstances, dispense with any requirement relating to the holding of or voting at meetings or obtaining votes, including any requirement as to quorums or as to the number or percentage of votes needed for approval, that would otherwise be imposed by the articles of incorporation, bylaws, or this Chapter.

(d)   Whenever practical any order issued pursuant to this section shall limit the subject matter of meetings or other forms of consent authorized to items, including amendments to the articles of incorporation or bylaws, the resolution of which will or may enable the corporation to continue managing its affairs without further resort to this section; provided, however, that an order under this section may also authorize the obtaining of whatever votes and approvals are necessary for the dissolution, merger, or sale of assets.

(e)   Any meeting or other method of obtaining the vote of members, delegates, or directors conducted pursuant to an order issued under this section, and that complies with all the provisions of the order, is for all purposes a valid meeting or vote, as the case may be, and shall have the same force and effect as if it complied with every requirement imposed by the articles of incorporation, bylaws, and this Chapter. (1993, c. 398, s. 1.)

Part 7. Miscellaneous.

§ 55A-1-70. Electronic transactions.

For purposes of applying Article 40 of Chapter 66 of the General Statutes to transactions under this Chapter, a corporation may agree to conduct a transaction by electronic means through provision in its articles of incorporation or bylaws or by action of its board of directors. (2008-37, s. 3.)

Article 2.

Organization.

§ 55A-2-01. Incorporators.

One or more persons may act as the incorporator or incorporators of a corporation by delivering articles of incorporation to the Secretary of State for filing. (1955, c. 1230; 1969, c. 875, s. 1; 1971, c. 1231, s. 1; 1993, c. 398, s. 1.)

§ 55A-2-02. Articles of incorporation.

(a)   The articles of incorporation shall set forth:

(1)   A corporate name for the corporation that satisfies the requirements of G.S. 55D-20 and G.S. 55D-21;

(2)   If the corporation is a charitable or religious corporation, a statement to that effect if it was incorporated on or after the effective date of this Chapter;

(3)   The street address, and the mailing address if different from the street address, of the corporation's initial registered office, the county in which the initial registered office is located, and the name of the corporation's initial registered agent at that address;

(4)   The name and address of each incorporator;

(5)   Whether or not the corporation will have members;

(6)   Provisions not inconsistent with law regarding the distribution of assets on dissolution; and

(7)   The street address, and the mailing address, if different from the street address, of the principal office, and the county in which the principal office is located.

(b)   The articles of incorporation may set forth any provision that under this Chapter is required or permitted to be set forth in the bylaws, and may also set forth:

31

(1)   The purpose or purposes for which the corporation is organized, which may be, either alone or in combination with other purposes, the transaction of any lawful activity;

(2)   The names and addresses of the individuals who are to serve as the initial directors;

(3)   Provisions not inconsistent with law regarding:

a.   Managing and regulating the affairs of the corporation;

b.   Defining, limiting, and regulating the powers of the corporation, its board of directors, and members (or any class of members); and

c.   The characteristics, qualifications, rights, limitations, and obligations attaching to each or any class of members;

(4)   A provision limiting or eliminating the personal liability of any director for monetary damages arising out of an action whether by or in the right of the corporation or otherwise for breach of any duty as a director. No such provision shall be effective with respect to (i) acts or omissions that the director at the time of the breach knew or believed were clearly in conflict with the best interests of the corporation, (ii) any liability under G.S. 55A-8-32 or G.S. 55A-8-33, (iii) any transaction from which the director derived an improper personal financial benefit, or (iv) acts or omissions occurring prior to the date the provision became effective. As used herein, the term "improper personal financial benefit" does not include a director's reasonable compensation or other reasonable incidental benefit for or on account of his service as a director, trustee, officer, employee, independent contractor, attorney, or consultant of the corporation. A provision permitted by this Chapter in the articles of incorporation, bylaws, or a contract or resolution indemnifying or agreeing to indemnify a director against personal liability shall be fully effective whether or not there is a provision in the articles of incorporation limiting or eliminating personal liability.

(c)   The articles of incorporation need not set forth any of the corporate powers enumerated in this Chapter. (1955, c. 1230; 1957, c. 979, s. 11; 1959, c. 1161, s. 5; 1985 (Reg. Sess., 1986), c. 801, ss. 3, 4; 1993, c. 398, s. 1; 1995, c. 539, s. 17; 2001-358, s. 20; 2001-387, ss. 173, 175(a); 2001-413, s. 6.)

§ 55A-2-03. Incorporation.

(a)   Unless a delayed effective date is specified, the corporate existence begins when the articles of incorporation are filed.

(b)   The Secretary of State's filing of the articles of incorporation is conclusive proof that the incorporators satisfied all conditions precedent to incorporation except in a proceeding by the State to cancel or revoke the incorporation or involuntarily dissolve the corporation. (1955, c. 1230; 1967, c. 13, s. 4; 1993, c. 398, s. 1.)

§ 55A-2-04. Reserved for future codification purposes.

§ 55A-2-05. Organization of corporation.

(a)   After incorporation:

(1)   If initial directors are named in the articles of incorporation, the initial directors shall hold an organizational meeting at the call of a majority of the directors to complete the organization of the corporation by appointing officers, adopting bylaws, and conducting any other business brought before the meeting.

(2)   If initial directors are not named in the articles of incorporation, the incorporator or incorporators shall hold an organizational meeting at the call of a majority of the incorporators (i) to elect directors and complete the organization of the corporation, or (ii) to elect a board of directors who shall complete the organization of the corporation.

(b)   Action required or permitted by this Chapter to be taken by incorporators at an organizational meeting may be taken without a meeting if the action taken is evidenced by one or more written consents describing the action taken and signed by each incorporator. If the incorporators act at a meeting, the notice and procedural provisions of G.S. 55A-8-22, 55A-8-23, and 55A-8-24 shall apply.

33

(c)   An organizational meeting may be held in or out of this State. (1955, c. 1230; 1969, c. 875, s. 2; 1985 (Reg. Sess., 1986), c. 801, s. 6; 1993, c. 398, s. 1.)

§ 55A-2-06. Bylaws.

(a)   The incorporators or board of directors of a corporation shall adopt initial bylaws for the corporation.

(b)   The bylaws may contain any provision for regulating and managing the affairs of the corporation that is not inconsistent with law or the articles of incorporation. (1955, c. 1230; 1993, c. 398, s. 1.)

§ 55A-2-07. Emergency bylaws.

(a)   Unless the articles of incorporation provide otherwise, the board of directors of a corporation may adopt, amend, or repeal bylaws to be effective only in an emergency defined in subsection (d) of this section. The emergency bylaws, which are subject to amendment or repeal by the members, may make all provisions necessary for managing the corporation during the emergency, including:

(1)   Procedures for calling a meeting of the board of directors;

(2)   Quorum requirements for the meeting; and

(3)   Designation of additional or substitute directors.

(b)   All provisions of the regular bylaws consistent with the emergency bylaws remain effective during the emergency. The emergency bylaws are not effective after the emergency ends.

(c)   Corporate action taken in good faith in accordance with the emergency bylaws binds the corporation, and the fact that the action was taken pursuant to emergency bylaws shall not be used to impose liability on a corporate director, officer, employee, or agent.

(d)   An emergency exists for purposes of this section if a quorum of the corporation's directors cannot readily be assembled because of some catastrophic event. (1993, c. 398, s. 1.)

Article 3.

Purposes and Powers.

§ 55A-3-01. Purposes.

(a)   Every corporation incorporated under this Chapter has the purpose of engaging in any lawful activity unless a more limited purpose is set forth in its articles of incorporation.

(b)   A corporation engaging in an activity that is subject to regulation under another statute of this State may incorporate under this Chapter only if permitted by, and subject to all limitations of, the other statute. (1955, c. 1230; 1993, c. 398, s. 1.)

§ 55A-3-02. General powers.

(a)   Unless its articles of incorporation or this Chapter provides otherwise, every corporation has perpetual duration and succession in its corporate name and has the same powers as an individual to do all things necessary or convenient to carry out its affairs, including without limitation, power:

(1)   To sue and be sued, complain and defend in its corporate name;

(2)   To have a corporate seal, which may be altered at will, and to use it, or a facsimile of it, by impressing or affixing it or in any other manner reproducing it;

(3)   To make and amend bylaws not inconsistent with its articles of incorporation or with the laws of this State, for regulating and managing the affairs of the corporation;

(4)   To purchase, receive, lease, or otherwise acquire, and own, hold, improve, use, and otherwise deal with, real or personal property, or any legal or equitable interest in property, wherever located;

(5)   To sell, convey, mortgage, pledge, lease, exchange, and otherwise dispose of all or any part of its property;

(6)   To purchase, receive, subscribe for, or otherwise acquire; own, hold, vote, use, sell, mortgage, lend, pledge, or otherwise dispose of; and deal in and with shares or other interests in, or obligations of, any other entity;

(7)   To make contracts and guarantees, incur liabilities, borrow money, issue its notes, bonds, and other obligations, and secure any of its obligations by mortgage or pledge of any of its property, franchises, or income;

(8)   To lend money, invest and reinvest its funds, and receive and hold real and personal property as security for repayment, except as limited by G.S. 55A-8-32;

(9)   To be a promoter, partner, member, associate or manager of any partnership, joint venture, trust, or other entity;

(10)   To conduct its affairs, locate offices, and exercise the powers granted by this Chapter within or without this State;

(11)   To elect or appoint directors, officers, employees, and agents of the corporation, define their duties, and fix their compensation;

(12)   To pay pensions and establish pension plans, pension trusts, and other benefit and incentive plans for any or all of its current or former directors, officers, employees, and agents;

(13)   To make donations for the public welfare or for charitable, religious, cultural, scientific, or educational purposes, and to make payments or donations not inconsistent with law for other purposes that further the corporate interest;

(14)   To impose dues, assessments, admission and transfer fees upon its members;

(15)   To establish conditions for admission of members, admit members and issue memberships;

(16)	To carry on a business;

(17)	To procure insurance for its benefit on the life or physical or mental ability of any director, officer or employee and, in the case of a charitable or religious corporation, any sponsor, contributor, pledgor, student or former student whose death or disability might cause financial loss to the corporation, and for these purposes the corporation is deemed to have an insurable interest in each such person; and to procure insurance for its benefit on the life or physical or mental ability of any other person in whom it has an insurable interest;

(18)	To engage in any lawful activity that will aid governmental policy;

(19)	To do all things necessary or convenient, not inconsistent with law, to further the activities and affairs of the corporation.

(b)	It shall not be necessary to set forth in the articles of incorporation any of the powers enumerated in this section. (1955, c. 1230; 1957, c. 783, s. 7; 1969, c. 875, s. 4; 1971, c. 1136, s. 1; 1977, c. 236, s. 1, c. 663; 1979, c. 1027; 1985, c. 505; 1985 (Reg. Sess., 1986), c. 801, ss. 8-14; 1993, c. 398, s. 1.)

§ 55A-3-03. Emergency powers.

(a)	In anticipation of or during an emergency defined in subsection (d) of this section, the board of directors of a corporation may:

(1)	Modify lines of succession to accommodate the incapacity of any director, officer, employee, or agent; and

(2)	Relocate the principal office, designate alternative principal offices or regional offices, or authorize the officers to do so.

(b)	During an emergency defined in subsection (d) of this section, unless emergency bylaws provide otherwise:

(1)	Notice of a meeting of the board of directors need be given only to those directors it is practicable to reach and may be given in any practicable manner, including by publication and radio; and

37

(2)   One or more officers of the corporation present at a meeting of the board of directors may be deemed to be directors for the meeting, in order of rank and within the same rank in order of seniority, as necessary to achieve a quorum.

(c)   Corporate action taken in good faith during an emergency under this section, to further the ordinary affairs of the corporation, binds the corporation and the fact that the action is taken pursuant to this section shall not be used to impose liability on a corporate director, officer, employee, or agent.

(d)   An emergency exists for purposes of this section if a quorum of the corporation's directors cannot readily be assembled because of some catastrophic event. (1993, c. 398, s. 1.)

§ 55A-3-04. Ultra vires.

(a)   Except as provided in subsection (b) of this section, the validity of corporate action shall not be challenged on the ground that the corporation lacks or lacked power to act.

(b)   A corporation's power to act may be challenged:

(1)   In a proceeding by a member or a director against the corporation to enjoin the act;

(2)   In a proceeding by the corporation, directly, derivatively, or through a receiver, trustee, or other legal representative, against an incumbent or former director, officer, employee, or agent of the corporation; or

(3)   In a proceeding by the Attorney General under G.S. 55A-14-30.

(c)   In a proceeding by a member or a director under subdivision (b)(1) of this section to enjoin an unauthorized corporate act, the court may enjoin or set aside the act, if equitable and if all affected persons are parties to the proceeding, and may award damages for loss (other than anticipated profits) suffered by the corporation or another party because of enjoining the unauthorized act. (1955, c. 1230; 1993, c. 398, s. 1.)

§ 55A-3-05. Exercise of corporate franchises not granted.

The Attorney General may upon the Attorney General's own information or upon complaint of a private party bring an action in the name of the State to restrain any person from exercising corporate franchises not granted. (1985 (Reg. Sess., 1986), c. 801, s. 5; 1993, c. 398, s. 1.)

§ 55A-3-06. Special powers; public parks and drives and certain recreational corporations.

Any corporation heretofore or hereafter formed for the purpose of creating and maintaining public parks and drives shall have full power and authority to lay out, manage, and control parks and drives within the State, under any rules and regulations as the corporation may prescribe and shall have power to purchase and hold property and take gifts or donations for such purpose. It may hold property and exercise such powers and trust for any town, city, township, or county, in connection with which the parks and drives shall be maintained. Any city, town, township, or county, holding such property, may vest and transfer the same to any such corporation for the purpose of controlling and maintaining the same as public parks and drives under any regulations and subject to any conditions as may be determined upon by the city, town, township, or county. All such lands as the corporation may acquire shall be held in trust as public parks and drives, and shall be held open to the public under any rules, laws, and regulations as the corporation may adopt through its board of directors, and it shall have power and authority to make and adopt all laws and regulations as it may determine upon for the reasonable management of such parks and drives. The terms "public parks and drives" as used in this section shall be construed so as to include playgrounds, recreational centers, and other recreational activities and facilities which may be provided and established under the sponsorship of any county, city, town, township, or school district in North Carolina and constructed or established with the assistance of the government of the United States or any agency thereof. (1955, c. 1230; 1973, c. 695, s. 9; 1993, c. 398, s. 1.)

§ 55A-3-07. Certain corporations subject to Public Records Act and Open Meetings Law.

Any of the following corporations organized under this Chapter is subject to the Public Records Act (Chapter 132 of the General Statutes) and the Open Meetings Law (Article 33C of Chapter 143 of the General Statutes):

(1)   A corporation organized under the terms of any consent decree and final judgment in any civil action calling on a state officer to create the corporation, for the purposes of receipt and distribution of funds allocated to the State of North Carolina to provide economic impact assistance on account of one industry.

(2)   A corporation organized upon the request of the State for the sole purpose of financing projects for public use. (1999-2, s. 7; 2001-84, s. 4.)

Article 4.

Names.

§§ 55A-4-01 through 55A-4-05: Repealed by Session Laws 2001-358, s. 23, effective January 1, 2002.

Article 5.

Office and Agent.

§ 55A-5-01. Registered office and registered agent.

Each corporation must maintain a registered office and registered agent as required by Article 4 of Chapter 55D of the General Statutes and is subject to service on the Secretary of State under that Article. (1955, c. 1230; 1957, c. 979, s. 20; 1993, c. 398, s. 1; 1995, c. 400, s. 1; 2000-140, s. 101(d); 2001-358, s. 48(a); 2001-387, s. 173; 2001-413, s. 6.)

§ 55A-5-02: Repealed by Session Laws 2001-358, s. 48.

§ 55A-5-02.1: Transferred to § 55A-16-23 by Session Laws 2001-358, s. 48(d).

§§ 55A-5-03 through 55A-5-04: Repealed by Session Laws 2001-358, s. 48(c), effective January 1, 2002.

Article 6.

Members and Memberships.

Part 1. Admission of Members.

§ 55A-6-01. Members.

(a)   A corporation may have one or more classes of members or may have no members.

(b)   No person shall be admitted as a member without the person's consent. (1955, c. 1230; 1993, c. 398, s. 1.)

§§ 55A-6-02 through 55A-6-19. Reserved for future codification purposes.

Part 2. Members' Rights and Obligations.

§ 55A-6-20. Designations, qualifications, rights, and obligations of members.

41

If a corporation has members, the designations, qualifications, rights, and obligations of members shall be set forth in or authorized by the articles of incorporation or bylaws, and may include any provisions not inconsistent with law or the articles of incorporation with respect to:

(1)   Conditions of admission and membership;

(2)   Voting rights and the manner of exercising voting rights;

(3)   The relative rights and obligations of members among themselves, to the corporation, and with respect to the property of the corporation;

(4)   The manner of terminating membership in the corporation;

(5)   The rights and obligations of the members and the corporation upon such termination;

(6)   The transferability or nontransferability of memberships; and

(7)   Any other matters.

Except as otherwise provided in or authorized by the articles of incorporation or bylaws, all members shall have the same designations, qualifications, rights, and obligations. (1955, c. 1230; 1985 (Reg. Sess., 1986), c. 801, s. 35; 1993, c. 398, s. 1.)

§ 55A-6-21. Prohibition of stock.

A corporation shall neither authorize nor issue shares of stock. (1955, c. 1230; 1985 (Reg. Sess., 1986), c. 801, s. 32; 1993, c. 398, s. 1.)

§ 55A-6-22. Member's liability to third parties.

A member of a corporation is not, as such, personally liable for the acts, debts, liabilities, or obligations of the corporation. (1993, c. 398, s. 1.)

42

§ 55A-6-23. Member's liability for dues, assessments, and fees.

A member may become liable to the corporation for dues, assessments, or fees; provided, however, that a provision in the articles of incorporation or bylaws or a resolution adopted by the board of directors authorizing or imposing dues, assessments, or fees does not, of itself, create liability. (1993, c. 398, s. 1.)

§ 55A-6-24. Creditor's action against member.

(a)   A creditor of a corporation shall not bring a proceeding to enforce any liability of a member to the corporation unless final judgment has been rendered in favor of the creditor against the corporation and execution has been returned unsatisfied in whole or in part or unless a proceeding against the corporation would be futile.

(b)   All creditors of the corporation, with or without reducing their claims to judgment, may intervene in any creditor's proceeding brought under subsection (a) of this section to collect and apply the proceeds of obligations owed to the corporation. Any or all members who are indebted to the corporatiyon may be joined in such proceeding. (1993, c. 398, s. 1.)

§§ 55A-6-25 through 55A-6-29. Reserved for future codification purposes.

Part 3. Resignation and Termination.

§ 55A-6-30. Resignation.

(a)   Any member may resign at any time.

(b)   The resignation of a member does not relieve the member from any obligations incurred or commitments made to the corporation prior to resignation. (1993, c. 398, s. 1.)

§ 55A-6-31. Termination, expulsion, and suspension.

(a)   No member of a corporation may be expelled or suspended, and no membership may be terminated or suspended, except in a manner that is fair and reasonable and is carried out in good faith.

(b)   Any proceeding challenging an expulsion, suspension, or termination shall be commenced within one year after the member receives notice of the expulsion, suspension, or termination.

(c)   A member who has been expelled or suspended may be liable to the corporation for dues, assessments, or fees as a result of obligations incurred or commitments made by the member prior to expulsion or suspension. (1955, c. 1230; 1993, c. 398, s. 1.)

§§ 55A-6-32 through 55A-6-39. Reserved for future codification purposes.

Part 4. Delegates.

§ 55A-6-40. Delegates.

(a)   A corporation may provide in its articles of incorporation or bylaws for delegates having some or all of the authority of members.

(b)   The articles of incorporation or bylaws may set forth provisions relating to:

(1)   The characteristics, qualifications, rights, limitations, and obligations of delegates, including their selection and removal;

(2)   Calling, noticing, holding, and conducting meetings of delegates; and

(3)   Carrying on corporate activities during and between meetings of delegates. (1993, c. 398, s. 1.)

Article 7.

Members' Meetings and Voting; Derivative Proceedings.

Part 1. Meetings and Action Without Meetings.

§ 55A-7-01. Annual and regular meetings.

(a)   A corporation having members with the right to vote for directors shall hold a meeting of such members annually.

(b)   A corporation with members may hold regular membership meetings at the times stated in or fixed in accordance with the bylaws.

(c)   Annual and regular membership meetings may be held in or out of this State at the place stated in or fixed in accordance with the bylaws. If no place is stated in or fixed in accordance with the bylaws, annual and regular meetings shall be held at the corporation's principal office.

(d)   At annual and regular meetings, the members shall consider and act upon such matters as may be raised consistent with the notice requirements of G.S. 55A-7-05 and G.S. 55A-7-22(d).

(e)   The failure to hold an annual or regular meeting at a time stated in or fixed in accordance with the corporation's bylaws does not affect the validity of any corporate action. (1955, c. 1230; 1993, c. 398, s. 1.)

§ 55A-7-02. Special meeting.

(a)   A corporation with members shall hold a special meeting of members:

(1)   On call of its board of directors or the person or persons authorized to do so by the articles of incorporation or bylaws; or

(2)   Within 30 days after the holders of at least ten percent (10%) of all the votes entitled to be cast on any issue proposed to be considered at the proposed special meeting sign, date, and deliver to the corporation's secretary

one or more written demands for the meeting describing the purpose or purposes for which it is to be held.

(b)   If not otherwise fixed under G.S. 55A-7-03 or G.S. 55A-7-07, the record date for determining members entitled to demand a special meeting is the date the first member signs the demand.

(c)   Special meetings of members may be held in or out of this State at the place stated in or fixed in accordance with the bylaws. If no place is stated or fixed in accordance with the bylaws, special meetings shall be held at the corporation's principal office.

(d)   Only those matters that are within the purpose or purposes described in the meeting notice required by G.S. 55A-7-05 may be acted upon at a special meeting of members. (1955, c. 1230; 1993, c. 398, s. 1.)

§ 55A-7-03. Court-ordered meeting.

(a)   The superior court of the county where a corporation's principal office, or, if there is none in this State, its registered office, is located may, after notice is given to the corporation and upon such further notice and opportunity to be heard, if any, as the court may deem appropriate under the circumstances, summarily order a meeting to be held:

(1)   On application of any member if an annual meeting was not held within 15 months after the corporation's last annual meeting; or

(2)   On application of a member who signed a demand for a special meeting valid under G.S. 55A-7-02, if the corporation has not held the meeting as required by that section.

(b)   The court may fix the time and place of the meeting, specify a record date for determining those persons entitled to notice of and to vote at the meeting, prescribe the form and content of the meeting notice, fix the quorum required for specific matters to be considered at the meeting (or direct that the votes represented at the meeting constitute a quorum for action on those matters), and enter other orders necessary to accomplish the purpose or purposes of the meeting.

(c)   If the court orders a meeting, it may also order the corporation to pay all or part of the member's costs (including reasonable attorneys' fees) incurred to obtain the order. (1993, c. 398, s. 1.)

§ 55A-7-04. Action by written consent.

(a)   Action required or permitted by this Chapter to be taken at a meeting of members may be taken without a meeting if the action is taken by all members entitled to vote on the action. The action shall be evidenced by one or more written consents describing the action taken, signed before or after such action by all members entitled to vote thereon, and delivered to the corporation for inclusion in the minutes or filing with the corporate records. To the extent the corporation has agreed pursuant to G.S. 55A-1-70, a member's consent to action taken without a meeting may be in electronic form and delivered by electronic means.

(b)   If not otherwise determined under G.S. 55A-7-03 or G.S. 55A-7-07, the record date for determining members entitled to take action without a meeting is the date the first member signs the consent under subsection (a) of this section.

(c)   A consent signed under this section has the effect of a meeting vote and may be described as such in any document. (1977, c. 193, s. 2; 1993, c. 398, s. 1; 2008-37, s. 4.)

§ 55A-7-05. Notice of meeting.

(a)   A corporation shall give notice of meetings of members by any means that is fair and reasonable and consistent with its bylaws.

(b)   Any notice that conforms to the requirements of subsection (c) is fair and reasonable, but other means of giving notice may also be fair and reasonable when all the circumstances are considered; provided, however, that notice of matters referred to in subdivision (c)(2) of this section shall be given as provided in subsection (c) of this section.

(c)   Notice is fair and reasonable if:

47

(1)   The corporation gives notice to all members entitled to vote at the meeting of the place, date, and time of each annual, regular, and special meeting of members no fewer than 10, or, if notice is mailed by other than first class, registered or certified mail, no fewer than 30, nor more than 60 days before the meeting date;

(2)   Notice of an annual or regular meeting includes a description of any matter or matters that shall be approved by the members under G.S. 55A-8-31, 55A-8-55, 55A-10-03, 55A-10-21, 55A-11-04, 55A-12-02, or 55A-14-02; and

(3)   Notice of special meeting includes a description of the matter or matters for which the meeting is called.

(d)   Unless the bylaws require otherwise, if an annual, regular, or special meeting of members is adjourned to a different date, time, or place, notice need not be given of the new date, time, or place, if the new date, time, or place is announced at the meeting before adjournment. If a new record date for the adjourned meeting is or must be fixed under G.S. 55A-7-07, however, notice of the adjourned meeting shall be given under this section to the members of record entitled to vote at the meeting as of the new record date.

(e)   When giving notice of an annual, regular, or special meeting of members, a corporation shall give notice of a matter a member intends to raise at the meeting if:

(1)   Requested in writing to do so by a person or persons entitled to call a special meeting pursuant to G.S. 55A-7-02; and

(2)   The request is received by the secretary or president of the corporation at least 10 days before the corporation gives notice of the meeting. (1955, c. 1230; 1993, c. 398, s. 1.)

§ 55A-7-06. Waiver of notice.

(a)   A member may waive any notice required by this Chapter, the articles of incorporation, or bylaws before or after the date and time stated in the notice. The waiver shall be in writing, be signed by the member entitled to the notice, and be delivered to the corporation for inclusion in the minutes or filing with the corporate records.

(b)   A member's attendance at a meeting:

(1)   Waives objection to lack of notice or defective notice of the meeting, unless the member at the beginning of the meeting objects to holding the meeting or conducting business at the meeting; and

(2)   Waives objection to consideration of a particular matter at the meeting that is not within the purpose or purposes described in the meeting notice, unless the member objects to considering the matter before it is voted upon. (1955, c. 1230; 1993, c. 398, s. 1.)

§ 55A-7-07. Record date.

(a)   The bylaws of a corporation may fix or provide the manner of fixing a date as the record date for determining the members entitled to notice of a members' meeting. If the bylaws do not fix or provide for fixing a record date, the board of directors may fix a future date as the record date. If no record date is fixed, members at the close of business on the business day preceding the day on which notice is given are entitled to notice of the meeting.

(b)   The bylaws of a corporation may fix or provide the manner of fixing a date as the record date for determining the members entitled to vote at a members' meeting. If the bylaws do not fix or provide for fixing a record date, the board of directors may fix a future date as the record date. If no record date is fixed, members on the date of the meeting who are otherwise eligible to vote are entitled to vote at the meeting.

(c)   The bylaws may fix or provide the manner for determining a date as the record date for the purpose of determining the members entitled to any rights in respect of any other lawful action. If the bylaws do not fix or provide for fixing a record date, the board may fix in advance the record date. If no record date is fixed, members at the close of business on the day on which the board adopts the resolution relating to such action, or the 60th day prior to the date of such action, whichever is later, are entitled to such rights.

(d)   A record date fixed under this section shall not be more than 70 days before the meeting or action for which a determination of members is required.

(e)   A determination of members entitled to notice of or to vote at a membership meeting is effective for any adjournment of the meeting unless the board fixes a new date for determining the right to notice or the right to vote, which it shall do if the meeting is adjourned to a date more than 120 days after the date fixed for the original meeting.

(f)   If a court orders a meeting adjourned to a date more than 120 days after the date fixed for the original meeting, it may provide that the original record date for notice or voting continues in effect or it may fix a new record date for notice or voting. (1993, c. 398, s. 1.)

§ 55A-7-08. Action by written ballot.

(a)   Unless prohibited or limited by the articles of incorporation or bylaws and without regard to the requirements of G.S. 55A-7-04, any action that may be taken at any annual, regular, or special meeting of members may be taken without a meeting if the corporation delivers a written ballot to every member entitled to vote on the matter. Any requirement that any vote of the members be made by written ballot may be satisfied by a ballot submitted by electronic transmission, including electronic mail, provided that such electronic transmission shall either set forth or be submitted with information from which it can be determined that the electronic transmission was authorized by the member or the member's proxy.

(b)   A written ballot shall:

(1)   Set forth each proposed action; and

(2)   Provide an opportunity to vote for or against each proposed action.

(c)   Approval by written ballot pursuant to this section shall be valid only when the number of votes cast by ballot equals or exceeds the quorum required to be present at a meeting authorizing the action, and the number of approvals equals or exceeds the number of votes that would be required to approve the matter at a meeting at which the same total number of votes were cast.

(d)   All solicitations for votes by written ballot shall indicate the time by which a ballot shall be received by the corporation in order to be counted.

(e)   Except as otherwise provided in the articles of incorporation or bylaws, a written ballot shall not be revoked. (1955, c. 1230; 1985 (Reg. Sess., 1986), c. 801, s. 35; 1993, c. 398, s. 1; 2008-37, s. 5.)

§§ 55A-7-09 through 55A-7-19. Reserved for future codification purposes.

Part 2. Voting.

§ 55A-7-20. Members' list for meeting.

(a)   After fixing a record date for a notice of a meeting, a corporation shall prepare an alphabetical list of the names of all its members who are entitled to notice of the meeting. The list shall show the address and number of votes each member is entitled to cast at the meeting. The corporation shall prepare on a current basis through the time of the membership meeting a list of members, if any, who are entitled to vote at the meeting, but not entitled to notice of the meeting. This list shall be prepared on the same basis as and be part of the list of members.

(b)   Beginning two business days after notice is given of the meeting for which the list was prepared and continuing through the meeting, the list of members shall be available at the corporation's principal office or at a reasonable place identified in the meeting notice in the city where the meeting will be held for inspection by any member for the purpose of communication with other members concerning the meeting. A member, personally or by or with his representatives, is entitled on written demand to inspect and, subject to the limitations of G.S. 55A-16-02(c) and G.S. 55A-16-05 and at his expense, to copy the list at a reasonable time during the period it is available for inspection.

(c)   The corporation shall make the list of members available at the meeting, and any member, personally or by or with his representatives, is entitled to inspect the list at any time during the meeting or any adjournment.

(d)   If the corporation refuses to allow a member or his representative to inspect or copy the list of members as permitted in subsections (b) and (c) of this section, the superior court of the county where a corporation's principal office (or, if there is none in this State, its registered office) is located, on

51

application of the member, after notice is given to the corporation and upon such further evidence, notice and opportunity to be heard, if any, as the court may deem appropriate under the circumstances, may summarily order the inspection or copying at the corporation's expense. The court may postpone the meeting for which the list was prepared until the inspection or copying is complete and may order the corporation to pay the member's costs, including reasonable attorneys' fees, incurred to obtain the order.

(e)   Refusal or failure to prepare or make available the members' list does not affect the validity of action taken at the meeting. (1993, c. 398, s. 1.)

§ 55A-7-21. Voting entitlement generally.

(a)   Unless the articles of incorporation or bylaws provide otherwise, each member is entitled to one vote on each matter voted on by the members.

(b)   Unless the articles of incorporation or bylaws provide otherwise, if a membership stands of record in the names of two or more persons, their acts with respect to voting shall have the following effect:

(1)   If only one votes, such act binds all; and

(2)   If more than one votes, the vote shall be divided on a pro rata basis.

(c)   An amendment to the articles of incorporation or bylaws on which members are entitled to vote, the purpose of which is to increase or decrease the number of votes any member is entitled to cast on any member action, shall be approved by the members entitled to vote on that action by a vote that would be sufficient to take the action before the amendment. (1955, c. 1230; 1985 (Reg. Sess., 1986), c. 801, s. 35; 1993, c. 398, s. 1; 1995, c. 400, s. 2.)

§ 55A-7-22. Quorum requirements.

(a)   Unless this Chapter, the articles of incorporation, or bylaws provide for a higher or lower quorum, ten percent (10%) of the votes entitled to be cast on a matter shall be represented at a meeting of members to constitute a quorum on that matter. Once a member is represented for any purpose at a meeting, the member is deemed present for quorum purposes for the remainder of the meeting and for any adjournment of that meeting unless a new record date is or must be set for that adjourned meeting.

(b)   A bylaw amendment to decrease the quorum for any member action may be approved by the members entitled to vote on that action or, unless prohibited by the bylaws, by the board of directors.

(c)   A bylaw amendment to increase the quorum required for any member action shall be approved by the members entitled to vote on that action.

(d)   Unless one-third or more of the votes entitled to be cast in the election of directors are represented in person or by proxy, the only matters that may be voted upon at an annual or regular meeting of members are those matters that are described in the meeting notice. (1955, c. 1230; 1993, c. 398, s. 1.)

§ 55A-7-23. Voting requirements.

(a)   Unless this Chapter, the articles of incorporation, or the bylaws require a greater vote or voting by class, if a quorum is present, the affirmative vote of a majority of the votes cast is the act of the members.

(b)   An amendment to the articles of incorporation or bylaws on which members are entitled to vote, the purpose of which is to increase or decrease the vote required for any member action, shall be approved by the members entitled to vote on that action by a vote that would be sufficient to take the action before the amendment. (1955, c. 1230; 1993, c. 398, s. 1; 1995, c. 400, s. 3.)

§ 55A-7-24. Proxies.

(a)   Unless the articles of incorporation or bylaws prohibit or limit proxy voting, a member may vote in person or by proxy. A member may appoint one or more proxies to vote or otherwise act for the member by signing an appointment form, either personally or by the member's attorney-in-fact. Without limiting G.S. 55A-1-70, an appointment in the form of an electronic record that bears the member's electronic signature and that may be directly reproduced in paper form by an automated process shall be deemed a valid appointment form

53

within the meaning of this section. In addition, if and to the extent permitted by the nonprofit corporation, a member may appoint one or more proxies by any kind of telephonic transmission, even if not accompanied by written communication, under circumstances or together with information from which the nonprofit corporation can reasonably assume that the appointment was made or authorized by the member.

(b)   An appointment of a proxy is effective when received by the secretary or other officer or agent authorized to tabulate votes. An appointment is valid for 11 months unless a different period is expressly provided in the appointment form.

(c)   An appointment of a proxy is revocable by the member unless the appointment form conspicuously states that it is irrevocable and the appointment is coupled with an interest. An appointment made irrevocable under this subsection shall be revocable when the interest with which it is coupled is extinguished. A transferee for value of an interest subject to an irrevocable appointment may revoke the appointment if he did not have actual knowledge of its irrevocability.

(d)   The death or incapacity of the member appointing a proxy does not affect the right of the corporation to accept the proxy's authority unless notice of the death or incapacity is received by the secretary or other officer or agent authorized to tabulate votes before the proxy exercises authority under the appointment.

(e)   A revocable appointment of a proxy is revoked by the person appointing the proxy:

(1)   Attending any meeting and voting in person; or

(2)   Signing and delivering to the secretary or other officer or agent authorized to tabulate proxy votes either a writing stating that the appointment of the proxy is revoked or a subsequent appointment form.

(f)   Subject to G.S. 55A-7-27 and to any express limitation on the proxy's authority appearing on the face of the appointment form, a corporation is entitled to accept the proxy's vote or other action as that of the member making the appointment. (1955, c. 1230; 1985 (Reg. Sess., 1986), c. 801, s. 35; 1993, c. 398, s. 1; 1999-139, s. 1; 2008-37, s. 6.)

§ 55A-7-25. Voting for directors; cumulative voting.

(a)   Unless otherwise provided in the articles of incorporation, the bylaws, or an agreement valid under G.S. 55A-7-30, directors are elected by a plurality of the votes cast by the members entitled to vote in the election at a meeting at which a quorum is present. If the articles of incorporation, bylaws, or an agreement valid under G.S. 55A-7-30 provides for cumulative voting by members, members may so vote, by multiplying the number of votes the members are entitled to cast by the number of directors for whom they are entitled to vote, and casting the product for a single candidate or distributing the product among two or more candidates.

(b)   Members otherwise entitled to vote cumulatively shall not vote cumulatively at a particular meeting unless:

(1)   The meeting notice or statement accompanying the notice states that cumulative voting will take place; or

(2)   A member or proxy who has the right to cumulate his votes announces in open meeting, before voting for directors starts, his intention to vote cumulatively; and if such announcement is made, the chair shall declare that all persons entitled to vote have the right to vote cumulatively, shall announce the number of votes entitled to be cast, and shall grant a recess of not less than one hour nor more than four hours, as the chair shall determine, or of such other period of time as is unanimously then agreed upon.

(c)   A director elected by cumulative voting may be removed by the members without cause if the requirements of G.S. 55A-8-08 are met unless the votes cast against removal would be sufficient to elect such director if voted cumulatively at an election at which the same total number of votes were cast and the entire number of directors elected at the time of the director's most recent election were then being elected. (1955, c. 1230; 1985 (Reg. Sess., 1986), c. 801, s. 35; 1993, c. 398, s. 1.)

§ 55A-7-26. Other methods of electing directors.

A corporation may provide in its articles of incorporation or bylaws for election of directors by members or delegates:

55

(1)   On the basis of chapter or other organizational unit;

(2)   By region or other geographic unit;

(3)   By preferential voting; or

(4)   By any other reasonable method. (1955, c. 1230; 1973, c. 192, ss. 1, 2; 1985, (Reg. Sess., 1986), c. 801, ss. 19, 21; 1993, c. 398, s. 1.)

§ 55A-7-27. Corporation's acceptance of votes.

(a)   If the name signed on a vote, consent, waiver, or proxy appointment corresponds to the name of a member, the corporation if acting in good faith is entitled to accept the vote, consent, waiver, or proxy appointment and give it effect as the act of the member.

(b)   If the name signed on a vote, consent, waiver, or proxy appointment does not correspond to the record name of a member, the corporation if acting in good faith is nevertheless entitled to accept the vote, consent, waiver, or proxy appointment and give it effect as the act of the member if:

(1)   The member is an entity and the name signed purports to be that of an officer or agent of the entity;

(2)   The name signed purports to be that of an attorney-in-fact of the member and, if the corporation requests it, evidence acceptable to the corporation of the signatory's authority to sign for the member is presented with respect to the vote, consent, waiver, or proxy appointment;

(3)   Two or more persons hold the membership as cotenants or fiduciaries and the name signed purports to be the name of at least one of the coholders and the person signing appears to be acting on behalf of all the coholders; or

(4)   In the case of a corporation other than a charitable or religious corporation:

a.   The name signed purports to be that of an administrator, executor, guardian, or conservator representing the member and, if the corporation requests it, evidence of fiduciary status acceptable to the corporation is presented with respect to the vote, consent, waiver, or proxy appointment;

b.   The name signed purports to be that of a receiver or trustee in bankruptcy of the member, and, if the corporation requests it, evidence of this status acceptable to the corporation is presented with respect to the vote, consent, waiver, or proxy appointment.

(c)   The corporation is entitled to reject a vote, consent, waiver, or proxy appointment if the secretary or other officer or agent authorized to tabulate votes, acting in good faith, has reasonable basis for doubt about the validity of the signature on it or about the signatory's authority to sign for the member.

(d)   The corporation and its officer or agent who accepts or rejects a vote, consent, waiver, or proxy appointment in good faith and in accordance with the standards of this section are not liable in damages to the member for the consequences of the acceptance or rejection.

(e)   Corporate action based on the acceptance or rejection of a vote, consent, waiver, or proxy appointment under this section is valid unless a court of competent jurisdiction determines otherwise. (1993, c. 398, s. 1; 1995, c. 509, s. 27.)

§ 55A-7-28. Reserved for future codification purposes.

§ 55A-7-29. Reserved for future codification purposes.

Part 3. Voting Agreements.

§ 55A-7-30. Voting agreements.

(a)   Two or more members may provide for the manner in which their voting rights will be exercised by signing an agreement for that purpose. The agreement may be valid for a period of up to 10 years. All or some of the parties to the agreement may extend it for more than 10 years from the date the first party signs the extension agreement, but the extension agreement binds only those parties signing it. For charitable or religious corporations, such agreements shall have a reasonable purpose not inconsistent with the corporation's charitable or religious purposes.

(b)   Subject to subsection (a) of this section, a voting agreement created under this section may be specifically enforceable.

(c)   The provisions of a voting agreement created under this section will bind a transferee of a membership covered by the agreement only if the transferee acquires the membership with knowledge of the provisions. (1993, c. 398, s. 1.)

§§ 55A-7-31 through 55A-7-39. Reserved for future codification purposes.

Part 4. Derivative Proceedings.

§ 55A-7-40. Derivative proceedings.

(a)   An action may be brought in a superior court of this State, which shall have exclusive original jurisdiction over actions brought hereunder, in the right of any domestic or foreign corporation by any member or director, provided that, in the case of an action by a member, the plaintiff or plaintiffs shall allege, and it shall appear, that each plaintiff-member was a member at the time of the transaction of which he complains.

(b)   The complaint shall allege with particularity the efforts, if any, made by the plaintiff to obtain the action the plaintiff desires from the directors or comparable authority and the reasons for the plaintiff's failure to obtain the action or for not making the effort. Whether or not a demand for action was made, if the corporation commences an investigation of the charges made in the demand or complaint, the court may stay any proceedings until the investigation is completed.

(c)   Upon motion of the corporation, the court may appoint a committee composed of two or more disinterested directors or other disinterested persons, acceptable to the corporation, to determine whether it is in the best interest of the corporation to pursue a particular legal right or remedy. The committee shall report its findings to the court. After considering the report and any other relevant evidence, the court shall determine whether the proceeding should be continued.

(d)   Such action shall not be discontinued, dismissed, compromised, or settled without the approval of the court. The court, in its discretion, may direct that notice, by publication or otherwise, shall be given to any directors, members, creditors, and other persons whose interests it determines will be substantially affected by the discontinuance, dismissal, compromise, or settlement. If notice is so directed to be given, the court may determine which one or more of the parties to the action shall bear the expense of giving the same, in such amount as the court shall determine and find to be reasonable in the circumstances, and the amount of the expense shall be awarded as costs of the action.

(e)   If the action on behalf of the corporation is successful, in whole or in part, whether by means of a compromise and settlement or by a judgment, the court may award the plaintiff the reasonable expenses of maintaining the action, including reasonable attorneys' fees, and shall direct the plaintiff to account to the corporation for the remainder of any proceeds of the action.

(f)   In any such action, the court, upon final judgment and a finding that the action was brought without reasonable cause, may require the plaintiff or plaintiffs to pay to the defendant or defendants the reasonable expenses, including attorneys' fees, incurred by them in the defense of the action.

(g)   In proceedings hereunder, no member shall be entitled to obtain or have access to any communication within the scope of the corporation's attorney-client privilege which could not be obtained by or would not be accessible to a party in an action other than on behalf of the corporation. (1985 (Reg. Sess., 1986), c. 801, s. 34; 1993, c. 398, s. 1.)

Article 8.

Directors and Officers.

Part 1. Board of Directors.

§ 55A-8-01. Requirement for and duties of board.

(a)   Except as provided in subsection (c) of this section, each corporation shall have a board of directors.

(b)   All corporate powers shall be exercised by or under the authority of, and the affairs of the corporation managed under the direction of, its board of directors, except as otherwise provided in the articles of incorporation.

(c)   A corporation may dispense with or limit the authority of a board of directors by describing in its articles of incorporation who will perform some or all of the duties of a board of directors; but no such limitation upon the authority which the board of directors would otherwise have shall be effective against other persons without actual knowledge of such limitation.

(d)   To the extent the articles of incorporation vests authority of the board of directors in an individual or group other than the board of directors, the individual or group in the exercise of such authority shall be deemed to be acting as the board of directors for all purposes of this Chapter. (1955, c. 1230; 1985 (Reg. Sess., 1986), c. 801, s. 18; 1993, c. 398, s. 1.)

§ 55A-8-02. Qualifications of directors.

The articles of incorporation or bylaws may prescribe qualifications for directors. A director need not be a resident of this State or a member of the corporation unless the articles of incorporation or bylaws so prescribe. (1955, c. 1230; 1985 (Reg. Sess., 1986), c. 801, s. 18; 1993, c. 398, s. 1.)

§ 55A-8-03. Number of directors.

(a)   A board of directors shall consist of one or more natural persons, with the number specified in or fixed in accordance with the articles of incorporation or bylaws.

(b)   The number of directors may be increased or decreased from time to time by amendment to or in the manner prescribed in the articles of incorporation or bylaws.

(c)   The articles of incorporation or bylaws may establish a variable range for the size of the board of directors by fixing a minimum and maximum number of directors. If a variable range is established, the number of directors may be fixed or changed from time to time, within the minimum and maximum, by the members entitled to vote for directors or (unless the articles of incorporation or an agreement valid under G.S. 55A-7-30 shall otherwise provide) the board of directors. If the corporation has members entitled to vote for directors, only such members may change the range for the size of the board or change from a fixed to a variable-range size board or vice versa. (1955, c. 1230; 1973, c. 192, ss. 1, 2; 1985 (Reg. Sess., 1986), c. 801, ss. 19-21; 1993, c. 398, s. 1.)

§ 55A-8-04. Election, designation, and appointment of directors.

(a)   If the corporation has members entitled to vote for directors, all the directors (except the initial directors) shall be elected at the first annual meeting of such members, and at each annual meeting thereafter, unless the articles of incorporation or bylaws provide some other time or method of election, or provide that some of the directors are appointed by some other person or are designated. If the articles of incorporation authorize dividing the members into classes, the articles of incorporation may also authorize the election of all or a specified number of directors by the members of one or more authorized classes.

(b)   If the corporation does not have members entitled to vote for directors, all the directors (except the initial directors) shall be elected, appointed, or designated as provided in the articles of incorporation or bylaws. If no method of designation or appointment is set forth in the articles of incorporation or bylaws, the directors (other than the initial directors) shall be elected by the board of directors.

(c)   If any member entitled to vote for directors so demands, election of directors by the members shall be by ballot, unless the articles of incorporation or bylaws otherwise provide. (1955, c. 1230; 1973, c. 192, ss. 1, 2; 1985 (Reg. Sess., 1986), c. 801, ss. 19-21; 1993, c. 398, s. 1.)

§ 55A-8-05. Terms of directors generally.

(a)   The articles of incorporation or bylaws may specify the terms of directors. In the absence of a contrary provision in the articles of incorporation or bylaws, the term of each director shall be one year, and directors may serve successive terms.

(b)   A decrease in the number of directors or term of office does not shorten an incumbent director's term.

(c)   Except as provided in the articles of incorporation or bylaws:

(1)   The term of a director filling a vacancy in the office of a director elected by members expires at the next election of directors by members; and

(2)   The term of a director filling any other vacancy expires at the end of the unexpired term that such director is filling.

(d)   Despite the expiration of a director's term, the director continues to serve until the director's successor is elected, designated, or appointed and qualifies, or until there is a decrease in the number of directors. (1955, c. 1230; 1973, c. 192, ss. 1, 2; 1985 (Reg. Sess., 1986), c. 801, ss. 19-21; 1993, c. 398, s. 1; 1995, c. 509, s. 28.)

§ 55A-8-06. Staggered terms for directors.

The articles of incorporation or bylaws may provide for staggering the terms of directors by dividing the total number of directors into groups. The terms of office of the several groups need not be uniform. (1955, c. 1230; 1973, c. 192, ss. 1, 2; 1985 (Reg. Sess., 1986), c. 801, ss. 19-21; 1993, c. 398, s. 1.)

§ 55A-8-07. Resignation of directors.

(a)   A director may resign at any time by communicating his resignation to the board of directors, its presiding officer, or to the corporation.

(b)   A resignation is effective when it is communicated unless the notice specifies a later effective date or subsequent event upon which it will become effective. (1993, c. 398, s. 1.)

§ 55A-8-08. Removal of directors elected by members or directors.

(a)   The members may remove one or more directors elected by them with or without cause unless the articles of incorporation provide that directors may be removed only for cause.

(b)   If a director is elected by a class, chapter or other organizational unit, or by region or other geographic grouping, the director may be removed only by that class, chapter, unit, or grouping.

(c)   Except as provided in subsection (i) of this section, a director may be removed under subsection (a) or (b) of this section, only if the number of votes cast to remove the director would be sufficient to elect the director at a meeting to elect directors.

(d)   If cumulative voting is authorized, a director shall not be removed:

(1)   If the number of votes; or

(2)   If the director was elected by a class, chapter, unit, or grouping of members, the number of votes of that class, chapter, unit, or grouping;

sufficient to elect the director under cumulative voting, if an election were then being held, is voted against the director's removal.

(e)   A director elected by members may be removed by the members only at a meeting called for the purpose of removing the director and the meeting notice shall state that the purpose, or one of the purposes, of the meeting is removal of the director.

(f)   In computing whether a director is protected from removal under subsections (b) through (d) of this section, it should be assumed that the votes against removal are cast in an election for the number of directors of the class to which the director to be removed belonged on the date of that director's election.

(g)   An entire board of directors may be removed under subsections (a) through (e) of this section.

63

(h)   A majority of the directors then in office or such greater number as is set forth in the articles of incorporation or bylaws may, subject to any limitation in the articles of incorporation or bylaws, remove any director elected by the board of directors; provided, however, that a director elected by the board to fill the vacancy of a director elected by the members may be removed by the members, but not the board.

(i)   Notwithstanding any other provision of this section, if, at the beginning of a director's term on the board of directors, the articles of incorporation or bylaws provide that the director may be removed by the board for missing a specified number of board meetings, the board may remove the director for failing to attend the specified number of meetings. The director may be removed only if a majority of the directors then in office vote for the removal.

(j)   Notwithstanding any other provision of this section, the articles of incorporation or bylaws may provide that directors elected after the effective date of such provision shall be removed automatically for missing a specified number of board meetings.

(k)   The articles of incorporation may:

(1)   Limit the application of this section in the case of a charitable or religious corporation; and

(2)   Set forth the vote and procedures by which the board of directors or any person may remove with or without cause a director elected by the members or the board. (1955, c. 1230; 1973, c. 192, ss. 1, 2; 1985 (Reg. Sess., 1986), c. 801, ss. 19-21; 1993, c. 398, s. 1.)

§ 55A-8-09. Removal of designated or appointed directors.

(a)   A designated director may be removed by an amendment to the articles of incorporation or bylaws deleting or changing the provision containing the designation.

(b)   Except as otherwise provided in the articles of incorporation or bylaws:

(1)   An appointed director may be removed with or without cause by the person appointing the director;

(2)   The person removing the director shall do so by giving written notice of the removal to the director and to the corporation; and

(3)   A removal is effective when the notice is effective unless the notice specifies a future effective date.

(c)   Notwithstanding any other provision of this section, the articles of incorporation or bylaws may provide that directors appointed after the effective date of such provision shall be removed automatically for missing a specified number of board meetings. (1955, c. 1230; 1973, c. 192, ss. 1, 2; 1985 (Reg. Sess., 1986), c. 801, ss. 19-21; 1993, c. 398, s. 1.)

§ 55A-8-10. Removal of directors by judicial proceeding.

(a)   The superior court of the county where a corporation's principal office (or, if there is none in this State, its registered office) is located may remove any director of the corporation from office in a proceeding commenced either by the corporation or by its members holding at least ten percent (10%) of the votes entitled to be cast of any class of members, if the court finds that:

(1)   The director engaged in fraudulent or dishonest conduct, or gross abuse of authority or discretion, with respect to the corporation, or a final judgment has been entered finding that the director has violated a duty set forth in G.S. 55A-8-30 through G.S. 55A-8-33, and

(2)   Removal is in the best interest of the corporation.

(b)   The court that removes a director may bar the director from serving on the board of directors for a period prescribed by the court.

(c)   If members commence a proceeding under subsection (a) of this section, the corporation shall be made a party defendant. (1993, c. 398, s. 1.)

§ 55A-8-11. Vacancy on board.

(a)   Unless the articles of incorporation or bylaws provide otherwise, and except as provided in subsections (b) and (c) of this section, if a vacancy occurs on a board of directors, including, without limitation, a vacancy resulting from an increase in the number of directors or from the failure by the members to elect the full authorized number of directors, the vacancy may be filled:

(1)   By the members entitled to vote for directors, if any, or if the vacant office was held by a director elected by a class, chapter or other organizational unit, or by region or other geographic grouping, by the members of that class, chapter, unit, or grouping;

(2)   By the board of directors; or

(3)   If the directors remaining in the office constitute fewer than a quorum of the board, by the affirmative vote of a majority of all the directors, or by the sole director, remaining in office.

(b)   Unless the articles of incorporation or bylaws provide otherwise, if a vacant office was held by an appointed director, only the person who appointed the director may fill the vacancy.

(c)   If a vacant office was held by a designated director, the vacancy shall be filled only as provided in the articles of incorporation or bylaws.

(d)   A vacancy that will occur at a specific later date (by reason of a resignation effective at a later date under G.S. 55A-8-07(b) or otherwise) may be filled before the vacancy occurs but the new director shall not take office until the vacancy occurs. (1955, c. 1230; 1993, c. 398, s. 1.)

§ 55A-8-12. Compensation of directors.

Unless the articles of incorporation provide otherwise, a board of directors may fix the compensation of directors. (1985 (Reg. Sess., 1986), c. 801, s. 26; 1993, c. 398, s. 1.)

§§ 55A-8-13 through 55A-8-19. Reserved for future codification purposes.

Part 2. Meetings and Action of the Board.

§ 55A-8-20. Regular and special meetings.

(a)   The board of directors may hold regular or special meetings in or out of this State.

(b)   Unless the articles of incorporation or bylaws provide otherwise, the board of directors may permit any or all directors to participate in a regular or special meeting by, or conduct the meeting through the use of, any means of communication by which all directors participating may simultaneously hear each other during the meeting. A director participating in a meeting by this means is deemed to be present in person at the meeting. (1955, c. 1230; 1973, c. 314, s. 3; 1985 (Reg. Sess., 1986), c. 801, ss. 24, 25; 1993, c. 398, s. 1.)

§ 55A-8-21. Action without meeting.

(a)   Unless the articles of incorporation or bylaws provide otherwise, action required or permitted by this Chapter to be taken at a board of directors' meeting may be taken without a meeting if the action is taken by all members of the board. The action shall be evidenced by one or more written consents signed by each director before or after such action, describing the action taken, and included in the minutes or filed with the corporate records reflecting the action taken. To the extent the corporation has agreed pursuant to G.S. 55A-1-70, a director's consent to action taken without meeting may be in electronic form and delivered by electronic means.

(b)   Action taken under this section is effective when the last director signs the consent, unless the consent specifies a different effective date.

(c)   A consent signed under this section has the effect of a meeting vote and may be described as such in any document. (1973, c. 314, s. 3; 1993, c. 398, s. 1; 2008-37, s. 7.)

§ 55A-8-22. Notice of meetings.

67

(a)   Unless the articles of incorporation or bylaws provide otherwise, regular meetings of the board of directors may be held without notice of the date, time, place, or purpose of the meeting.

(b)   Special meetings of the board of directors shall be held upon such notice as is provided in the articles of incorporation or bylaws, or in the absence of any such provision, upon notice sent by any usual means of communication not less than five days before the meeting. The notice need not describe the purpose of the special meeting unless required by: (i) this Chapter, (ii) the articles of incorporation, or (iii) the bylaws.

(c)   Unless the articles of incorporation or bylaws provide otherwise, the presiding officer of the board, the president or twenty percent (20%) of the directors then in office may call and give notice of a meeting of the board. (1955, c. 1230; 1985 (Reg. Sess., 1986), c. 801, ss. 24, 25; 1993, c. 398, s. 1.)

§ 55A-8-23. Waiver of notice.

(a)   A director may waive any notice required by this Chapter, the articles of incorporation, or bylaws before or after the date and time stated in the notice. Except as provided by subsection (b) of this section, the waiver shall be in writing, signed by the director entitled to the notice, and filed with the minutes or corporate records.

(b)   A director's attendance at or participation in a meeting waives any required notice to him of the meeting unless the director at the beginning of the meeting (or promptly upon his arrival) objects to holding the meeting or transacting business at the meeting and does not thereafter vote for or assent to action taken at the meeting. (1955, c. 1230; 1985 (Reg. Sess., 1986), c. 801, ss. 24, 25; 1993, c. 398, s. 1; 1995, c. 509, s. 29.)

§ 55A-8-24. Quorum and voting.

(a)   Except as otherwise provided in: (i) this Chapter, (ii) the articles of incorporation, or (iii) the bylaws, a quorum of a board of directors consists of a majority of the directors in office immediately before a meeting begins. In no

68

event may the articles of incorporation or bylaws authorize a quorum of fewer than one-third of the number of directors in office.

(b)   If a quorum is present when a vote is taken, the affirmative vote of a majority of directors present is the act of the board unless: (i) this Chapter, (ii) the articles of incorporation, or (iii) the bylaws require the vote of a greater number of directors.

(c)   A director who is present at a meeting of the board of directors or a committee of the board of directors when corporate action is taken is deemed to have assented to the action taken unless:

(1)   He objects at the beginning of the meeting (or promptly upon his arrival) to holding it or transacting business at the meeting;

(2)   His dissent or abstention from the action taken is entered in the minutes of the meeting; or

(3)   He files written notice of his dissent or abstention with the presiding officer of the meeting before its adjournment or with the corporation immediately after adjournment of the meeting. The right of dissent or abstention is not available to a director who votes in favor of the action taken. (1955, c. 1230; 1985 (Reg. Sess., 1986), c. 801, s. 33; 1993, c. 398, s. 1.)

§ 55A-8-25. Committees of the board.

(a)   Unless the articles of incorporation or bylaws provide otherwise, a board of directors may create one or more committees of the board and appoint members of the board to serve on them. Each committee shall have two or more members, who serve at the pleasure of the board.

(b)   The creation of a committee and appointment of members to it shall be approved by the greater of:

(1)   A majority of all the directors in office when the action is taken; or

(2)   The number of directors required by the articles of incorporation or bylaws to take action under G. S. 55A-8-24.

(c)   G.S. 55A-8-20 through G.S. 55A-8-24, which govern meetings, action without meetings, notice and waiver of notice, and quorum and voting requirements of the board, apply to committees of the board and their members as well.

(d)   To the extent specified by the board of directors or in the articles of incorporation or bylaws, each committee of the board may exercise the board's authority under G.S. 55A-8-01.

(e)   A committee of the board shall not, however:

(1)   Authorize distributions;

(2)   Recommend to members or approve dissolution, merger or the sale, pledge, or transfer of all or substantially all of the corporation's assets;

(3)   Elect, appoint or remove directors, or fill vacancies on the board of directors or on any of its committees; or

(4)   Adopt, amend, or repeal the articles of incorporation or bylaws.

(f)   The creation of, delegation of authority to, or action by a committee does not alone constitute compliance by a director with the standards of conduct described in G.S. 55A-8-30. (1955, c. 1230; 1969, c. 875, s. 5; 1985 (Reg. Sess., 1986), c. 801, ss. 22, 23; 1993, c. 398, s. 1.)

§§ 55A-8-26 through 55A-8-29. Reserved for future codification purposes.

Part 3. Standards of Conduct.

§ 55A-8-30. General standards for directors.

(a)   A director shall discharge his duties as a director, including his duties as a member of a committee:

(1)   In good faith;

(2)　　　With the care an ordinarily prudent person in a like position would exercise under similar circumstances; and

(3)　　　In a manner the director reasonably believes to be in the best interests of the corporation.

(b)　　　In discharging his duties, a director is entitled to rely on information, opinions, reports, or statements, including financial statements and other financial data, if prepared or presented by:

(1)　　　One or more officers or employees of the corporation whom the director reasonably believes to be reliable and competent in the matters presented;

(2)　　　Legal counsel, public accountants, or other persons as to matters the director reasonably believes are within their professional or expert competence; or

(3)　　　A committee of the board of which he is not a member if the director reasonably believes the committee merits confidence.

(c)　　　A director is not entitled to the benefit of subsection (b) of this section if he has actual knowledge concerning the matter in question that makes reliance otherwise permitted by subsection (b) of this section unwarranted.

(d)　　　A director is not liable for any action taken as a director, or any failure to take any action, if he performed the duties of his office in compliance with this section.

(e)　　　A director's personal liability for monetary damages for breach of a duty as a director may be limited or eliminated only to the extent provided in G.S. 55A-8-60 or permitted in G.S. 55A-2-02(b)(4), and a director may be entitled to indemnification against liability and expenses pursuant to Part 5 of Article 8 of this Chapter.

(f)　　　A director shall not be deemed to be a trustee with respect to the corporation or with respect to any property held or administered by the corporation, including without limit, property that may be subject to restrictions imposed by the donor or transferor of such property. (1985 (Reg. Sess., 1986), c. 801, s. 29; 1993, c. 398, s. 1.)

§ 55A-8-31. Director conflict of interest.

(a)   A conflict of interest transaction is a transaction with the corporation in which a director of the corporation has a direct or indirect interest. A conflict of interest transaction is not voidable by the corporation solely because of the director's interest in the transaction if any one of the following is true:

(1)   The material facts of the transaction and the director's interest were disclosed or known to the board of directors or a committee of the board and the board or committee authorized, approved, or ratified the transaction;

(2)   The material facts of the transaction and the director's interest were disclosed or known to the members entitled to vote and they authorized, approved, or ratified the transaction; or

(3)   The transaction was fair to the corporation.

(b)   For purposes of this section, a director of the corporation has an indirect interest in a transaction if:

(1)   Another entity in which he has a material financial interest or in which he is a general partner is a party to the transaction; or

(2)   Another entity of which he is a director, officer, or trustee is a party to the transaction and the transaction is or should be considered by the board of directors of the corporation.

(c)   For purposes of subdivision (a)(1) of this section, a conflict of interest transaction is authorized, approved, or ratified if it receives the affirmative vote of a majority of the directors on the board of directors (or on the committee) who have no direct or indirect interest in the transaction, but a transaction shall not be authorized, approved, or ratified under this section by a single director. If a majority of the directors who have no direct or indirect interest in the transaction vote to authorize, approve, or ratify the transaction, a quorum is present for the purpose of taking action under this section. The presence of, or a vote cast by, a director with a direct or indirect interest in the transaction does not affect the validity of any action taken under subdivision (a)(1) of this section if the transaction is otherwise authorized, approved, or ratified as provided in that subdivision.

72

(d)   For purposes of subdivision (a)(2) of this section, a conflict of interest transaction is authorized, approved, or ratified by the members if it receives a majority of the votes entitled to be counted under this subsection. Votes cast by or voted under the control of a director who has a direct or indirect interest in the transaction, and votes cast by or voted under the control of an entity described in subdivision (b)(1) of this section, shall not be counted in a vote of members to determine whether to authorize, approve, or ratify a conflict of interest transaction under subdivision (a)(2) of this section. The vote of these members, however, is counted in determining whether the transaction is approved under other sections of this Chapter. A majority of the votes, whether or not present, that are entitled to be cast in a vote on the transaction under this subsection constitutes a quorum for the purpose of taking action under this section.

(e)   The articles of incorporation, bylaws, or a resolution of the board may impose additional requirements on conflict of interest transactions. (1985 (Reg. Sess., 1986), c. 801, s. 26; 1993, c. 398, s. 1.)

§ 55A-8-32. Loans to or guaranties for directors and officers.

No loan, guaranty, or other form of security shall be made or provided by a corporation to or for the benefit of its directors or officers, except that loans, guaranties, or other forms of security may be made to full-time employees of the corporation who are also directors or officers by action of its board of directors in accordance with G.S. 55A-8-31(a)(1). (1955, c. 1230; 1985 (Reg. Sess., 1986), c. 801, s. 17; 1993, c. 398, s. 1.)

§ 55A-8-33. Liability for unlawful loans or distributions.

(a)   The liabilities imposed by this section are in addition to any other liabilities imposed by law upon directors of a corporation.

(b)   A director who votes for or assents to the making of a loan or guaranty or other form of security is personally liable to the corporation for the repayment or return of the money or value loaned, with interest thereon at the legal rate until paid, or for any liability of the corporation upon the guaranty, if it is established that he did not perform his duties in compliance with G.S. 55A-8-30 or that the loan or guaranty was made in violation of G.S. 55A-8-32.

73

(c)   A director who votes for or assents to a distribution made in violation of Article 13 of this Chapter, Article 14 of this Chapter, or the articles of incorporation is personally liable to the corporation for the amount of the distribution that exceeds what could have been distributed without violating Article 13 of this Chapter, Article 14 of this Chapter, or the articles of incorporation if it is established that he did not perform his duties in compliance with G.S. 55A-8-30. In any proceeding commenced under this section, a director has all of the defenses ordinarily available to a director.

(d)   A director held liable under subsection (b) or (c) of this section is entitled to:

(1)   Contribution from every other director who could be held liable under subsection (b) or (c) of this section for the unlawful loan or distribution; and

(2)   Reimbursement from each person for the amount he accepted knowing the unlawful loan or distribution was made in violation of G.S. 55A-8-32, Article 13 of this Chapter, or Article 14 of this Chapter, or the articles of incorporation.

(e)   No action shall be brought against the directors for liability under this section after three years from the time when the cause of action was discovered or ought to have been discovered. (1985 (Reg. Sess., 1986), c. 801, s. 33; 1993, c. 398, s. 1.)

§§ 55A-8-34 through 55A-8-39. Reserved for future codification purposes.

Part 4. Officers.

§ 55A-8-40. Officers.

(a)   A corporation has the officers described in its bylaws or appointed by the board of directors in accordance with the bylaws.

(b)   A duly appointed officer may appoint one or more officers or assistant officers if authorized by the bylaws or the board of directors.

(c)   The secretary or any assistant secretary or any one or more other officers designated by the bylaws or the board of directors shall have the responsibility and authority to maintain and authenticate the records of the corporation.

(d)   The same individual may simultaneously hold more than one office in a corporation, but no individual may act in more than one capacity where action of two or more officers is required.

(e)   Whenever a specific office is referred to in this Chapter, it shall be deemed to include any person who, individually or collectively with one or more other persons, holds or occupies such office. (1955, c. 1230; 1985 (Reg. Sess., 1986), c. 801, s. 28; 1993, c. 398, s. 1.)

§ 55A-8-41. Duties of officers.

Each officer has the authority and duties set forth in the bylaws or, to the extent consistent with the bylaws, the authority and duties prescribed by the board of directors or by direction of an officer authorized by the board of directors to prescribe the authority and duties of other officers. (1955, c. 1230; 1985 (Reg. Sess., 1986), c. 801, s. 28; 1993, c. 398, s. 1.)

§ 55A-8-42. Standards of conduct for officers.

(a)   An officer with discretionary authority shall discharge his duties under that authority:

(1)   In good faith;

(2)   With the care an ordinarily prudent person in a like position would exercise under similar circumstances; and

(3)   In a manner the officer reasonably believes to be in the best interests of the corporation.

(b)   In discharging his duties, an officer is entitled to rely on information, opinions, reports, or statements, including financial statements and other financial data, if prepared or presented by:

(1)   One or more officers or employees of the corporation whom the officer reasonably believes to be reliable and competent in the matters presented; or

(2)   Legal counsel, public accountants, or other persons as to matters the officer reasonably believes are within the person's professional or expert competence.

(c)   An officer is not entitled to the benefit of subsection (b) of this section if the officer has actual knowledge concerning the matter in question that makes reliance otherwise permitted by subsection (b) of this section unwarranted.

(d)   An officer is not liable for any action taken as an officer, or any failure to take any action, if the officer performed the duties of his office in compliance with this section.

(e)   An officer may be entitled to immunity under Part 6 of Article 8 of this Chapter or to indemnification against liability and expenses pursuant to Part 5 of Article 8 of this Chapter. (1985 (Reg. Sess., 1986), c. 801, s. 29; 1993, c. 398, s. 1.)

§ 55A-8-43. Resignation and removal of officers.

(a)   An officer may resign at any time by communicating his resignation to the corporation. A resignation is effective when it is communicated unless it specifies in writing a later effective date. If a resignation is made effective at a later date and the corporation accepts the future effective date, its board of directors may fill the pending vacancy before the effective date if the board of directors provides that the successor does not take office until the effective date.

(b)   A board of directors may remove any officer at any time with or without cause. (1955, c. 1230; 1993, c. 398, s. 1.)

§ 55A-8-44. Contract rights of officers.

76

(a)   The appointment of an officer does not itself create contract rights.

(b)   An officer's removal does not affect the officer's contract rights, if any, with the corporation. An officer's resignation does not affect the corporation's contract rights, if any, with the officer. (1955, c. 1230; 1993, c. 398, s. 1.)

§§ 55A-8-45 through 55A-8-49. Reserved for future codification purposes.

Part 5. Indemnification.

§ 55A-8-50. Policy statement and definitions.

(a)   It is the public policy of this State to enable corporations organized under this Chapter to attract and maintain responsible, qualified directors, officers, employees, and agents, and, to that end, to permit corporations organized under this Chapter to allocate the risk of personal liability of directors, officers, employees, and agents through indemnification and insurance as authorized in this Part.

(b)   Definitions in this Part:

(1)   "Corporation" includes any domestic or foreign corporation absorbed in a merger which, if its separate existence had continued, would have had the obligation or power to indemnify its directors, officers, employees, or agents, so that a person who would have been entitled to receive or request indemnification from such corporation if its separate existence had continued shall stand in the same position under this Part with respect to the surviving corporation.

(2)   "Director" means an individual who is or was a director of a corporation or an individual who, while a director of a corporation, is or was serving at the corporation's request as a director, officer, partner, trustee, employee, or agent of another foreign or domestic business or nonprofit corporation, partnership, joint venture, trust, employee benefit plan, or other enterprise. A director is considered to be serving an employee benefit plan at the corporation's request if the director's duties to the corporation also impose duties on, or otherwise

77

involve services by, the director to the plan or to participants in or beneficiaries of the plan. "Director" includes, unless the context requires otherwise, the estate or personal representative of a director.

(3)   "Expenses" means expenses of every kind incurred in defending a proceeding, including counsel fees.

(4)   "Liability" means the obligation to pay a judgment, settlement, penalty, fine (including an excise tax assessed with respect to an employee benefit plan), or reasonable expenses actually incurred with respect to a proceeding.

(5)   "Officer," "employee," or "agent" includes, unless the context requires otherwise, the estate or personal representative of a person who acted in that capacity.

(6)   "Official capacity" means: (i) when used with respect to a director, the office of director in a corporation; and (ii) when used with respect to an individual other than a director, as contemplated in G.S. 55A-8-56, the office in a corporation held by the officer or the employment or agency relationship undertaken by the employee or agent on behalf of the corporation. "Official capacity" does not include service for any other foreign or domestic business or nonprofit corporation or any partnership, joint venture, trust, employee benefit plan, or other enterprise.

(7)   "Party" includes an individual who was, is, or is threatened to be made a named defendant or respondent in a proceeding.

(8)   "Proceeding" means any threatened, pending, or completed action, suit, or proceeding whether civil, criminal, administrative, or investigative and whether formal or informal. (1993, c. 398, s. 1.)

§ 55A-8-51. Authority to indemnify.

(a)   Except as provided in subsection (d) of this section, a corporation may indemnify an individual made a party to a proceeding because the individual is or was a director against liability incurred in the proceeding if the individual:

(1)   Conducted himself in good faith;

(2)   Reasonably believed (i) in the case of conduct in his official capacity with the corporation, that his conduct was in its best interests; and (ii) in all other cases, that his conduct was at least not opposed to its best interests; and

(3)   In the case of any criminal proceeding, had no reasonable cause to believe his conduct was unlawful.

(b)   A director's conduct with respect to an employee benefit plan for a purpose the director reasonably believed to be in the interests of the participants in and beneficiaries of the plan is conduct that satisfies the requirement of clause (ii) of subdivision (a)(2) of this section.

(c)   The termination of a proceeding by judgment, order, settlement, conviction, or upon a plea of no contest or its equivalent is not, of itself, determinative that the director did not meet the standard of conduct described in this section.

(d)   A corporation shall not indemnify a director under this section:

(1)   In connection with a proceeding by or in the right of the corporation in which the director was adjudged liable to the corporation; or

(2)   In connection with any other proceeding charging improper personal benefit to the director, whether or not involving action in his official capacity, in which the director was adjudged liable on the basis that personal benefit was improperly received by the director.

(e)   Indemnification permitted under this section in connection with a proceeding by or in the right of the corporation that is concluded without a final adjudication on the issue of liability is limited to reasonable expenses incurred in connection with the proceeding.

(f)   The authorization, approval, or favorable recommendation by the board of directors of a corporation of indemnification, as permitted by this section, shall not be deemed an act or corporate transaction in which a director has a conflict of interest, and no such indemnification shall be void or voidable on such ground. (1977, c. 236, s. 2; 1985 (Reg. Sess., 1986), c. 801, ss. 15, 16; 1993, c. 398, s. 1.)

§ 55A-8-52. Mandatory indemnification.

Unless limited by its articles of incorporation, a corporation shall indemnify a director who was wholly successful, on the merits or otherwise, in the defense of any proceedings to which the director was a party because he is or was a director of the corporation against reasonable expenses actually incurred by the director in connection with the proceeding. (1977, c. 236, s. 2; 1993, c. 398, s. 1.)

§ 55A-8-53. Advance for expenses.

Expenses incurred by a director in defending a proceeding may be paid by the corporation in advance of the final disposition of such proceeding as authorized by the board of directors in the specific case or as authorized or required under any provision in the articles of incorporation or bylaws or by any applicable resolution or contract upon receipt of an undertaking by or on behalf of the director to repay such amount unless it shall ultimately be determined that the director is entitled to be indemnified by the corporation against such expenses. (1977, c. 236, s. 2; 1985 (Reg. Sess., 1986), c. 801, ss. 15, 16; 1993, c. 398, s. 1.)

§ 55A-8-54. Court-ordered indemnification.

Unless a corporation's articles of incorporation provide otherwise, a director of the corporation who is a party to a proceeding may apply for indemnification to the court conducting the proceeding or to another court of competent jurisdiction. On receipt of an application, the court, after giving any notice the court considers necessary, may order indemnification if it determines:

(1)   The director is entitled to mandatory indemnification under G.S. 55A-8-52, in which case the court shall also order the corporation to pay the director's reasonable expenses incurred to obtain court-ordered indemnification; or

(2)   The director is fairly and reasonably entitled to indemnification, in whole or in part, in view of all the relevant circumstances, whether or not the director met the standard of conduct set forth in G.S. 55A-8-51 or was adjudged liable as described in G.S. 55A-8-51(d), but if the director was adjudged so liable,

80

such indemnification is limited to reasonable expenses incurred. (1977, c. 236, s. 2; 1993, c. 398, s. 1.)

§ 55A-8-55. Determination and authorization of indemnification.

(a)   A corporation shall not indemnify a director under G.S. 55A-8-51 unless authorized in the specific case after a determination has been made that indemnification of the director is permissible in the circumstances because the director has met the standard of conduct set forth in G.S. 55A-8-51.

(b)   The determination shall be made:

(1)   By the board of directors by majority vote of a quorum consisting of directors not at the time parties to the proceeding;

(2)   If a quorum cannot be obtained under subdivision (1) of this subsection, by a majority vote of a committee duly designated by the board of directors (in which designation directors who are parties may participate), consisting solely of two or more directors not at the time parties to the proceeding;

(3)   By special legal counsel (i) selected by the board of directors or its committee in the manner prescribed in subdivision (1) or (2) of this subsection; or (ii) if a quorum of the board cannot be obtained under subdivision (1) of this subsection and a committee cannot be designated under subdivision (2) of this subsection, selected by majority vote of the full board (in which selection directors who are parties may participate); or

(4)   By the members, but directors who are at the time parties to the proceeding shall not vote on the determination.

(c)   Authorization of indemnification and evaluation as to reasonableness of expenses shall be made in the same manner as the determination that indemnification is permissible, except that if the determination is made by special legal counsel, authorization of indemnification and evaluation as to reasonableness of expenses shall be made by those entitled under subdivision (b)(3) of this section to select counsel. (1977, c. 236, s. 2; 1993, c. 398, s. 1.)

81

§ 55A-8-56. Indemnification of officers, employees, and agents.

Unless a corporation's articles of incorporation provide otherwise:

(1)   An officer of the corporation is entitled to mandatory indemnification under G.S. 55A-8-52, and is entitled to apply for court-ordered indemnification under G.S. 55A-8-54, in each case to the same extent as a director;

(2)   The corporation may indemnify and advance expenses under this Part to an officer, employee, or agent of the corporation to the same extent as to a director; and

(3)   A corporation may also indemnify and advance expenses to an officer, employee, or agent to the extent, consistent with public policy, that may be provided by its articles of incorporation, bylaws, general or specific action of its board of directors, or contract. (1977, c. 236, s. 2; 1993, c. 398, s. 1.)

§ 55A-8-57. Additional indemnification and insurance.

(a)   In addition to and separate and apart from the indemnification provided for in G.S. 55A-8-51, 55A-8-52, 55A-8-54, 55A-8-55, and 55A-8-56, a corporation may in its articles of incorporation or bylaws or by contract or resolution indemnify or agree to indemnify any one or more of its directors, officers, employees, or agents against liability and expenses in any proceeding (including without limitation a proceeding brought by or on behalf of the corporation itself) arising out of their status as such or their activities in any of the foregoing capacities; provided, however, that a corporation shall not indemnify or agree to indemnify a person against liability or expenses the person may incur on account of his activities which were at the time taken, known, or believed by the person to be clearly in conflict with the best interests of the corporation or if the person received an improper personal benefit. A corporation may likewise and to the same extent indemnify or agree to indemnify any person who, at the request of the corporation, is or was serving as a director, officer, partner, trustee, employee, or agent of another foreign or domestic corporation, partnership, joint venture, trust, or other enterprise or as a trustee or administrator under an employee benefit plan. Any provision in any articles of incorporation, bylaw, contract, or resolution permitted under this section may include provisions for recovery from the corporation of reasonable costs, expenses, and attorneys' fees in connection with the enforcement of rights to indemnification granted therein and may further include provisions establishing reasonable procedures for determining and enforcing the rights granted therein.

(b)   A corporation may purchase and maintain insurance on behalf of an individual who is or was a director, officer, employee, or agent of the corporation, or who, while a director, officer, employee, or agent of the corporation, is or was serving at the request of the corporation as a director, officer, partner, trustee, employee, or agent of another foreign or domestic corporation, partnership, joint venture, trust, employee benefit plan, or other enterprise, against liability asserted against or incurred by him in that capacity or arising from his status as a director, officer, employee, or agent, whether or not the corporation would have power to indemnify him against the same liability under any provision of this Chapter. (1977, c. 236, s. 2; 1985 (Reg. Sess., 1986), c. 801, ss. 15, 16; 1993, c. 398, s. 1.)

§ 55A-8-58. Application of Part.

(a)   If articles of incorporation limit indemnification or advance for expenses, indemnification and advance for expenses are valid only to the extent consistent with the articles of incorporation.

(b)   This Part does not limit a corporation's power to pay or reimburse expenses incurred by a director in connection with appearing as a witness in a proceeding at a time when the director has not been made a named defendant or respondent to the proceeding. (1993, c. 398, s. 1.)

§ 55A-8-59. Reserved for future codification purposes.

Part 6. Immunity.

§ 55A-8-60. Immunity.

(a)   In addition to the immunity that is authorized in G.S. 55A-2-02(b)(4), a person serving as a director or officer of a nonprofit corporation shall be immune

83

individually from civil liability for monetary damages, except to the extent covered by insurance, for any act or failure to act arising out of this service, except where the person:

(1)   Is compensated for his services beyond reimbursement for expenses;

(2)   Was not acting within the scope of his official duties;

(3)   Was not acting in good faith;

(4)   Committed gross negligence or willful or wanton misconduct that resulted in the damage or injury;

(5)   Derived an improper personal financial benefit from the transaction;

(6)   Incurred the liability from the operation of a motor vehicle; or

(7)   Is a defendant in an action brought under G.S. 55A-8-33.

The immunity in this subsection may be limited or eliminated by a provision in the articles of incorporation, but only with respect to acts or omissions occurring on or after the effective date of such provision.

(b)   The immunity in subsection (a) of this section is personal to the directors and officers, and does not immunize the corporation against liability for the acts or omissions of the directors or officers.

(c)   Without diminishing the applicability of any other provisions of this Chapter, "nonprofit corporation" as referred to in this section shall include any credit union chartered under the laws of this State, the laws of any other state, or under the laws of the United States. (1987, c. 799, s. 3; 1989, c. 472; 1993, c. 398, s. 1.)

Article 10.

Amendment of Articles of Incorporation and Bylaws.

Part 1. Amendment of Articles of Incorporation.

§ 55A-10-01. Authority to amend.

(a)   A corporation may amend its articles of incorporation at any time to add or change a provision that is required or permitted in the articles of incorporation or to delete a provision not required in the articles of incorporation. Whether a provision is required or permitted in the articles of incorporation is determined as of the effective date of the amendment.

(b)   A member of the corporation does not have a vested property right resulting from any provision in the articles of incorporation, including provisions relating to management, control, distribution entitlement, or purpose or duration of the corporation. (1955, c. 1230; 1993, c. 398, s. 1.)

§ 55A-10-02. Amendment by board of directors.

(a)   Unless the articles of incorporation provide otherwise, a corporation's board of directors may adopt one or more amendments to the corporation's articles of incorporation without member approval:

(1)   To delete the names and addresses of the initial directors;

(2)   To delete the name and address of the initial registered agent or registered office, if a statement of change is on file with the Secretary of State;

(3)   To change the corporate name by substituting the word "corporation", "incorporated", "company", "limited", or the abbreviation "corp.", "inc.", "co.", or "ltd.", for a similar word or abbreviation in the name, or by adding, deleting or changing a geographical attribution to the name; or

(4)   To make any other change expressly permitted by this Chapter to be made by director action.

(b)   If a corporation has no members entitled to vote thereon, its incorporators, until directors have been chosen, and thereafter its board of directors, may adopt one or more amendments to the corporation's articles of incorporation subject to any approval required pursuant to G.S. 55A-10-30. The corporation shall provide at least five days' written notice of any meeting at which an amendment is to be voted upon. The notice shall state that the purpose, or one of the purposes, of the meeting is to consider a proposed

85

amendment to the articles of incorporation and contain or be accompanied by a copy or summary of the amendment or state the general nature of the amendment. The amendment shall be approved by a majority of the directors in office at the time the amendment is adopted. (1955, c. 1230; 1981, c. 372; 1985 (Reg. Sess., 1986), c. 801, ss. 36, 37; 1993, c. 398, s. 1.)

§ 55A-10-03. Amendment by directors and members.

(a)   If the corporation has members entitled to vote thereon, then, unless this Chapter, the articles of incorporation, bylaws, the members (acting pursuant to subsection (b) of this section), or the board of directors (acting pursuant to subsection (c) of this section) require a greater vote or voting by class, an amendment to a corporation's articles of incorporation to be adopted shall be approved:

(1)   By the board or in lieu thereof in writing by the number or proportion of members entitled under G.S. 55A-7-02(a)(2) to call a special meeting to consider such amendment;

(2)   By the members entitled to vote thereon by two-thirds of the votes cast or a majority of the votes entitled to be cast on the amendment, whichever is less; and

(3)   In writing by any person or persons whose approval is required by a provision of the articles of incorporation authorized by G.S. 55A-10-30.

(b)   The members entitled to vote thereon may condition the amendment's adoption on receipt of a higher percentage of affirmative votes or on any other basis.

(c)   If the board initiates an amendment to the articles of incorporation or board approval is required by subsection (a) of this section to adopt an amendment to the articles of incorporation, the board may condition the amendment's adoption on receipt of a higher percentage of affirmative votes or any other basis.

(d)   If the board or the members seek to have the amendment approved by the members entitled to vote thereon at a membership meeting, the corporation shall give notice of the membership meeting to those members in accordance with G.S. 55A-7-05. The notice shall state that the purpose, or one of the purposes, of the meeting is to consider the proposed amendment and contain or be accompanied by a copy or summary of the amendment.

(e)   If the board or the members seek to have the amendment approved by the members entitled to vote thereon by written consent or written ballot, the material soliciting the approval shall contain or be accompanied by a copy or summary of the amendment. (1955, c. 1230; 1981, c. 372; 1985 (Reg. Sess., 1986), c. 801, ss. 36, 37; 1993, c. 398, s. 1; 1995, c. 400, s. 4.)

§ 55A-10-04. Class voting by members on amendments.

(a)   The members of a class in a charitable or religious corporation are entitled to vote as a class on a proposed amendment to the articles of incorporation if the amendment would affect the rights of that class as to voting in a manner that is different from the manner in which the amendment would affect another class.

(b)   The members of a class in a corporation other than a charitable or religious corporation are entitled to vote as a class on a proposed amendment to the articles of incorporation if the amendment would:

(1)   Affect the rights, privileges, preferences, restrictions, or conditions of that class as to voting, dissolution, redemption, or transfer of memberships in a manner that is different from the manner in which the amendment would affect another class;

(2)   Affect the rights, privileges, preferences, restrictions, or conditions of that class as to voting, dissolution, redemption, or transfer of memberships by changing the rights, privileges, preferences, restrictions, or conditions of another class;

(3)   Increase or decrease the number of memberships authorized for that class;

(4)   Increase the number of memberships authorized for another class;

(5)   Effect an exchange, reclassification, or termination of the memberships of that class; or

(6)   Authorize a new class of memberships.

(c)   If a class is to be divided into two or more classes as a result of an amendment to the articles of incorporation, the amendment shall be approved by the members of each class that would be created by the amendment.

(d)   If a class vote is required to approve an amendment to the articles of incorporation of a corporation, the amendment shall be approved by the members of the class by two-thirds of the votes cast by the class or a majority of the votes entitled to be cast by the class on the amendment, whichever is less.

(e)   A class of members is entitled to the voting rights granted by this section although the articles of incorporation and bylaws provide that the class shall not vote on the proposed amendment. (1993, c. 398, s. 1.)

§ 55A-10-05. Articles of amendment.

A corporation amending its articles of incorporation shall deliver to the Secretary of State for filing articles of amendment setting forth:

(1)   The name of the corporation;

(2)   The text of each amendment adopted;

(3)   The date of each amendment's adoption;

(4)   If approval of members was not required, a statement to that effect and a brief explanation of why member action was not required, and a statement that the amendment was approved by a sufficient vote of the board of directors or incorporators;

(5)   If approval by members was required, a statement that member approval was obtained as required by this Chapter;

(6)   If approval of the amendment by some person or persons other than the members, the board, or the incorporators is required pursuant to G.S. 55A-10-30, a statement that the approval was obtained. (1955, c. 1230; 1993, c. 398, s. 1.)

§ 55A-10-06. Restated articles of incorporation.

(a) A corporation's board of directors may restate its articles of incorporation at any time with or without approval by members or any other person.

(b) The restated articles of incorporation may include one or more amendments to the articles of incorporation. If the restated articles of incorporation include an amendment requiring approval by the members or any other person, it shall be adopted as provided in G.S. 55A-10-03.

(c) If the board of directors submits restated articles of incorporation for member action, the corporation shall notify in writing each member entitled to vote on the proposed amendment of the membership meeting in accordance with G.S. 55A-7-05. The notice shall (i) state that the purpose, or one of the purposes, of the meeting is to consider the proposed restated articles of incorporation, (ii) contain or be accompanied by a copy of the proposed restated articles of incorporation, and (iii) identify any amendment or other change they would make in the articles of incorporation.

(d) If the restated articles of incorporation include an amendment requiring approval pursuant to G.S. 55A-10-30, the board of directors shall submit the restated articles of incorporation for such approval.

(e) A corporation restating its articles of incorporation shall deliver to the Secretary of State for filing articles of restatement which shall:

(1) Set forth the name of the corporation;

(2) Attach as an exhibit thereto the text of the restated articles of incorporation;

(3) State whether the restated articles of incorporation contain an amendment to the articles of incorporation requiring member approval and, if they do not, that the board of directors adopted the restated articles of incorporation;

(4)   If the restated articles of incorporation contain an amendment to the articles of incorporation requiring member approval, state that member approval was obtained as required by this Chapter; and

(5)   If the restated articles of incorporation contain an amendment to the articles of incorporation requiring approval by a person whose approval is required pursuant to G.S. 55A-10-30, state that such approval was obtained.

(f)   Duly adopted restated articles of incorporation supersede the original articles of incorporation and all amendments to them.

(g)   The Secretary of State may certify restated articles of incorporation, as the articles of incorporation currently in effect, without including the other information required by subsection (e) of this section. (1965, c. 762; 1993, c. 398, s. 1.)

§ 55A-10-07. Effect of amendment.

An amendment to articles of incorporation does not affect a cause of action existing against or in favor of the corporation, a proceeding to which the corporation is a party, any requirement or limitation imposed upon the corporation or any property held by it by virtue of any restriction or condition upon which such property is held by the corporation or the existing rights of persons other than members of the corporation. An amendment changing a corporation's name does not abate a proceeding brought by or against the corporation in its former name. (1955, c. 1230; 1985 (Reg. Sess., 1986), c. 801, s. 38; 1993, c. 398, s. 1.)

§§ 55A-10-08 through 55A-10-19. Reserved for future codification purposes.

Part 2. Bylaws.

§ 55A-10-20. Amendment by directors.

If a corporation has no members entitled to vote thereon, its incorporators, until directors have been chosen, and thereafter its board of directors, may adopt one or more amendments to the corporation's bylaws subject to any approval required pursuant to G.S. 55A-10-30. The corporation shall provide at least five days' written notice of any meeting of directors at which an amendment is to be voted upon. The notice shall state that the purpose, or one of the purposes, of the meeting is to consider a proposed amendment to the bylaws and contain or be accompanied by a copy or summary of the amendment or state the general nature of the amendment. The amendment shall be approved by a majority of the directors in office at the time the amendment is adopted. (1955, c. 1230; 1993, c. 398, s. 1.)

§ 55A-10-21. Amendment by directors and members.

(a)   If the corporation has members entitled to vote thereon, then, unless this Chapter, the articles of incorporation, bylaws, the members (acting pursuant to subsection (b) of this section), or the board of directors (acting pursuant to subsection (c) of this section) require a greater vote or voting by class, an amendment to a corporation's bylaws to be adopted shall be approved:

(1)   By the board or in lieu thereof in writing by the number or proportion of members entitled under G.S. 55A-7-02(a)(2) to call a special meeting to consider such amendment;

(2)   By the members entitled to vote thereon by two-thirds of the votes cast or a majority of the votes entitled to be cast on the amendment, whichever is less; and

(3)   In writing by any person or persons whose approval is required by a provision of the articles of incorporation authorized by G.S. 55A-10-30.

(b)   The members entitled to vote thereon may condition the amendment's adoption on its receipt of a higher percentage of affirmative votes or on any other basis.

(c)   If the board initiates an amendment to the bylaws or board approval is required by subsection (a) of this section to adopt an amendment to the bylaws, the board may condition the amendment's adoption on receipt of a higher percentage of affirmative votes or on any other basis.

(d)   If the board or the members seek to have the amendment approved by the members entitled to vote thereon at a membership meeting, the corporation shall give notice of the membership meeting to those members in accordance with G.S. 55A-7-05. The notice shall state that the purpose, or one of the purposes, of the meeting is to consider the proposed amendment and contain or be accompanied by a copy or summary of the amendment.

(e)   If the board or the members seek to have the amendment approved by the members entitled to vote thereon by written consent or written ballot, the material soliciting the approval shall contain or be accompanied by a copy or summary of the amendment. (1955, c. 1230; 1993, c. 398, s. 1; 2002-27, s. 1.)

§ 55A-10-22. Class voting by members on amendments.

(a)   The members of a class in a charitable or religious corporation are entitled to vote as a class on a proposed amendment to the bylaws if the amendment would affect the rights of that class as to voting in a manner that is different from the manner in which such amendment would affect another class.

(b)   The members of a class in a corporation other than a charitable or religious corporation are entitled to vote as a class on a proposed amendment to the bylaws if the amendment would:

(1)   Affect the rights, privileges, preferences, restrictions, or conditions of that class as to voting, dissolution, redemption, or transfer of memberships in a manner that is different from the manner in which such amendment would affect another class;

(2)   Affect the rights, privileges, preferences, restrictions, or conditions of that class as to voting, dissolution, redemption, or transfer of memberships by changing the rights, privileges, preferences, restrictions, or conditions of another class;

(3)   Increase or decrease the number of memberships authorized for that class;

(4)   Increase the number of memberships authorized for another class;

92

(5)   Effect an exchange, reclassification, or termination of all or part of the memberships of that class; or

(6)   Authorize a new class of memberships.

(c)   If a class is to be divided into two or more classes as a result of an amendment to the bylaws, the amendment shall be approved by the members of each class that would be created by the amendment.

(d)   If a class vote is required to approve an amendment to the bylaws, the amendment shall be approved by the members of the class by two-thirds of the votes cast by the class or a majority of the votes entitled to be cast by the class on the amendment, whichever is less.

(e)   A class of members is entitled to the voting rights granted by this section although the articles of incorporation and bylaws provide that the class shall not vote on the proposed amendment. (1993, c. 398, s. 1.)

§§ 55A-10-23 through 55A-10-29. Reserved for future codification purposes.

Part 3. Articles of Incorporation and Bylaws.

§ 55A-10-30. Approval by third persons.

The articles of incorporation or bylaws may require an amendment to the articles of incorporation or bylaws to be approved in writing by a specified person or persons other than the board of directors. Such a provision in the articles of incorporation or bylaws may only be amended with the approval in writing of such person or persons. (1993, c. 398, s. 1; 1995, c. 509, s. 30.)

Article 11.

Merger.

§ 55A-11-01. Approval of plan of merger.

(a)   Subject to the limitations set forth in G.S. 55A-11-02, one or more nonprofit corporations may merge into another nonprofit corporation, if the plan of merger is approved as provided in G.S. 55A-11-03.

(b)   The plan of merger shall set forth:

(1)   The name of each corporation planning to merge and the name of the surviving corporation into which each other corporation plans to merge;

(2)   The terms and conditions of the merger; and

(3)   The manner and basis, if any, of converting memberships of each merging corporation into memberships, obligations, or securities of the surviving or any other corporation or into cash or other property in whole or part.

(c)   The plan of merger may set forth:

(1)   Any amendments to the articles of incorporation or bylaws of the surviving corporation to be effected by the merger; and

(2)   Other provisions relating to the merger.

(d)   The provisions of the plan of merger, other than the provisions referred to in subdivisions (b)(1) and (c)(1) of this section, may be made dependent on facts objectively ascertainable outside the plan of merger if the plan of merger sets forth the manner in which the facts will operate upon the affected provisions. The facts may include any of the following:

(1)   Statistical or market indices, market prices of any security or group of securities, interest rates, currency exchange rates, or similar economic or financial data.

(2)   A determination or action by the corporation or by any other person, group, or body.

(3)   The terms of, or actions taken under, an agreement to which the corporation is a party, or any other agreement or document. (1955, c. 1230; 1993, c. 398, s. 1; 1995, c. 400, s. 5; 2005-268, s. 38.)

§ 55A-11-02. Limitations on mergers by charitable or religious corporations.

(a)   Without the prior approval of the superior court in a proceeding in which the Attorney General has been given written notice, a charitable or religious corporation may merge only with any of the following:

(1)   A charitable or religious corporation.

(2)   A foreign corporation that would qualify under this Chapter as a charitable or religious corporation.

(3)   A wholly owned foreign or domestic corporation (business or nonprofit) which is not a charitable or religious corporation, or an unincorporated entity, provided the charitable or religious corporation is the survivor in the merger and continues to be a charitable or religious corporation after the merger.

(4)   A business or nonprofit corporation (foreign or domestic) other than a charitable or religious corporation, or an unincorporated entity, provided that: (i) on or prior to the effective date of the merger, assets with a value equal to the greater of the fair market value of the net tangible and intangible assets (including goodwill) of the charitable or religious corporation or the fair market value of the charitable or religious corporation if it were to be operated as a business concern are transferred or conveyed to one or more persons who would have received its assets under G.S. 55A-14-03(a)(1) and (2) had it dissolved; (ii) it shall return, transfer or convey any assets held by it upon condition requiring return, transfer or conveyance, which condition occurs by reason of the merger, in accordance with such condition; and (iii) the merger is approved by a majority of directors of the charitable or religious corporation who are not and will not become members, as "member" is defined in G.S. 55A-1-40(16) or G.S. 57D-1-03, partners, limited partners, or shareholders in or directors, managers, officers, employees, agents, or consultants of the survivor in the merger.

(b)   At least 30 days before consummation of any merger of a charitable or religious corporation pursuant to subdivision (a)(4) of this section, notice, including a copy of the proposed plan of merger, shall be delivered to the Attorney General. This notice shall include all the information the Attorney General determines is required for a complete review of the proposed

95

transaction. The Attorney General may require an additional 30-day period to review the proposed transaction by providing written notice to the charitable or religious corporation prior to the expiration of the initial notice period. During this 30-day period, the transaction may not be finalized.

(c)   Without the prior written consent of the Attorney General, or approval of the superior court in a proceeding in which the Attorney General has been given notice, no member of a charitable or religious corporation may receive or retain any property as a result of a merger other than an interest as a member, as "member" is defined in G.S. 55A-1-40(16), in the survivor of the merger. The Attorney General may consent to the transaction, or the court shall approve the transaction, if it is fair and not contrary to the public interest. (1993, c. 398, s. 1; c. 553, s. 83(a); 1995, c. 400, s. 6; 1999-204, s. 1; 1999-369, s. 2.4; 2013-157, s. 5.)

§ 55A-11-03. Action on plan.

(a)   Unless this Chapter, the articles of incorporation, bylaws, or the board of directors or members (acting pursuant to subsection (c) of this section) require a greater vote or voting by class, a plan of merger to be adopted shall be approved for each constituent corporation:

(1)   By the board;

(2)   By the members entitled to vote thereon, if any, by two-thirds of the votes cast or a majority of the votes entitled to be cast on the plan of merger, whichever is less; and

(3)   In writing by any person or persons whose approval is required by a provision of the articles of incorporation authorized by G.S. 55A-10-30 for an amendment to the articles of incorporation or bylaws.

(b)   If the corporation does not have members entitled to vote thereon, the merger shall be approved by a majority of the directors then in office. The corporation shall provide at least five days' written notice of any directors' meeting at which the approval will be considered. The notice shall state that the purpose, or one of the purposes, of the meeting is to consider the proposed merger.

(c)   The board may condition its approval of the proposed merger, and the members entitled to vote thereon may condition their approval of the merger, on receipt of a higher percentage of affirmative votes or on any other basis.

(d)   If the board seeks to have the plan approved by the members entitled to vote thereon at a membership meeting, the corporation shall give notice of the membership meeting to those members in accordance with G.S. 55A-7-05. The notice shall state that the purpose, or one of the purposes, of the meeting is to consider the plan of merger and contain or be accompanied by a copy or summary of the plan. The copy or summary of the plan for members of the surviving corporation shall include any provision that, if contained in a proposed amendment to the articles of incorporation or bylaws, would entitle members to vote on the provision. The copy or summary of the plan for members of the disappearing corporation shall include a copy or summary of the articles of incorporation and bylaws that will be in effect immediately after the merger takes effect.

(e)   If the board seeks to have the plan approved by the members entitled to vote thereon by written consent or written ballot, the material soliciting the approval shall contain or be accompanied by a copy or summary of the plan. The copy or summary of the plan for members of the surviving corporation shall include any provision that, if contained in a proposed amendment to the articles of incorporation or bylaws, would entitle members to vote on the provision. The copy or summary of the plan for members of the disappearing corporation shall include a copy or summary of the articles of incorporation and bylaws that will be in effect immediately after the merger takes effect.

(f)   Voting by a class of members is required on a plan of merger if the plan contains a provision that, if contained in a proposed amendment to articles of incorporation or bylaws, would entitle the class of members to vote as a class on the proposed amendment under G.S. 55A-10-04 or G.S. 55A-10-22. The plan is approved by a class of members by two-thirds of the votes cast by the class or a majority of the votes entitled to be cast by the class, whichever is less.

(g)   After a merger is adopted but before the articles of merger become effective, the plan of merger (i) may be amended as provided in the plan of merger, or (ii) may be abandoned, subject to any contractual rights, as provided in the plan of merger, or, if there is no such provision, as determined by the board of directors without further action by the members or other persons who approved the plan of merger. (1955, c. 1230; 1993, c. 398, s. 1; 2005-268, s. 39.)

§ 55A-11-04. Articles of merger.

(a)   After a plan of merger has been authorized as required by this Chapter, the surviving corporation shall deliver to the Secretary of State for filing articles of merger setting forth:

(1)   The name and state or country of incorporation of each merging corporation.

(2)   The name of the merging corporation that will survive the merger and, if the surviving corporation is not authorized to transact business or conduct affairs in this State, a designation of its mailing address and a commitment to file with the Secretary of State a statement of any subsequent change in its mailing address.

(3)   If the surviving corporation is a domestic corporation, any amendment to the articles of incorporation of the corporation provided in the plan of merger.

(4)   A statement that the plan of merger has been approved by each merging corporation in the manner required by law.

(a1)   If the plan of merger is amended after the articles of merger have been filed but before the articles of merger become effective and any statement in the articles of merger becomes incorrect as a result of the amendment, the surviving corporation shall deliver to the Secretary of State for filing prior to the time the articles of merger become effective an amendment to the articles of merger correcting the incorrect statement. If the articles of merger are abandoned after the articles of merger are filed but before the articles of merger become effective, the surviving corporation shall deliver to the Secretary of State for filing prior to the time the articles of merger become effective an amendment reflecting abandonment of the plan of merger.

(b)   A merger takes effect when the articles of merger become effective.

(c)   Certificates of merger shall also be registered as provided in G.S. 47-18.1.

(d)   In the case of a merger pursuant to G.S. 55A-11-06 or G.S. 55A-11-08, references in subsections (a) and (a1) of this section to "corporation" shall include a domestic corporation, a foreign nonprofit corporation, a domestic business corporation, and a foreign business corporation as applicable. (1955, c. 1230; 1967, c. 823, s. 22; 1993, c. 398, s. 1; 2005-268, s. 40; 2006-264, s. 44(d).)

§ 55A-11-05. Effect of merger.

(a)   When a merger pursuant to G.S. 55A-11-01, 55A-11-06, or 55A-11-08 takes effect:

(1)   Each other merging corporation merges into the surviving corporation and the separate existence of each merging corporation except the surviving corporation ceases.

(2)   The title to all real estate and other property owned by each merging corporation is vested in the surviving corporation without reversion or impairment subject to any and all conditions to which the property was subject prior to the merger.

(3)   The surviving corporation has all liabilities and obligations of each merging corporation.

(4)   A proceeding pending by or against any merging corporation may be continued as if the merger did not occur or the surviving corporation may be substituted in the proceeding for a merging corporation whose separate existence ceases in the merger.

(5)   If a domestic corporation survives the merger, its articles of incorporation are amended to the extent provided in the articles of merger.

(6)   If a foreign corporation or a foreign business corporation survives the merger, it is deemed:

a.   To agree that it may be served with process in this State in any proceeding for enforcement (i) of any obligation of any merging domestic

99

corporation and (ii) of any obligation of the surviving foreign corporation or foreign business corporation arising from the merger.

b.   To have appointed the Secretary of State as its agent for service of process in any proceeding for enforcement as specified in sub-subdivision a. of this subdivision. Service of process on the Secretary of State shall be made by delivering to, and leaving with, the Secretary of State, or with any clerk authorized by the Secretary of State to accept service of process, duplicate copies of the process and the fee required by G.S. 55A-1-22(b). Upon receipt of service of process on behalf of a surviving foreign corporation or foreign business corporation in the manner provided for in this section, the Secretary of State shall immediately mail a copy of the process by registered or certified mail, return receipt requested, to the surviving foreign corporation or foreign business corporation. If the surviving foreign corporation or foreign business corporation is authorized to transact business or conduct affairs in this State, the address for mailing shall be its principal office designated in the latest document filed with the Secretary of State that is authorized by law to designate the principal office, or if there is no principal office on file, its registered office. If the surviving foreign corporation or foreign business corporation is not authorized to transact business or conduct affairs in this State, the address for mailing shall be the mailing address designated pursuant to G.S. 55A-11-04(a)(2).

The merger shall not affect the liability or absence of liability of any member of a merging corporation for acts, omissions, or obligations of any merging corporation made or incurred prior to the effectiveness of the merger.

(b)   In the case of a merger pursuant to G.S. 55A-11-06 or G.S. 55A-11-08, references in subsection (a) of this section to "corporation" shall include a domestic corporation, a foreign nonprofit corporation, a domestic business corporation, and a foreign business corporation, as applicable. (1955, c. 1230; 1967, c. 950, s. 2; 1993, c. 398, s. 1; 1999-369, s. 2.5; 2005-268, s. 41; 2006-264, s. 44(e).)

§ 55A-11-06. Merger with foreign corporation.

(a)   Except as provided in G.S. 55A-11-02, one or more foreign corporations may merge with one or more domestic nonprofit corporations if:

(1)   The merger is permitted by the law of the state or country under whose law each foreign corporation is incorporated and each foreign corporation complies with that law in effecting the merger;

(2)   The foreign corporation complies with G.S. 55A-11-04 if it is the surviving corporation of the merger; and

(3)   Each domestic nonprofit corporation complies with the applicable provisions of G.S. 55A-11-01 through G.S. 55A-11-03 and, if it is the surviving corporation of the merger, with G.S. 55A-11-04.

(b)   Repealed by Session Laws 2005, c. 268, s. 42.

(c)   This section does not limit the power of a foreign corporation to acquire all or part of the memberships of one or more classes of a domestic nonprofit corporation through a voluntary exchange or otherwise. (1973, c. 314, s. 4; 1985 (Reg. Sess., 1986), c. 801, s. 39; 1993, c. 398, s. 1; 1995, c. 400, s. 7; 2001-387, ss. 36, 37; 2005-268, s. 42; 2006-226, s. 16(c); 2006-264, s. 44(f).)

§ 55A-11-07. Devises and gifts.

Any devise, gift, grant, or promise contained in a will or other instrument of donation, subscription, or conveyance, that is made to a constituent corporation and that takes effect or remains payable after the merger, inures to the survivor in the merger unless the will or other instrument otherwise specifically provides. (1993, c. 398, s. 1; 1999-369, s. 2.6; 2011-284, s. 53.)

§ 55A-11-08. Merger with business corporation.

(a)   One or more domestic or foreign business corporations may merge with one or more domestic nonprofit corporations if:

(1)   Each domestic business corporation complies with the applicable provisions of G.S. 55-11-01, 55-11-03, and 55-11-04;

(2)   In a merger involving one or more foreign business corporations, the merger is permitted by the law of the state or country under whose law each

foreign business corporation is incorporated and each foreign business corporation complies with that law in effecting the merger;

(3)   The domestic or foreign business corporation complies with G.S. 55A-11-04 if it is the surviving corporation; and

(4)   Each domestic nonprofit corporation complies with the applicable provisions of G.S. 55A-11-01 through G.S. 55A-11-03 and, if it is the surviving corporation, with G.S. 55A-11-04.

(b)   Repealed by Session Laws 2005, c. 268, s. 43.

(c)   This section does not limit the power of a domestic or foreign business corporation to acquire all or part of the memberships of one or more classes of a domestic nonprofit corporation through a voluntary exchange or otherwise. (1995, c. 400, s. 8; 2001-387, ss. 38, 39; 2005-268, s. 43.)

§ 55A-11-09. Merger with unincorporated entity.

(a)   As used in this section, "business entity" means a domestic business corporation (including a professional corporation as defined in G.S. 55B-2), a foreign business corporation (including a foreign professional corporation as defined in G.S. 55B-16), a domestic or foreign nonprofit corporation, a domestic or foreign limited liability company, a domestic or foreign limited partnership, a registered limited liability partnership or foreign limited liability partnership as defined in G.S. 59-32, or any other partnership as defined in G.S. 59-36 whether or not formed under the laws of this State.

(b)   One or more domestic nonprofit corporations may merge with one or more unincorporated entities and, if desired, one or more foreign nonprofit corporations, domestic business corporations, or foreign business corporations if:

(1)   The merger is permitted by the laws of the state or country governing the organization and internal affairs of each of the other merging business entities;

(2)   Each merging domestic nonprofit corporation and each other merging business entity comply with the requirements of this section and, to the extent applicable, the laws referred to in subdivision (1) of this subsection; and

(3)   The merger complies with G.S. 55A-11-02, if applicable.

(c)   Each merging domestic nonprofit corporation and each other merging business entity shall approve a written plan of merger containing:

(1)   For each merging business entity, its name, type of business entity, and the state or country whose laws govern its organization and internal affairs;

(2)   The name of the merging business entity that shall survive the merger;

(3)   The terms and conditions of the merger;

(4)   The manner and basis for converting the interests in each merging business entity into interests, obligations, or securities of the surviving business entity or into cash or other property in whole or in part; and

(5)   If the surviving business entity is a domestic nonprofit corporation, any amendments to its articles of incorporation that are to be made in connection with the merger.

(c1)   The plan of merger may contain other provisions relating to the merger.

(c2)   The provisions of the plan of merger, other than the provisions referred to in subdivisions (1), (2), and (5) of subsection (c) of this section, may be made dependent on facts objectively ascertainable outside the plan of merger if the plan of merger sets forth the manner in which the facts will operate upon the affected provisions. The facts may include any of the following:

(1)   Statistical or market indices, market prices of any security or group of securities, interest rates, currency exchange rates, or similar economic or financial data.

(2)   A determination or action by the domestic nonprofit corporation or by any other person, group, or body.

(3)   The terms of, or actions taken under, an agreement to which the domestic nonprofit corporation is a party, or any other agreement or document.

103

(c3)   In the case of a merging domestic nonprofit corporation, approval of the plan of merger requires that the plan of merger be adopted as provided in G.S. 55A-11-03. If any member of a merging domestic nonprofit corporation has or will have personal liability for any existing or future obligation of the surviving business entity solely as a result of holding an interest in the surviving business entity, then in addition to the requirements of G.S. 55A-11-03, approval of the plan of merger by the domestic nonprofit corporation shall require the affirmative vote or written consent of the member. In the case of each other merging business entity, the plan of merger must be approved in accordance with the laws of the state or country governing the organization and internal affairs of such merging business entity.

(c4)   After a plan of merger has been approved by a domestic nonprofit corporation but before the articles of merger become effective, the plan of merger (i) may be amended as provided in the plan of merger, or (ii) may be abandoned (subject to any contractual rights) as provided in the plan of merger or, if there is no such provision, as determined by the board of directors.

(d)   After a plan of merger has been approved by each merging domestic nonprofit corporation and each other merging business entity as provided in subsection (c) of this section, the surviving business entity shall deliver articles of merger to the Secretary of State for filing. The articles of merger shall set forth:

(1)   Repealed by Session Laws 2005-268, s. 45.

(2)   For each merging business entity, its name, type of business entity, and the state or country whose laws govern its organization and internal affairs.

(3)   The name of the merging business entity that will survive the merger and, if the surviving business entity is not authorized to transact business or conduct affairs in this State, a designation of its mailing address and a commitment to file with the Secretary of State a statement of any subsequent change in its mailing address.

(3a)   If the surviving business entity is a domestic corporation, any amendment to its articles of incorporation as provided in the plan of merger.

(4)   A statement that the plan of merger has been approved by each merging business entity in the manner required by law.

104

(5)   Repealed by Session Laws 2005-268, s. 45.

If the plan of merger is amended after the articles of merger have been filed but before the articles of merger become effective, and any statement in the articles of merger becomes incorrect as a result of the amendment, the surviving business entity shall deliver to the Secretary of State for filing prior to the time the articles of merger become effective an amendment to the articles of merger correcting the incorrect statement. If the articles of merger are abandoned after the articles of merger are filed but before the articles of merger become effective, the surviving business entity shall deliver to the Secretary of State for filing prior to the time the articles of merger become effective an amendment reflecting abandonment of the plan of merger.

Certificates of merger shall also be registered as provided in G.S. 47-18.1.

(e)   A merger takes effect when the articles of merger become effective. When a merger takes effect:

(1)   Each other merging business entity merges into the surviving business entity and the separate existence of each merging business entity except the surviving business entity ceases;

(2)   The title to all real estate and other property owned by each merging business entity is vested in the surviving business entity without reversion or impairment;

(3)   The surviving business entity has all liabilities of each merging business entity;

(4)   A proceeding pending by or against any merging business entity may be continued as if the merger did not occur, or the surviving business entity may be substituted in the proceeding for a merging business entity whose separate existence ceases in the merger;

(5)   If a domestic nonprofit corporation is the surviving business entity, its articles of incorporation shall be amended to the extent provided in the articles of merger;

(6)   The interests in each merging business entity that are to be converted into interests, obligations, or securities of the surviving business entity or into

105

the right to receive cash or other property are thereupon so converted, and the former holders of the interests are entitled only to the rights provided to them in the plan of merger or, in the case of former holders of shares in a domestic business corporation, any rights they may have under Article 13 of Chapter 55 of the General Statutes; and

(7)   If the surviving business entity is not a domestic business corporation, the surviving business entity is deemed to agree that it will promptly pay to the shareholders of any merging domestic business corporation exercising appraisal rights the amount, if any, to which they are entitled under Article 13 of Chapter 55 of the General Statutes and otherwise to comply with the requirements of Article 13 as if it were a surviving domestic business corporation in the merger.

The merger shall not affect the liability or absence of liability of any holder of an interest in a merging business entity for any acts, omissions, or obligations of any merging business entity made or incurred prior to the effectiveness of the merger. The cessation of separate existence of a merging business entity in the merger shall not constitute a dissolution or termination of the merging business entity.

(e1)   If the surviving business entity is not a domestic limited liability company, a domestic business corporation, a domestic nonprofit corporation, or a domestic limited partnership, when the merger takes effect the surviving business entity is deemed:

(1)   To agree that it may be served with process in this State in any proceeding for enforcement of (i) any obligation of any merging domestic limited liability company, domestic business corporation, domestic nonprofit corporation, domestic limited partnership, or other partnership as defined in G.S. 59-36 that is formed under the laws of this State, (ii) the appraisal rights of shareholders of any merging domestic business corporation under Article 13 of Chapter 55 of the General Statutes, and (iii) any obligation of the surviving business entity arising from the merger; and

(2)   To have appointed the Secretary of State as its agent for service of process in any such proceeding. Service on the Secretary of State of any such process shall be made by delivering to and leaving with the Secretary of State, or with any clerk authorized by the Secretary of State to accept service of process, duplicate copies of such process and the fee required by G.S. 55A-1-22(b). Upon receipt of service of process on behalf of a surviving business entity

106

in the manner provided for in this section, the Secretary of State shall immediately mail a copy of the process by registered or certified mail, return receipt requested, to the surviving business entity. If the surviving business entity is authorized to transact business or conduct affairs in this State, the address for mailing shall be its principal office designated in the latest document filed with the Secretary of State that is authorized by law to designate the principal office or, if there is no principal office on file, its registered office. If the surviving business entity is not authorized to transact business or conduct affairs in this State, the address for mailing shall be the mailing address designated pursuant to subdivision (3) of subsection (d) of this section.

(f)   This section does not apply to a merger that does not include a merging unincorporated entity. (1999-369, s. 2.7; 2000-140, s. 48; 2001-387, ss. 40, 41, 42; 2001-487, s. 62(f); 2005-268, ss. 44, 45, 46; 2007-385, s. 3; 2011-347, ss. 13, 14.)

§ 55A-11-10. Merger with certain charitable or religious corporation or hospital authority.

(a)   A hospital authority created by a city may merge into a charitable or religious corporation having its principal office in the county in which the city is located, under a plan of merger approved by the city and the county and by a majority of the members of the board of commissioners of such authority and by or for the corporation as provided in G.S. 55A-11-03.

This section applies only to the merger of a hospital authority formed by a city in a county with a population of less than 150,000 as of the most recent U.S. Census and either (i) a charitable or religious corporation formed on or before September 29, 2005 having its principal office located in such county as of September 29, 2005, or (ii) a hospital authority formed after September 29, 2005 by the county in which the city is located.

(b)   A hospital authority created by a city may merge into a hospital authority created by the county in which the city is located, pursuant to a plan of merger approved by the city and the county and by a majority of the members of the board of commissioners of each authority.

(c)   The plan of merger shall include all of the following:

107

(1)   The name of the city hospital authority and the charitable or religious corporation or the county hospital authority planning to merge and the name of the surviving charitable or religious corporation or county hospital authority into which such city hospital authority plans to merge.

(2)   The terms and conditions of the merger.

(3)   Any amendments to the articles or certificate of incorporation or bylaws of the surviving charitable or religious corporation or the surviving county hospital authority to be effected by the merger.

(4)   Other provisions relating to the merger.

(d)   After the plan of merger is approved, the surviving charitable or religious corporation or the surviving county hospital authority shall deliver to the Secretary of State for filing articles of merger that include all of the following:

(1)   The plan of merger.

(2)   In the case of a merger of a city hospital authority into a charitable or religious corporation, a statement that the plan of merger was approved by the city and by a majority of the members of the board of commissioners of the city hospital authority and the statements required under G.S. 55A-11-04(a)(2), (3), or (4); or

(3)   In the case of a merger of a city hospital authority into a county hospital authority, a statement that the plan of merger was approved by the city and the county and a majority of each of the boards of commissioners of the authorities.

(e)   A merger takes effect upon the effective date of the articles of merger.

(f)   Certificates of merger shall also be registered as provided in G.S. 47-18.1.

(g)   All of the following shall occur upon an effective merger under this section:

(1)   The separate existence of the city hospital authority that merges into the charitable or religious corporation or into the county hospital authority ceases.

(2)   The title to all real estate and other property owned by the hospital authority is vested in the surviving charitable or religious corporation or in the surviving county hospital authority without reversion or impairment subject to any and all conditions to which the property was subject prior to the merger.

(3)   The surviving charitable or religious corporation or the surviving county hospital authority has all liabilities and obligations of the city hospital authority and the charitable or religious corporation or the county hospital authority party to the merger.

(4)   A proceeding pending by or against the city hospital authority and the charitable or religious corporation or the county hospital authority party to the merger may be continued as if the merger did not occur or the surviving charitable or religious corporation or the surviving county hospital authority may be substituted in the proceeding for the city hospital authority whose existence ceased.

(5)   The articles or certificate of incorporation and bylaws of the surviving charitable or religious corporation or the surviving county hospital authority are amended to the extent provided in the plan of merger.

(6)   Any devise, gift, grant, or promise contained in a will or other instrument of donation, subscription, or conveyance that is made to a city hospital authority that has merged into a charitable or religious corporation or into a county hospital authority and that takes effect or remains payable after the merger, inures to the surviving charitable or religious corporation or the surviving county hospital authority unless the will or other instrument otherwise specifically provides.

(h)   A merger pursuant to the provisions of this section will not be deemed to be a sale or conveyance of a hospital facility under or pursuant to G.S. 131E-8, 131E-13, or 131E-14 of the Municipal Hospital Act (Part 1, Article 2, Chapter 131E of the General Statutes) and G.S. 131E-13(d) will not be applicable to such merger. (2005-449, ss. 1, 2; 2011-284, s. 54.)

Article 12.

Transfer of Assets.

§ 55A-12-01. Sale of assets in regular course of activities and mortgage of assets.

(a)   A corporation may on the terms and conditions and for the consideration determined by the board of directors:

(1)   Sell, lease, exchange, or otherwise dispose of all, or substantially all, of its property in the usual and regular course of its activities; or

(2)   Mortgage, pledge, dedicate to the repayment of indebtedness (whether with or without recourse), or otherwise encumber any or all of its property whether or not in the usual and regular course of its activities.

(b)   Unless the articles of incorporation require it, approval of the members or any other person of a transaction described in subsection (a) of this section is not required. (1955, c. 1230; 1985 (Reg. Sess., 1986), c. 801, s. 40; 1993, c. 398, s. 1.)

§ 55A-12-02. Sale of assets other than in regular course of activities.

(a)   A corporation may sell, lease, exchange, or otherwise dispose of all, or substantially all, of its property other than in the usual and regular course of its activities on the terms and conditions and for the consideration determined by the corporation's board of directors if the proposed transaction is authorized by subsection (b) of this section.

(b)   Unless this Chapter, the articles of incorporation, bylaws, or the board of directors or members (acting pursuant to subsection (d) of this section) require a greater vote or voting by class, the proposed transaction to be authorized shall be approved:

(1)   By the board;

(2)   By the members entitled to vote thereon by two-thirds of the votes cast or a majority of the votes entitled to be cast on the proposed transaction, whichever is less; and

(3)   In writing by any person or persons whose approval is required by a provision of the articles of incorporation authorized by G.S. 55A-10-30 for an amendment to the articles of incorporation or bylaws.

(c)   If the corporation does not have members entitled to vote thereon, the transaction shall be approved by a vote of a majority of the directors then in office. The corporation shall provide at least five days' written notice of any directors' meeting at which such approval will be considered. The notice shall state that the purpose, or one of the purposes, of the meeting is to consider the sale, lease, exchange, or other disposition of all, or substantially all, of the property or assets of the corporation and contain or be accompanied by a description of the transaction.

(d)   The board may condition its approval of the proposed transaction, and the members entitled to vote thereon may condition their approval of the transaction, on receipt of a higher percentage of affirmative votes or on any other basis.

(e)   If the corporation seeks to have the transaction approved by the members entitled to vote thereon at a membership meeting, the corporation shall give notice of the membership meeting to those members in accordance with G.S. 55A-7-05. The notice shall state that the purpose, or one of the purposes, of the meeting is to consider the sale, lease, exchange, or other disposition of all, or substantially all, of the property or assets of the corporation and contain or be accompanied by a description of the transaction.

(f)   If the board seeks to have the transaction approved by the members entitled to vote thereon by written consent or written ballot, the material soliciting the approval shall contain or be accompanied by a description of the transaction.

(g)   A charitable or religious corporation shall give written notice to the Attorney General 30 days before it sells, leases, exchanges, or otherwise disposes of all, or a majority of, its property if the transaction is not in the usual and regular course of its activities unless the Attorney General has given the corporation a written waiver of this subsection. This notice shall include all the information the Attorney General determines is required for a complete review of the proposed transaction. The Attorney General may require an additional 30-day period to review the proposed transaction by providing written notice to the charitable or religious corporation prior to the expiration of the initial notice period. During this 30-day period, the transaction may not be finalized.

111

(h)   After a sale, lease, exchange, or other disposition of property is authorized, the transaction may be abandoned (subject to any contractual rights), without further action by the members or any other person who approved the transaction, in accordance with the procedure set forth in the resolution proposing the transaction or, if none is set forth, in the manner determined by the board of directors. (1955, c. 1230; 1985 (Reg. Sess., 1986), c. 801, s. 40; 1993, c. 398, s. 1; 1999-204, s. 2.)

Article 13.

Distributions.

§ 55A-13-01. Prohibited distributions.

Except as authorized by G.S. 55A-13-02 or Article 14 of this Chapter, a corporation shall not make any distributions. (1955, c. 1230; 1985 (Reg. Sess., 1986), c. 801, s. 32; 1993, c. 398, s. 1.)

§ 55A-13-02. Authorized distributions.

(a)   A corporation may pay reasonable amounts to its members, directors, or officers for services rendered or other value received and may confer benefits upon its members in conformity with its purposes.

(b)   Subject to the provisions of subsection (d) of this section:

(1)   A corporation may make distributions to any entity that is exempt under section 501(c)(3) of the Internal Revenue Code of 1986 or any successor section, or that is organized exclusively for one or more of the purposes specified in section 501(c)(3) of the Internal Revenue Code of 1986 or any successor section and that upon dissolution shall distribute its assets to a charitable or religious corporation, the United States, a state or an entity that is exempt under section 501(c)(3) of the Internal Revenue Code of 1986 or any successor section.

112

(2)   Any corporation other than a charitable or religious corporation may make distributions to any domestic or foreign corporation.

(3)   Except as otherwise prohibited by statute, a corporation not operated for profit, the membership of which is limited to the owners or occupants of real property in a condominium, cooperative housing corporation, or other real property development, having as its primary purposes the management, operation, preservation, maintenance, and repair of common areas and improvements upon the real property owned by the members and the corporation or organization, may make distribution to its members of excess or surplus membership dues, fees, or assessments remaining after the payment of or provisions for common expenses and any prepayment of reserves; provided that these distributions are in proportion to the dues, fees, or assessments collected from the members.

(c)   Subject to the provisions of subsection (d) of this section, a corporation other than a charitable or religious corporation may make distributions to purchase its memberships.

(d)   A corporation shall not make any distribution under subsection (b) or (c) of this section if at the time of or as a result of such distribution:

(1)   The corporation would not be able to pay its debts as they become due in the usual course of business; or

(2)   The corporation's total assets would be less than the sum of its total liabilities. (1955, c. 1230; 1985 (Reg. Sess., 1986), c. 801, s. 32; 1993, c. 398, s. 1; 1999-369, s. 7.)

Article 14.

Dissolution.

Part 1. Voluntary Dissolution.

§ 55A-14-01. Dissolution by incorporators or directors prior to commencement of activities.

113

(a)   A corporation that has not admitted members entitled to vote on dissolution, has not commenced activities, and has no assets may be dissolved by action of its board of directors or a majority of its incorporators, if there are no directors, by delivering to the Secretary of State for filing articles of dissolution that set forth:

(1)   The name of the corporation;

(2)   The names and addresses of its officers, if any;

(3)   The names and addresses of its directors, if any, or if none, the names and addresses of its incorporators;

(4)   The date of its incorporation;

(5)   That the corporation has not admitted members entitled to vote on dissolution, has not commenced activities, and has no assets;

(6)   That no debt of the corporation remains unpaid; and

(7)   That a majority of the incorporators or directors authorized the dissolution.

(b)   Upon the filing of articles of dissolution under this section, the corporation becomes nonexistent and is cancelled as if such corporation had never been created. (1955, c. 1230; 1973, c. 314, s. 5; 1985 (Reg. Sess., 1986), c. 801, ss. 41, 43; 1993, c. 398, s. 1.)

§ 55A-14-02. Dissolution by directors, members, and third persons.

(a)   Unless this Chapter, the articles of incorporation, bylaws, or the board of directors or members (acting pursuant to subsection (c) of this section) require a greater vote or voting by class, dissolution is authorized if a plan of dissolution meeting the requirements of G.S. 55A-14-03 is approved:

(1)   By the board;

(2)   By the members entitled to vote thereon, if any, by two-thirds of the votes cast or a majority of the votes entitled to be cast on the plan of dissolution, whichever is less; and

(3)   In writing by any person or persons whose approval is required by a provision of the articles of incorporation authorized by G.S. 55A-10-30 for an amendment to the articles of incorporation or bylaws.

(b)   If the corporation does not have members entitled to vote thereon, dissolution shall be approved by a vote of a majority of the directors then in office. The corporation shall provide at least five days' written notice of any directors' meeting at which such approval will be considered. The notice shall state that the purpose, or one of the purposes, of the meeting is to consider dissolution of the corporation and contain or be accompanied by a copy or summary of the plan of dissolution.

(c)   The board of directors may condition its approval of the proposed dissolution, and the members entitled to vote thereon may condition their approval of the dissolution on receipt of a higher percentage of affirmative votes or on any other basis.

(d)   If the board of directors seeks to have dissolution approved by the members entitled to vote thereon at a membership meeting, the corporation shall give notice of the membership meeting to those members in accordance with G.S. 55A-7-05. The notice shall state that the purpose, or one of the purposes, of the meeting is to consider dissolving the corporation and contain or be accompanied by a copy or summary of the plan of dissolution.

(e)   If the board seeks to have dissolution approved by the members entitled to vote thereon by written consent or written ballot, the material soliciting the approval shall contain or be accompanied by a copy or summary of the plan of dissolution. (1955, c. 1230; 1973, c. 314, s. 5; 1985 (Reg. Sess., 1986), c. 801, s. 41; 1993, c. 398, s. 1.)

§ 55A-14-03. Plan of dissolution.

(a)   The plan of dissolution approved pursuant to G.S. 55A-14-02 shall provide that all liabilities and obligations of the corporation be paid and discharged, or adequate provisions be made therefor, and that the remainder of the corporation's assets be distributed as follows:

(1)　　Assets held by the corporation upon condition requiring return, transfer, or conveyance, which condition occurs by reason of the dissolution, shall be returned, transferred, or conveyed in accordance with such requirements;

(2)　　Other assets, if any, of a charitable or religious corporation shall, subject to the articles of incorporation or bylaws, be transferred or conveyed to one or more of the following: the United States, a state, a charitable or religious corporation, or a person that is exempt under section 501(c)(3) of the Internal Revenue Code of 1986 or any successor section;

(3)　　Other assets, if any, of a corporation that is not a charitable or religious corporation shall, subject to the articles of incorporation and bylaws, be distributed as provided in the plan of dissolution.

(b)　　The plan of dissolution may set forth other provisions relating to the dissolution. (1955, c. 1230; 1993, c. 398, s. 1.)

§ 55A-14-04. Articles of dissolution.

(a)　　At any time after dissolution is authorized pursuant to G.S. 55A-14-02, the corporation may dissolve by delivering to the Secretary of State for filing articles of dissolution setting forth:

(1)　　The name of the corporation;

(2)　　The names and addresses of its officers;

(3)　　The names and addresses of its directors;

(4)　　The plan of dissolution as required by G.S. 55A-14-03;

(5)　　The date dissolution was authorized;

(6)　　If approval by members was not required, a statement to that effect and a statement that the plan of dissolution was approved by a sufficient vote of the board of directors;

116

(7)   If approval by members was required, a statement that the plan of dissolution was approved as required by this Chapter; and

(8)   If approval of dissolution by some person or persons other than the members or the board of directors is required pursuant to G.S. 55A-14-02(a)(3), a statement that the approval was obtained.

(b)   A corporation is dissolved upon the effective date of its articles of dissolution. (1955, c. 1230; 1973, c. 314, s. 7; 1993, c. 398, s. 1.)

§ 55A-14-05. Revocation of dissolution.

(a)   A corporation may revoke its dissolution authorized under G.S. 55A-14-02 within 120 days of its effective date.

(b)   Revocation of dissolution shall be authorized in the same manner as the dissolution was authorized unless an authorization under G.S. 55A-14-02 permitted revocation by action of the board of directors alone, in which event the board of directors may revoke the dissolution without action by the members or any other person.

(c)   After the revocation of dissolution is authorized, the corporation may revoke the dissolution by delivering to the Secretary of State for filing articles of revocation of dissolution, together with a copy of its articles of dissolution, that set forth:

(1)   The name of the corporation;

(2)   The effective date of the dissolution that was revoked;

(3)   The date that the revocation of dissolution was authorized;

(4)   If the corporation's board of directors revoked the dissolution, a statement to that effect;

(5)   If the corporation's board of directors revoked a dissolution authorized by the members alone or in conjunction with another person or persons, a

117

statement that revocation was permitted by action by the board of directors alone pursuant to that authorization; and

(6)   If member or third person action was required to revoke the dissolution, a statement that the action was taken as required.

(d)   Revocation of dissolution is effective upon the effective date of the articles of revocation of dissolution.

(e)   When the revocation of dissolution is effective, it relates back to and takes effect as of the effective date of the dissolution and the corporation resumes carrying on its activities as if dissolution had never occurred, subject to the rights of any person who reasonably relied to his prejudice upon the filing of the articles of dissolution. (1955, c. 1230; 1993, c. 398, s. 1.)

§ 55A-14-06. Effect of dissolution.

(a)   A dissolved corporation continues its corporate existence but shall not carry on any activities except those appropriate to wind up and liquidate its affairs, including:

(1)   Preserving and protecting its assets;

(2)   Discharging or making provision for discharging its liabilities and obligations;

(3)   Disposing of its remaining assets in accordance with its plan of dissolution; and

(4)   Doing every other act necessary to wind up and liquidate its assets and affairs.

(b)   Dissolution of a corporation does not:

(1)   Transfer title to the corporation's property;

(2)   Subject its directors or officers to standards of conduct different from those prescribed in Article 8 of this Chapter;

118

(3)   Change quorum or voting requirements for its board of directors or members; change provisions for selection, resignation, or removal of its directors or officers or both; or change provisions for amending its bylaws;

(4)   Prevent commencement of a proceeding by or against the corporation in its corporate name;

(5)   Abate or suspend a proceeding pending by or against the corporation on the effective date of dissolution; or

(6)   Terminate the authority of the registered agent of the corporation. (1955, c. 1230; 1993, c. 398, s. 1.)

§ 55A-14-07. Known claims against dissolved corporation.

(a)   A dissolved corporation may dispose of the known claims against it by following the procedure described in this section.

(b)   The dissolved corporation shall notify its known claimants in writing of the dissolution at any time after its effective date. The written notice shall:

(1)   Describe information that shall be included in a claim;

(2)   Provide a mailing address where a claim may be sent;

(3)   State the deadline, which shall not be fewer than 120 days from the effective date of the written notice, by which the dissolved corporation shall receive the claim; and

(4)   State that the claim will be barred if not received by the deadline.

(c)   A claim against the dissolved corporation is barred:

(1)   If the corporation does not receive the claim by the deadline from a claimant who received written notice under subsection (b) of this section; or

(2)   If a claimant whose claim was rejected by written notice from the dissolved corporation does not commence a proceeding to enforce the claim within 90 days from the date of receipt of the rejection notice.

119

(d)   For purposes of this section, "claim" does not include a contingent liability or a claim based on an event occurring after the effective date of dissolution. (1955, c. 1230; 1973, c. 314, s. 5; 1985 (Reg. Sess., 1986), c. 801, s. 41; 1993, c. 398, s. 1.)

§ 55A-14-08. Unknown and certain other claims against dissolved corporation.

(a)   A dissolved corporation may also publish notice of its dissolution and request that persons with claims against the corporation present them in accordance with the notice.

(b)   The notice shall:

(1)   Be published one time in a newspaper of general circulation in the county where the dissolved corporation's principal office (or, if there is none in this State, its registered office) is or was last located;

(2)   Describe the information that shall be included in a claim and provide a mailing address where the claim may be sent; and

(3)   State that a claim against the corporation will be barred unless a proceeding to enforce the claim is commenced within five years after the publication of the notice.

(c)   If the dissolved corporation publishes a newspaper notice in accordance with subsection (b) of this section, the claim of each of the following claimants is barred unless the claimant commences a proceeding to enforce the claim against the dissolved corporation within five years after the publication date of the newspaper notice:

(1)   A claimant who did not receive written notice under G.S. 55A-14-07;

(2)   A claimant whose claim was timely sent to the dissolved corporation but not acted on;

(3)   A claimant whose claim is contingent or based on an event occurring after the effective date of dissolution.

(d)   Nothing in this section shall bar:

(1)   Any claim alleging the liability of the corporation; or

(2)   Any proceeding or action to establish the liability of the corporation; or

(3)   The recovery on any judgment against the corporation

to the extent that the corporation is protected by insurance coverage with respect to such claim, proceeding, or judgment. (1955, c. 1230; 1973, c. 314, s. 5; 1985 (Reg. Sess., 1986), c. 801, s. 41; 1993, c. 398, s. 1.)

§ 55A-14-09. Enforcement of claims.

(a)   A claim under G.S. 55A-14-07 or G.S. 55A-14-08 may be enforced:

(1)   Against the dissolved corporation, to the extent of its undistributed assets, including coverage under any applicable insurance policy, or

(2)   If the assets have been distributed in liquidation, against any person, other than a creditor of the corporation, to whom the corporation distributed its property to the extent of the distributee's pro rata share of the claim or the corporate assets distributed to such person in liquidation, whichever is less, but the distributee's total liability for all claims under this section shall not exceed the total amount of assets distributed to the distributee.

(b)   Nothing in G.S. 55A-14-07 or G.S. 55A-14-08 shall extend any applicable period of limitation. (1985 (Reg. Sess., 1986), c. 801, s. 33; 1993, c. 398, s. 1.)

§§ 55A-14-10 through 55A-14-19. Reserved for future codification purposes.

Part 2. Administrative Dissolution.

§ 55A-14-20. Grounds for administrative dissolution.

121

The Secretary of State may commence a proceeding under G.S. 55A-14-21 to dissolve administratively a corporation if:

(1)   The corporation does not pay within 60 days after they are due any penalties, fees, or other payments due under this Chapter;

(2)   Repealed by Session Laws 1995, c. 539, s. 24.

(3)   The corporation is without a registered agent or registered office in this State for 60 days or more;

(4)   The corporation does not notify the Secretary of State within 60 days that its registered agent or registered office has been changed, that its registered agent has resigned, or that its registered office has been discontinued;

(5)   The corporation's period of duration stated in its articles of incorporation expires;

(6)   The corporation knowingly fails or refuses to answer truthfully and fully within the time prescribed in this Chapter interrogatories propounded by the Secretary of State in accordance with the provisions of this Chapter; or

(7)   The corporation does not designate the address of its principal office with the Secretary of State or does not notify the Secretary of State within 60 days that the principal office has changed. (1993, c. 398, s. 1; 1995, c. 539, ss. 24, 25.)

§ 55A-14-21. Procedure for and effect of administrative dissolution.

(a)   If the Secretary of State determines that one or more grounds exist under G.S. 55A-14-20 for dissolving a corporation, the Secretary of State shall mail the corporation written notice of the Secretary of State's determination.

(b)   If the corporation does not correct each ground for dissolution or demonstrate to the reasonable satisfaction of the Secretary of State that each ground determined by the Secretary of State does not exist within 60 days after notice is mailed, the Secretary of State shall administratively dissolve the corporation by signing a certificate of dissolution that recites the ground or grounds for dissolution and its effective date. The Secretary of State shall file the original of the certificate and mail a copy to the corporation.

(c)   The provisions of G.S. 55A-14-06, 55A-14-07, and 55A-14-08 apply to a corporation administratively dissolved.

(d)   The administrative dissolution of a corporation does not terminate the authority of its registered agent. (1993, c. 398, s. 1.)

§ 55A-14-22. Reinstatement following administrative dissolution.

(a)   A corporation administratively dissolved under G.S. 55A-14-21 may apply to the Secretary of State for reinstatement. The application shall:

(1)   Recite the name of the corporation and the effective date of its administrative dissolution; and

(2)   State that the ground or grounds for dissolution either did not exist or have been eliminated.

(a1)   If, at the time the corporation applies for reinstatement, the name of the corporation is not distinguishable from the name of another entity authorized to be used under G.S. 55D-21, then the corporation must change its name to a name that is distinguishable upon the records of the Secretary of State from the name of the other entity before the Secretary of State may prepare a certificate of reinstatement.

(b)   If the Secretary of State determines that the application contains the information required by subsection (a) of this section, that the information is correct, and that the name of the corporation complies with G.S. 55D-21 and any other applicable section, the Secretary of State shall cancel the certificate of dissolution and prepare a certificate of reinstatement that recites the Secretary of State's determination and the effective date of reinstatement, file the original of the certificate, and mail a copy to the corporation.

(c)   When the reinstatement is effective, it relates back to and takes effect as of the effective date of the administrative dissolution and the corporation resumes carrying on its activities as if the administrative dissolution had never

123

occurred, subject to the rights of any person who reasonably relied to his prejudice upon the certificate of dissolution. (1993, c. 398, s. 1; 1996, 2nd Ex. Sess., c. 17, s. 15.1(d); 1997-485, s. 2; 2001-390, s. 9; 2001-413, ss. 7.2, 7.3.)

§ 55A-14-23. Appeal from denial of reinstatement.

(a)   If the Secretary of State denies a corporation's application for reinstatement following administrative dissolution, the Secretary of State shall serve the corporation under G.S. 55D-33 with a written notice that explains the reason or reasons for denial.

(b)   The corporation may appeal the denial of reinstatement to the Superior Court of Wake County within 30 days after service of the notice of denial is perfected. The appeal is commenced by filing a petition with the court and with the Secretary of State requesting the court to set aside the dissolution. The petition shall have attached to it copies of the Secretary of State's certificate of dissolution, the corporation's application for reinstatement, and the Secretary of State's notice of denial. No service of process on the Secretary of State is required except for the filing of the petition as set forth in this subsection. The appeal to the superior court shall be determined by a judge of the superior court upon such further evidence, notice, and opportunity to be heard, if any, as the court may deem appropriate under the circumstances. The corporation shall have the burden of establishing that it is entitled to reinstatement.

(c)   Upon consideration of the petition and any response made by the Secretary of State, the court may, prior to entering final judgment, order the Secretary of State to reinstate the dissolved corporation or may take other action the court considers appropriate.

(d)   The court's final decision may be appealed as in other civil proceedings. (1993, c. 398, s. 1; 2001-358, ss. 5A(c), 48(e); 2001-387, ss. 173, 175(a); 2001-413, s. 6.)

§ 55A-14-24. Inapplicability of Administrative Procedure Act.

The Administrative Procedure Act shall not apply to any proceeding or appeal provided for in G.S. 55A-14-20 through G.S. 55A-14-23. (1993, c. 398, s. 1.)

§§ 55A-14-25 through 55A-14-29. Reserved for future codification purposes.

Part 3. Judicial Dissolution.

§ 55A-14-30. Grounds for judicial dissolution.

(a)   The superior court may dissolve a corporation:

(1)   In a proceeding by the Attorney General if it is established that:

a.   The corporation obtained its articles of incorporation through fraud; or

b.   The corporation has, after written notice by the Attorney General given at least 20 days prior thereto, continued to exceed or abuse the authority conferred upon it by law;

(2)   In a proceeding by a member or director, if it is established that:

a.   The directors are deadlocked in the management of the corporate affairs, and the members, if any, are unable to break the deadlock;

b.   The directors or those in control of the corporation have acted, are acting, or will act in a manner that is illegal, oppressive, or fraudulent;

c.   The members are deadlocked in voting power and have failed, for a period that includes at least two consecutive annual meeting dates, to elect successors to directors whose terms have, or would otherwise have, expired;

d.   The corporate assets are being misapplied or wasted; or

e.   The corporation is no longer able to carry out its purposes.

(3)   In a proceeding by a creditor if it is established that:

a.   The creditor's claim has been reduced to judgment and execution on the judgment has been returned unsatisfied; or

b.   The corporation has admitted in writing that the creditor's claim is due and owing and the corporation is insolvent.

(4)   In a proceeding by the corporation to have its voluntary dissolution continued under court supervision.

(b)   Prior to dissolving a corporation, the court shall consider whether:

(1)   There are reasonable alternatives to dissolution;

(2)   Dissolution is in the public interest, if the corporation is a charitable or religious corporation; and

(3)   Dissolution is reasonably necessary for the protection of the rights or interests of the members, if any. (1955, c. 1230; 1985 (Reg. Sess., 1986), c. 801, s. 42; 1993, c. 398, s. 1.)

§ 55A-14-31. Procedure for judicial dissolution.

(a)   Venue for a proceeding to dissolve a corporation lies in the county where a corporation's principal office, or, if there is none in this State, its registered office, is or was last located.

(b)   It is not necessary to make directors or members parties to a proceeding to dissolve a corporation unless relief is sought against them individually.

(c)   A court in a proceeding brought to dissolve a corporation may issue injunctions, appoint a receiver with all powers and duties the court directs, take other action required to preserve the corporate assets wherever located, and carry on the activities of the corporation. (1955, c. 1230; 1985 (Reg. Sess., 1986), c. 801, s. 42; 1993, c. 398, s. 1.)

§ 55A-14-32. Receivership.

(a)   A court in a judicial proceeding brought to dissolve a corporation may appoint one or more receivers to wind up and liquidate, or to manage, the affairs of the corporation. The court shall hold a hearing, after notifying all parties to the proceeding and any interested persons designated by the court, before appointing a receiver. The court appointing a receiver has exclusive jurisdiction over the corporation and all of its property wherever located.

(b)   The court may appoint an individual or a domestic or foreign business or nonprofit corporation (authorized to transact business in this State) as a receiver. The court may require the receiver to post bond, with or without sureties, in an amount the court directs.

(c)   The court shall describe the powers and duties of the receiver in its appointing order, which may be amended from time to time. Such powers may include without limitation the power:

(1)   To dispose of all or any part of the assets of the corporation wherever located, at a public or private sale, if authorized by the court;

(2)   To sue and defend in his own name as receiver of the corporation in all courts of this State; and

(3)   To exercise all of the powers of the corporation, through or in place of its board of directors or officers, to the extent necessary to manage the affairs of the corporation in the best interests of its members and creditors.

(d)   The court from time to time during the receivership may order compensation paid and expense disbursements or reimbursements made to the receiver and his counsel from the assets of the corporation or proceeds from the sale of the assets. (1955, c. 1230; 1993, c. 398, s. 1.)

§ 55A-14-33. Decree of dissolution.

(a)   If, after a hearing, the court determines that one or more grounds for judicial dissolution described in G.S. 55A-14-30 exist, it may enter a decree dissolving the corporation and specifying the effective date of the dissolution, and the clerk of the court shall deliver a certified copy of the decree to the Secretary of State, who shall file it.

(b)   After entering the decree of dissolution, the court shall direct the winding up and liquidation of the corporation's affairs in accordance with G.S. 55A-14-06 and the notification of its claimants in accordance with G.S. 55A-14-07 and G.S. 55A-14-08. The corporation's name becomes available for use by another entity as provided in G.S. 55D-21. (1955, c. 1230; 1967, c. 823, s. 23; 1985 (Reg. Sess., 1986), c. 801, s. 42; 1993, c. 398, s. 1; 2001-358, s. 24; 2001-387, ss. 173, 175(a); 2001-413, s. 6.)

§§ 55A-14-34 through 55A-14-39. Reserved for future codification purposes.

Part 4. Miscellaneous.

§ 55A-14-40. Disposition of amounts due to unavailable members and creditors.

Upon liquidation of a corporation, the portion of the assets distributable to a creditor or member who is unknown or cannot be found shall be disposed of in accordance with Chapter 116B of the General Statutes. (1955, c. 1230; 1981, c. 682, s. 13; 1993, c. 398, s. 1.)

Article 14A.

Reorganization.

§ 55A-14A-01. Fundamental changes in reorganization proceedings.

(a)   Whenever a plan of reorganization of a corporation is confirmed by decree or order of a court of competent jurisdiction in proceedings for the reorganization of the corporation pursuant to the provisions of any applicable statute of the United States relating to reorganization of corporations, the corporation may put into effect and carry out the plan and the decrees and orders of the court relative thereto and may take any action provided in the plan or directed by the decrees and orders without further action by its directors or members. Such action may be taken, as may be directed by the decrees or orders, by the trustee or trustees of the corporation appointed in the reorganization proceedings, or by designated officers of the corporation, or by a master or other representative appointed by the court, with like effect as if taken by unanimous action of the directors and members of the corporation. In particular and without limiting the generality or effect of the foregoing, the corporation may:

(1)   Amend its articles of incorporation or bylaws, or both, so long as the articles of incorporation and bylaws as amended contain only such provisions as might be lawfully contained therein at the time of making such amendment;

(2)   Constitute or reconstitute and classify or reclassify its board of directors, and name, constitute or appoint directors and officers in place of or in addition to all or any of the directors or officers then in office;

(3)   Make any change in its memberships or securities or cancel any or all of its outstanding memberships or securities;

(4)   Dissolve and liquidate;

(5)   Effect a merger;

(6)   Transfer all or part of its assets;

(7)   Change its registered office or registered agent, or both;

(8)   Authorize the issuance of bonds, debentures, or other obligations of the corporation and fix the terms and conditions thereof.

(b)   Any articles of amendment, statement of change of registered office or registered agent, restated articles of incorporation, articles of merger, articles of dissolution, or any other document appropriate to complete any action permitted by this section shall be executed and filed in accordance with the provisions of this Chapter on behalf of the corporation by such person or persons as may be authorized to take such action pursuant to subsection (a) of this section.

(c)   This section does not apply after entry of a final decree in the reorganization proceeding even though the court retains jurisdiction of the proceeding for limited purposes unrelated to consummation of the reorganization plan. (1993, c. 398, s. 1.)

Article 15.

Foreign Corporations.

Part 1. Certificate of Authority.

§ 55A-15-01. Authority to conduct affairs required.

(a)   A foreign corporation shall not conduct affairs in this State until it obtains a certificate of authority from the Secretary of State.

(b)   Without excluding other activities which might not constitute conducting affairs in this State, a foreign corporation shall not be considered to be conducting affairs in this State solely for the purposes of this Chapter, by reason of carrying on in this State any one or more of the following activities:

(1)   Maintaining or defending any action or suit or any administrative or arbitration proceeding, or affecting the settlement thereof or the settlement of claims or disputes;

(2)   Holding meetings of its directors or members or carrying on other activities concerning its internal affairs;

(3)   Maintaining bank accounts or borrowing money in this State, with or without security, even if such borrowings are repeated and continuous transactions;

(4)   Maintaining offices or agencies for the transfer, exchange, and registration of memberships or securities, or appointing and maintaining trustees or despositories with relation to those securities;

(5)   Soliciting or procuring orders, whether by mail or through employees or agents or otherwise, where the orders require acceptance without this State before becoming binding contracts;

(6)   Making or investing in loans with or without security including servicing of mortgages or deeds of trust through independent agencies within the State, the conducting of foreclosure proceedings and sale, the acquiring of property at foreclosure sale, and the management and rental of such property for a reasonable time while liquidating its investment, provided no office or agency therefor is maintained in this State;

(7)   Taking security for or collecting debts due to it or enforcing any rights in property securing the same;

(8)   Conducting affairs in interstate commerce;

(9)   Conducting an isolated transaction completed within a period of six months and not in the course of a number of repeated transactions of like nature;

(10)   Selling through independent contractors;

(11)   Owning, without more, real or personal property. (1955, c. 1230; 1993, c. 398, s. 1.)

§ 55A-15-02. Consequences of conducting affairs without authority.

(a)   No foreign corporation conducting affairs in this State without permission obtained through a certificate of authority under this Chapter or through domestication under prior acts shall be permitted to maintain any action or proceeding in any court of this State unless the foreign corporation has obtained a certificate of authority prior to trial.

An issue arising under this subsection must be raised by motion and determined by the trial judge prior to trial.

(b)   A foreign corporation failing to obtain a certificate of authority as required by this Chapter or by prior acts then applicable shall be liable to the State for the years or parts thereof during which it conducted affairs in this State without a certificate of authority in an amount equal to all fees and taxes which would have been imposed by law upon the corporation had it duly applied for and received such permission, plus interest and all penalties imposed by law for failure to pay such fees and taxes. In addition, the foreign corporation shall be liable for a civil penalty of ten dollars ($10.00) for each day, but not to exceed a total of one thousand dollars ($1,000) for each year or part thereof, it conducts affairs in this State without a certificate of authority. The Attorney General may bring actions to recover all amounts due the State under the provisions of this subsection. The clear proceeds of civil penalties provided for in this subsection shall be remitted to the Civil Penalty and Forfeiture Fund in accordance with G.S. 115C-457.2.

131

(c)   Notwithstanding subsection (a) of this section, the failure of a foreign corporation to obtain a certificate of authority does not impair the validity of its corporate acts or prevent it from defending any proceeding in this State.

(d)   The Secretary of State is hereby directed to require that every foreign corporation conducting affairs in this State comply with the provisions of this Chapter. The Secretary of State is authorized to employ such assistants as shall be deemed necessary in the Secretary of State's office for the purpose of enforcing the provisions of this Article and for making such investigations as shall be necessary to ascertain foreign corporations now conducting affairs in this State which may have failed to comply with the provisions of this Chapter. (1955, c. 1230; 1993, c. 398, s. 1; 1998-215, s. 118; 1999-151, s. 2.)

§ 55A-15-03. Application for certificate of authority.

(a)   A foreign corporation may apply for a certificate of authority to conduct affairs in this State by delivering an application to the Secretary of State for filing. The application shall set forth:

(1)   The name of the foreign corporation or, if its name is unavailable for use in this State, a corporate name that satisfies the requirements of Article 3 of Chapter 55D of the General Statutes;

(2)   The name of the state or country under whose law it is incorporated;

(3)   Its date of incorporation and period of duration;

(4)   The street address, and mailing address if different from the street address, of its principal office;

(5)   The street address, and the mailing address if different from the street address, of its registered office in this State, the county in which the registered office is located, and the name of its registered agent at that office;

(6)   The names and usual business addresses of its current officers; and

(7)   Whether it has members.

(b)   The foreign corporation shall deliver with the completed application a certificate of existence (or a document of similar import) duly authenticated by the Secretary of State or other official having custody of corporate records in the state or country under whose law it is incorporated.

(c)   If the Secretary of State finds that the application conforms to law, the Secretary of State shall when all fees have been tended as prescribed in this Chapter:

(1)   Endorse on the application and an exact or conformed copy thereof the word "filed" and the hour, day, month, and year of the filing thereof;

(2)   File in the Secretary of State's office the application and the certificate of existence (or document of similar import as described in subsection (b) of this section);

(3)   Issue a certificate of authority to conduct affairs in this State to which the Secretary of State shall affix the exact or conformed copy of the application; and

(4)   Send to the foreign corporation or its representative the certificate of authority, together with the exact or conformed copy of the application affixed thereto. (1955, c. 1230; 1957, c. 979, s. 14; 1969, c. 875, s. 8; 1993, c. 398, s. 1; 2001-358, s. 21; 2001-387, ss. 169(b), 173, 175(a); 2001-413, s. 6.)

§ 55A-15-04. Amended certificate of authority.

(a)   A foreign corporation authorized to conduct affairs in this State shall obtain an amended certificate of authority from the Secretary of State if it changes:

(1)   Its corporate name;

(2)   The period of its duration; or

(3)   The state or country of its incorporation.

(b)   A foreign corporation may apply for an amended certificate of authority by delivering an application to the Secretary of State for filing that sets forth:

133

(1)   The name of the foreign corporation and the name in which the corporation is authorized to conduct affairs in North Carolina if different;

(2)   The name of the state or country under whose law it is incorporated;

(3)   The date it was originally authorized to conduct affairs in this State; and

(4)   A statement of the change or changes being made.

Except for the content of the application, the requirements of G.S. 55A-15-03 for obtaining an original certificate of authority apply to obtaining an amended certificate under this section. (1955, c. 1230; 1993, c. 398, s. 1.)

§ 55A-15-05. Effect of certificate of authority.

(a)   A certificate of authority authorizes the foreign corporation to which it is issued to conduct affairs in this State subject, however, to the right of the State to revoke the certificate as provided in this Chapter. A foreign corporation, however, is not eligible or entitled to qualify in this State as executor, administrator, or guardian, or as trustee under the will of any person domiciled in this State at the time of his death.

(b)   Except as otherwise provided by this Chapter, a foreign corporation with a valid certificate of authority has the same but no greater rights and has the same but no greater privileges as, and is subject to the same duties, restrictions, penalties, and liabilities now or later imposed on, a domestic corporation of like character. (1955, c. 1230; 1993, c. 398, s. 1.)

§ 55A-15-06: Repealed by Session Laws 2001-358, s. 22, effective January 1, 2002.

§ 55A-15-07. Registered office and registered agent of foreign corporation.

Each foreign corporation authorized to conduct affairs in this State must maintain a registered office and registered agent as required by Article 4 of

Chapter 55D of the General Statutes and is subject to service on the Secretary of State under that Article. (1955, c. 1230; 1993, c. 398, s. 1; 2000-140, s. 101(e); 2001-358, s. 48(b); 2001-387, ss. 173, 175(a); 2001-413, s. 6.)

§§ 55A-15-08 through 55A-15-10: Repealed by Session Laws 2001-358, s. 48(c), effective January 1, 2002.

§§ 55A-15-11 through 55A-15-19. Reserved for future codification purposes.

Part 2. Withdrawal.

§ 55A-15-20. Withdrawal of foreign corporation.

(a)   A foreign corporation authorized to conduct affairs in this State shall not withdraw from this State until it obtains a certificate of withdrawal from the Secretary of State.

(b)   A foreign corporation authorized to conduct affairs in this State may apply for a certificate of withdrawal by delivering an application to the Secretary of State for filing. The application shall set forth:

(1)   The name of the foreign corporation and the name of the state or country under whose law it is incorporated;

(2)   That it is not conducting affairs in this State and that it surrenders its authority to conduct affairs in this State;

(3)   That the corporation revokes the authority of its registered agent to accept service of process and consents that service of process in any action or proceeding based upon any cause of action arising in this State, or arising out of affairs conducted in this State, during the time the corporation was authorized to conduct affairs in this State may thereafter be made on such corporation by service thereof on the Secretary of State;

(4)   A mailing address to which the Secretary of State may mail a copy of any process served on the Secretary of State under subdivision (3) of this subsection; and

(5)   A commitment to file with the Secretary of State a statement of any subsequent change in its mailing address.

(c)   If the Secretary of State finds that the application conforms to law, the Secretary of State shall:

(1)   Endorse on the application and an exact or conformed copy thereof the word "filed", and the hour, day, month, and year of the filing thereof;

(2)   File the application in the Secretary of State's office;

(3)   Issue a certificate of withdrawal to which the Secretary of State shall affix the exact or conformed copy of the application; and

(4)   Send to the foreign corporation or its representative the certificate of withdrawal together with the exact or conformed copy of the application affixed thereto.

(d)   After the withdrawal of the foreign corporation is effective, service of process on the Secretary of State in accordance with subsection (b) of this section shall be made by delivering to and leaving with the Secretary of State, or any clerk authorized by the Secretary of State to accept service of process, duplicate copies of the process and the fee required by G.S. 55A-1-22(b). Upon receipt of process in the manner provided in this subsection, the Secretary of State shall immediately mail a copy of the process by registered or certified mail, return receipt requested, to the foreign corporation at the mailing address designated pursuant to subsection (b) of this section. (1955, c. 1230; 1973, c. 476, s. 193; 1993, c. 398, s. 1; 1995, c. 400, s. 9; 2001-387, ss. 44, 45.)

§ 55A-15-21. Withdrawal of foreign corporation by reason of a merger, consolidation, or conversion.

(a)   Whenever a foreign corporation authorized to conduct affairs in this State ceases its separate existence as a result of a statutory merger or consolidation permitted by the laws of the state or country under which it was

136

incorporated, or converts into another entity as permitted by those laws, the surviving or resulting entity shall apply for a certificate of withdrawal for the foreign corporation by delivering to the Secretary of State for filing a copy of the articles of merger, consolidation, or conversion or a certificate reciting the facts of the merger, consolidation, or conversion duly authenticated by the secretary of state or other official having custody of corporate records in the state or country under the laws of which the foreign corporation was incorporated. If the surviving or resulting entity is not authorized to conduct affairs or transact business in this State, the articles or certificate shall be accompanied by an application which must set forth:

(1)   The name of the foreign corporation authorized to conduct affairs in this State, the type of entity and the name of the surviving or resulting entity, and a statement that the surviving or resulting entity is not authorized to conduct affairs or transact business in this State;

(2)   A statement that the surviving or resulting entity consents that service of process based upon any cause of action arising in this State, or arising out of affairs conducted in this State, during the time the foreign corporation was authorized to conduct affairs in this State may thereafter be made by service thereof on the Secretary of State;

(3)   A mailing address to which the Secretary of State may mail a copy of any process served on the Secretary of State under subdivision (a)(2) of this section; and

(4)   A commitment to file with the Secretary of State a statement of any subsequent change in its mailing address.

(b)   If the Secretary of State finds that the articles or certificate and the application for withdrawal, if required, conform to law the Secretary of State shall:

(1)   Endorse on the articles or certificate and the application for withdrawal, if required, the word "filed", and the hour, day, month, and year of filing thereof;

(2)   File the articles or certificate and the application, if required;

(3)   Issue a certificate of withdrawal; and

137

(4)   Send to the surviving or resulting entity or its representative the certificate of withdrawal, together with the exact or conformed copy of the application, if required, affixed thereto.

(c)   After the withdrawal of the foreign corporation is effective, service of process on the Secretary of State in accordance with subsection (a) of this section shall be made by delivering to and leaving with the Secretary of State, or any clerk authorized by the Secretary of State to accept service of process, duplicate copies of the process and the fee required by G.S. 55A-1-22(b). Upon receipt of process in the manner provided in this subsection, the Secretary of State shall immediately mail a copy of the process by registered or certified mail, return receipt requested, to the foreign corporation at the mailing address designated pursuant to subsection (a) of this section. (1993, c. 398, s. 1; 1999-369, s. 2.8; 2001-387, ss. 46, 47; 2001-487, s. 62(g).)

§§ 55A-15-22 through 55A-15-29. Reserved for future codification purposes.

Part 3. Revocation of Certificate of Authority.

§ 55A-15-30. Grounds for revocation.

(a)   The Secretary of State may commence a proceeding under G.S. 55A-15-31 to revoke the certificate of authority of a foreign corporation authorized to conduct affairs in this State if:

(1)   Repealed by Session Laws 1995, c. 539, s. 28.

(2)   The foreign corporation does not pay within 60 days after they are due any penalties, fees, or other payments due under this Chapter;

(3)   The foreign corporation is without a registered agent or registered office in this State for 60 days or more;

(4)   The foreign corporation does not inform the Secretary of State under G.S. 55D-31 or G.S. 55D-32 that its registered agent or registered office has changed, that its registered agent has resigned, or that its registered office has been discontinued within 60 days of the change, resignation, or discontinuance;

138

(5)   An incorporator, director, officer, or agent of the foreign corporation signs a document he knew was false in any material respect with intent that the document be delivered to the Secretary of State for filing;

(6)   The Secretary of State receives a duly authenticated certificate from the secretary of state or other official having custody of corporate records in the state or country under whose law the foreign corporation is incorporated stating that it has been dissolved or disappeared as the result of a merger;

(7)   The corporation is exceeding the authority conferred upon it by this Chapter; or

(8)   The corporation knowingly fails or refuses to answer truthfully and fully within the time prescribed in this Chapter interrogatories propounded by the Secretary of State in accordance with the provisions of this Chapter.

(b)   Nothing herein shall be deemed to repeal or modify any provision of the Revenue Act relating to the suspension of the certificate of authority of foreign corporations for failure to comply with the provisions thereof. (1955, c. 1230; 1993, c. 398, s. 1; 1995, c. 509, s. 32; c. 539, s. 28; 2001-358, s. 48(f); 2001-387, ss. 173, 175(a); 2001-413, s. 6.)

§ 55A-15-31. Procedure and effect of revocation.

(a)   If the Secretary of State determines that one or more grounds exist under G.S. 55A-15-30 for revocation of a certificate of authority, the Secretary of State shall mail to the foreign corporation written notice of the Secretary of State's determination.

(b)   If the foreign corporation does not correct each ground for revocation or demonstrate to the reasonable satisfaction of the Secretary of State that each ground determined by the Secretary of State does not exist within 60 days after notice is mailed, the Secretary of State may revoke the foreign corporation's certificate of authority by signing a certificate of revocation that recites the ground or grounds for revocation and its effective date. The Secretary of State shall file the original of the certificate and mail a copy to the foreign corporation.

(c)   The authority of a foreign corporation to conduct affairs in this State ceases on the date shown on the certificate revoking its certificate of authority.

(d)   The Secretary of State's revocation of a foreign corporation's certificate of authority appoints the Secretary of State the foreign corporation's agent for service of process in any proceeding based on a cause of action arising in this State or arising out of affairs conducted in this State during the time the foreign corporation was authorized to conduct affairs in this State. The Secretary of State shall then proceed in accordance with G.S. 55D-33.

(e)   Revocation of a foreign corporation's certificate of authority does not terminate the authority of the registered agent of the corporation.

(f)   The corporation shall not be granted a new certificate of authority until each ground for revocation has been substantially corrected to the reasonable satisfaction of the Secretary of State. (1955, c. 1230; 1993, c. 398, s. 1; 1995, c. 400, s. 10; 2001-358, s. 48(g); 2001-387, ss. 173, 175(a); 2001-413, s. 6.)

§ 55A-15-32. Appeal from revocation.

(a)   A foreign corporation may appeal the Secretary of State's revocation of its certificate of authority to the Superior Court of Wake County within 30 days after service of the certificate of revocation is mailed. The appeal is commenced by filing a petition with the court and with the Secretary of State requesting the court to set aside the revocation. The petition shall have attached to it copies of the corporation's certificate of authority and the Secretary of State's certificate of revocation. No service of process on the Secretary of State is required except for the filing of the petition as set forth in this subsection. The appeal to the superior court shall be determined by a judge of the superior court upon such further evidence, notice, and opportunity to be heard, if any, as the court may deem appropriate under the circumstances. The foreign corporation shall have the burden of establishing that it is entitled to have the revocation set aside.

(b)   Upon consideration of the petition and any response made by the Secretary of State, the court may, prior to entering final judgment, order the Secretary of State to set aside the revocation or may take any other action the court considers appropriate.

(c)   The court's final decision may be appealed as in other civil proceedings. (1993, c. 398, s. 1; c. 553, s. 83(b); 2001-358, s. 5A(d); 2001-387, ss. 173, 175(a); 2001-413, s. 6.)

§ 55A-15-33. Inapplicability of Administrative Procedure Act.

The Administrative Procedure Act shall not apply to any proceeding or appeal provided for in G.S. 55A-15-30 through G.S. 55A-15-32. (1995, c. 400, s. 11.)

Article 16.

Records and Reports.

Part 1. Records.

§ 55A-16-01. Corporate records.

(a)   A corporation shall keep as permanent records minutes of all meetings of its members and board of directors, a record of all actions taken by the members or directors without a meeting pursuant to G.S. 55A-7-04, 55A-7-08, or 55A-8-21, and a record of all actions taken by committees of the board of directors in place of the board of directors on behalf of the corporation.

(b)   A corporation shall maintain appropriate accounting records.

(c)   A corporation or its agent shall maintain a record of its members, in a form that permits preparation of a list of the names and addresses of all members, in alphabetical order by class, showing the number of votes each member is entitled to cast.

(d)   A corporation shall maintain its records in written form or in another form capable of conversion into written form within a reasonable time.

(e)   A corporation shall keep a copy of the following records at its principal office:

(1)   Its articles of incorporation or restated articles of incorporation and all amendments to them currently in effect;

(2)   Its bylaws or restated bylaws and all amendments to them currently in effect;

(3)   Resolutions adopted by its members or board of directors relating to the number or classification of directors or to the characteristics, qualifications, rights, limitations, and obligations of members or any class or category of members;

(4)   The minutes of all membership meetings, and records of all actions taken by the members without a meeting pursuant to G.S. 55A-7-04 or G.S. 55A-7-08, for the past three years;

(5)   All written communications to members generally within the past three years, and the financial statements, if any, that have been furnished or would have been required to be furnished to a member upon demand under G.S. 55A-16-20 during the past three years;

(6)   A list of the names and business or home addresses of its current directors and officers; and

(7)   Repealed by Session Laws 1995, c. 539, s. 29, effective July 29, 1995. (1955, c. 1230; 1969, c. 875, s. 6; 1985 (Reg. Sess., 1986), c. 801, s. 31; 1993, c. 398, s. 1; 1995, c. 539, s. 29.)

§ 55A-16-02. Inspection of records by members.

(a)   A member is entitled to inspect and copy, at a reasonable time and location specified by the corporation, any of the records of the corporation described in G.S. 55A-16-01(e) if the member gives the corporation written notice of his demand at least five business days before the date on which the member wishes to inspect and copy.

(b)   A member is entitled to inspect and copy, at a reasonable time and reasonable location specified by the corporation, any of the following records of the corporation if the member meets the requirements of subsection (c) of this

142

section and gives the corporation written notice of his demand at least five business days before the date on which the member wishes to inspect and copy:

(1)   Excerpts from any records required to be maintained under G.S. 55A-16-01(a), to the extent not subject to inspection under G.S. 55A-16-02(a);

(2)   Accounting records of the corporation; and

(3)   Subject to G.S. 55A-16-05, the membership list.

(c)   A member may inspect and copy the records identified in subsection (b) of this section only if:

(1)   The member's demand is made in good faith and for a proper purpose;

(2)   The member describes with reasonable particularity the purpose and the records the member desires to inspect; and

(3)   The records are directly connected with this purpose.

(d)   This section does not affect:

(1)   The right of a member to inspect records under G.S. 55A-7-20 or, if the member is in litigation with the corporation, to inspect the records to the same extent as any other litigant; or

(2)   The power of a court, independently of this Chapter, to compel the production of corporate records for examination.

(e)   A member of a corporation that has the power to elect, appoint, or designate a majority of the directors of another domestic or foreign corporation, whether nonprofit or business, shall have inspection rights with respect to the records of that other corporation. (1955, c. 1230; 1985 (Reg. Sess., 1986), c. 801, s. 31; 1993, c. 398, s. 1.)

§ 55A-16-03. Scope of inspection rights.

(a)   A member's agent or attorney has the same inspection and copying rights as the member the agent or attorney represents.

(b)   The right to copy records under G.S. 55A-16-02 includes, if reasonable, the right to receive copies made by photographic, xerographic, electronic, magnetic, or other means.

(c)   The corporation may impose a reasonable charge, covering the costs of labor and material, for producing for inspection or copying any records provided to the member. The charge shall not exceed the estimated cost of production or reproduction of the records.

(d)   The corporation may comply with a member's demand to inspect the record of members under G.S. 55A-16-02(b)(3) by providing the member with a list of its members that was compiled no earlier than the date of the member's demand. (1955, c. 1230; 1985 (Reg. Sess., 1986), c. 801, s. 31; 1993, c. 398, s. 1.)

§ 55A-16-04. Court-ordered inspection.

(a)   If a corporation does not allow a member who complies with G.S. 55A-16-02(a) to inspect and copy any records required by that subsection to be available for inspection, the superior court in the county where the corporation's principal office (or, if there is none in this State, its registered office) is located may, upon application of the member, summarily order inspection and copying of the records demanded at the corporation's expense.

(b)   If a corporation does not within a reasonable time allow a member to inspect and copy any other record, the member who complies with G.S. 55A-16-02(b) and (c) may apply to the superior court in the county where the corporation's principal office (or, if there is none in this State, its registered office) is located for an order to permit inspection and copying of the records demanded. The court shall dispose of an application under this subsection on an expedited basis.

(c)   If the court orders inspection and copying of the records demanded, it shall also order the corporation to pay the member's cost (including reasonable attorneys' fees) incurred to obtain the order unless the corporation proves that it

144

refused inspection in good faith because it had a reasonable basis for doubt about the right of the member to inspect the records demanded.

(d)   If the court orders inspection and copying of the records demanded, it may impose reasonable restrictions on the use or distribution of the records by the demanding member. (1993, c. 398, s. 1.)

§ 55A-16-05. Limitations on use of membership list.

Without consent of the board of directors, a membership list or any part thereof shall not be obtained or used by any person for any purpose unrelated to a member's interest as a member. Without limiting the generality of the foregoing, and without the consent of the board, a membership list or any part thereof shall not be:

(1)   Used to solicit money or property unless such money or property will be used solely to solicit the votes of the members in an election to be held by the corporation;

(2)   Used for any commercial purpose; or

(3)   Sold to or purchased by any person. (1993, c. 398, s. 1; 1995, c. 509, s. 33.)

§§ 55A-16-06 through 55A-16-19. Reserved for future codification purposes.

Part 2. Reports.

§ 55A-16-20. Financial statements for members.

(a)   Except as provided in the articles of incorporation or bylaws of a charitable or religious corporation, a corporation upon written demand from a member shall furnish that member its latest annual financial statements, if any, which may be consolidated or combined statements of the corporation and one or more of its subsidiaries or affiliates, as appropriate, that include a balance sheet as of the end of the fiscal year and statement of operations for that year. If financial statements are prepared for the corporation on the basis of generally accepted accounting principles, the annual financial statements shall also be prepared on that basis.

(b)   If annual financial statements are reported upon by a public accountant, the accountant's report shall accompany them. If not, the statements must be accompanied by the statement of the president or the person responsible for the corporation's financial accounting records:

(1)   Stating the president's or other person's reasonable belief as to whether the statements were prepared on the basis of generally accepted accounting principles and, if not, describing the basis of preparation; and

(2)   Describing any respects in which the statements were not prepared on a basis of accounting consistent with the statements prepared for the preceding year. (1993, c. 398, s. 1.)

§ 55A-16-21. Notice of indemnification to members.

If a corporation indemnifies or advances expenses to a director under G.S. 55A-8-51, 55A-8-52, 55A-8-53, 55A-8-54, or 55A-8-57 in connection with a proceeding by or in the right of the corporation, the corporation shall give notice of the indemnification or advance in writing to the members with or before the notice of the next meeting of members. (1993, c. 398, s. 1.)

§ 55A-16-22: Repealed by Session Laws 1995, c. 539, s. 8.

§ 55A-16-23. Principal office address.

(a)   Any corporation that does not designate the street address and the mailing address, if different from the street address, of the corporation's principal office and the county of location in an annual report or its articles of incorporation shall file a Designation of Principal Office Address form with the Secretary of State that contains that information.

(b)   A corporation may change its principal office by delivering to the Secretary of State for filing a Corporation's Statement of Change of Principal Office form that sets forth:

(1)   The street address, and the mailing address if different from the street address, of the corporation's current principal office and the county in which it is located; and

(2)   The street address, and the mailing address if different from the street address, of the new principal office and the county in which it is located. (1995, c. 539, s. 21; 2001-358, s. 48(d); 2001-387, ss. 173, 175(a); 2001-413, s. 6.)

§ 55A-16-24. Financial statements for the public.

(a)   Notwithstanding any provisions in the articles of incorporation or bylaws, a corporation that receives over five thousand dollars ($5,000) of public funding within a fiscal year, including the amount of grants or loans and the value of any in-kind donations, from a local government, the State, or the federal government shall provide its latest annual financial statements upon written demand from any member of the public. The statements shall be substantively similar to those required under G.S. 55A-16-20 but shall contain additional details about the amount of public funds received and how those funds were used. Additionally, a corporation that receives public funding shall provide, upon written demand from any member of the public, a copy of its most recently completed and filed Internal Revenue Service Form 990 or Form 990-EZ, except of any information not required for public disclosure pursuant to 26 U.S.C. § 6104(d)(3), or a copy of the message confirming the corporation's submission of Internal Revenue Service Form 990-N. A corporation may comply with the provisions of this section by maintaining on its public Web site a financial report as described in this section and a copy of its most recent Internal Revenue Service Form 990, Form 990-EZ, or Form 990-N submission confirmation or by having such materials posted, as part of a database of similar documents of other tax-exempt organization, on a Web site established and maintained by another entity, provided that the entity does not charge a fee to access the information and provided that the corporation provides a link on its public Web site to the Web site maintained by the other entity.

147

(b)   Exceptions. - The following corporations already required to report information shall not be subject to subsection (a) of this section, but shall provide information on their public Web site to whom the corporation reports its information and how to access that information:

(1)   A corporation required to report to the North Carolina Medical Care Commission of the Department of Health and Human Services.

(2)   A corporation required to report to the Local Government Commission of the Department of State Treasurer.

(3)   A private college that meets the definition of "institution" under G.S. 116-22 and is required to report to the State under G.S. 143C-6-23. (2012-169, s. 1.)

Article 17.

Transition and Curative Provisions.

§ 55A-17-01. Applicability of Chapter.

(a)   The provisions of this Chapter relating to domestic corporations shall apply to:

(1)   All corporations heretofore or hereafter organized under this Chapter.

(2)   All nonprofit corporations without capital stock heretofore or hereafter organized under any other act, unless there is some other specific statutory provision particularly applicable to such corporations or inconsistent with some provisions of this Chapter, in which case that other provision prevails. Nothing herein shall apply to hospital and medical service corporations as defined in Article 65 of Chapter 58 of the General Statutes which were incorporated prior to July 1, 1957, or repeal or modify the provisions of G.S. 54-138.

(b)   The provisions of this Chapter relating to foreign corporations shall apply to all corporations conducting affairs in this State for purposes for which a corporation might be organized under this Chapter. A foreign corporation authorized to conduct affairs in this State on July 1, 1994, is subject to this Chapter but is not required to obtain a new certificate of authority to conduct affairs under this Chapter. (1955, c. 1230; 1967, c. 659; 1991, c. 720, s. 76; 1993, c. 398, s. 1; 1995, c. 400, s. 12.)

§ 55A-17-02. Certain religious, etc., associations deemed incorporated.

In all cases where a religious, educational, or charitable association has been formed prior to January 1, 1894, and has since that date been acting as a corporation, exercising the powers and performing the duties of religious, educational, or charitable corporations as prescribed by the laws of this State, then such association shall be conclusively presumed to have been duly and regularly organized and existing as a corporation under the laws of this State on January 1, 1894, and all of its acts as a corporation from and after said date, if otherwise valid, are hereby declared to be valid corporate acts. (1955, c. 1230; 1993, c. 398, s. 1.)

§ 55A-17-03. Saving provisions.

(a)   The existence of corporations formed before the effective date of this Chapter, shall not be impaired by the enactment of this Chapter nor by any change made by this Chapter in the requirements for the formation of corporations nor by any amendment or repeal by this Chapter of the laws under which they were formed or created, and, except as otherwise expressly provided in this Chapter, the repeal of a prior act by this Chapter shall not affect any liability or penalty incurred, under the provisions of such act, prior to the repeal thereof.

(b)   Any proceeding or corporate action commenced prior to the effective date of this Chapter, may be completed in accordance with the law then in effect. (1993, c. 398, s. 1.)

149

§ 55A-17-04. Severability.

If any provision of this Chapter or its application to any person or circumstance is held invalid by a court of competent jurisdiction, the invalidity does not affect other provisions or applications of the Chapter that can be given effect without the invalid provision or application, and to this end the provisions of the Chapter are severable. (1993, c. 398, s. 1.)

§ 55A-17-05. Validation of amendments to corporate charters extending corporate existence; limitation of actions; intent.

(a)   In every case where a corporation chartered under either the general or private laws of the State of North Carolina has continued or shall continue to act and conduct affairs as a corporation after the expiration of its period of existence as theretofore fixed in its charter and has thereafter filed in the office of the Secretary of State an amendment to its charter to extend or renew its corporate existence, such amendment is hereby validated and made effective for all intents and purposes to the same extent and with the same effect as if the amendment has been made within the period of such corporation's existence as theretofore fixed in its charter.

(b)   No action or proceeding shall be brought or defense or counterclaim pleaded later than July 1, 1958, in which either the continued existence of the corporation or the validity of any of the contracts, acts, deeds, rights, privileges, powers, franchises, and titles of the corporation is attacked or otherwise questioned on the grounds that the amendment was not filed within the period of the corporation's existence as theretofore fixed in its charter.

(c)   In no event shall the limitation provided in subsection (b) of this section bar any action, proceeding, defense, or counterclaim based upon grounds other than those mentioned in subsection (b) of this section, unless the grounds set out in subsection (b) of this section are an essential part thereof. (1957, c. 509; 1993, c. 398, s. 1.)

Chapter 55B.

Professional Corporation Act.

§ 55B-1. Title.

This Chapter may be cited as "The Professional Corporation Act." (1969, c. 718, s. 1.)

§ 55B-2. Definitions.

As used in this Chapter, the following words shall, unless the context requires otherwise, have the following meanings:

(1)   "Disqualified person" means a licensed person who for any reason becomes legally disqualified to render the same professional services which are or were being rendered by the professional corporation of which such person is an officer, director, shareholder or employee.

(2)   "Licensee" means any natural person who is duly licensed by the appropriate licensing board to render the same professional services which will be rendered by the professional corporation of which he is, or intends to become, an officer, director, shareholder or employee.

(3)   "Licensing board" means a board which is charged with the licensing and regulating of the profession or practice in this State in which the professional corporation is organized to engage.

(4)   The term "licensing board," as the same applies to attorneys at law, shall mean the Council of the North Carolina State Bar, and it shall include the North Carolina State Board of Law Examiners only to the extent that the North Carolina Board of Law Examiners is authorized to issue licenses for the practice of law under the supervision of the Council of the North Carolina State Bar.

(5)   "Professional corporation" means a corporation which is engaged in rendering the professional services as herein specified and defined, pursuant to a certificate of registration issued by the Licensing Board regulating the profession or practice, and which has as its shareholders only those individuals permitted by G.S. 55B-6 of this Chapter to be shareholders and which designates itself as may be required by this statute, and which is organized under the provisions of this Chapter and of Chapter 55, the North Carolina Business Corporation Act.

(6)   The term "professional service" means any type of personal or professional service of the public which requires as a condition precedent to the rendering of such service the obtaining of a license from a licensing board as herein defined, and pursuant to the following provisions of the General Statutes: Chapter 83A, "Architects"; Chapter 84, "Attorneys-at-Law"; Chapter 93, "Public Accountants"; and the following Articles in Chapter 90: Article 1, "Practice of Medicine," Article 2, "Dentistry," Article 6, "Optometry," Article 7, "Osteopathy," Article 8, "Chiropractic," Article 9A, "Nursing Practice Act," with regard to registered nurses, Article 11, "Veterinarians," Article 12A, "Podiatrists," Article 18A, "Practicing Psychologists," Article 18C, "Marriage and Family Therapy Licensure," Article 18D, "Occupational Therapy," Article 22, "Licensure Act for Speech and Language Pathologists and Audiologists," and Article 24, "Licensed Professional Counselors"; Chapter 89C, "Engineering and Land Surveying"; Chapter 89A, "Landscape Architects"; Chapter 90B, "Social Worker Certification and Licensure Act" with regard to Licensed Clinical Social Workers as defined by G.S. 90B-3; Chapter 89E, "Geologists"; Chapter 89B, "Foresters"; and Chapter 89F, "North Carolina Soil Scientist Licensing Act". (1969, c. 718, s. 2; 1971, c. 196, s. 1; 1977, c. 53; c. 855, s. 1; 1979, c. 460; 1989 (Reg. Sess., 1990), c. 1024, s. 3; 1991, c. 205, s. 1; 1995, c. 382, s. 2; 1997-421, s. 2; 2000-115, s. 4; 2001-487, s. 40(d); 2003-117, s. 3; 2004-199, s. 19; 2004-203, s. 4.)

§ 55B-3. North Carolina Business Corporation Act applicable; other applicable law.

(a)   Chapter 55 of the General Statutes, the North Carolina Business Corporation Act, applies to professional corporations, including their organization, and professional corporations shall enjoy the powers and privileges and shall be subject to the duties, restrictions and liabilities of other corporations, except insofar as the same may be limited or enlarged by this Chapter. If any provision of this Chapter conflicts with the provisions of Chapter 55 of the General Statutes, the North Carolina Business Corporation Act, the provisions of this Chapter shall prevail.

(b)   A document required or permitted by this Chapter to be filed by the Secretary of State shall be filed under Chapter 55D of the General Statutes, Filings, Names, and Registered Agents for Corporations, Nonprofit Corporations, Limited Liability Companies, Limited Partnerships, and Limited Partnerships. (1969, c. 718, s. 3; 1989 (Reg. Sess., 1990), c. 1024, s. 3; 2001-358, s. 11; 2001-387, ss. 173, 175(a); 2001-413, s. 6.)

§ 55B-4. Formation of corporation.

A professional corporation under this Chapter may be formed pursuant to the provisions of Chapter 55, the North Carolina Business Corporation Act, with the following limitations:

(1)   At least one incorporator shall be a "licensee" as hereinabove defined in G.S. 55B-2(2).

(2)   All of the shares of stock of the corporation shall be owned and held by a licensee, or licensees, as hereinabove defined in G.S. 55B-2(2), except as otherwise permitted in G.S. 55B-6.

(3)   At least one director and one officer shall be a "licensee" as hereinabove defined in G.S. 55B-2(2).

(4)   The articles of incorporation, in addition to the requirements of Chapter 55, shall designate the personal services to be rendered by the professional corporation and shall be accompanied by a certification by the appropriate licensing board that the ownership of the shares of stock is in compliance with the requirements of G.S. 55B-4(2) and G.S. 55B-6. (1969, c. 718, s. 4; 1977, c. 855, s. 1; 1989 (Reg. Sess., 1990), c. 1024, s. 3; 1991, c. 205, s. 2; 1995, c. 351, s. 15.)

§ 55B-5. Corporate name.

The corporate name used by professional corporations under this Chapter, except as limited by the licensing acts of the respective professions, shall be governed by the provisions of Chapter 55D, provided that professional corporations may use the words "Professional Association, P.A.," "Professional Corporation," or "P.C." in lieu of the corporate designations specified in Chapter 55D, and provided further that licensing boards by regulations may make further corporate name requirements or limitations for the respective professions, but such regulations may not prohibit the continued use of any corporate name duly adopted in conformity with the General Statutes and with the pertinent licensing board regulations in effect at the date of such adoption. (1969, c. 718, s. 5;

1983, c. 22; 1989 (Reg. Sess., 1990), c. 1024, s. 3; 2001-358, s. 25; 2001-387, ss. 173, 175(a); 2001-413, s. 6.)

§ 55B-6. Capital stock.

(a)   Except as provided in subsections (a1) and (b) of this section, a professional corporation may issue shares of its capital stock only to a licensee as defined in G.S. 55B-2, and a shareholder may voluntarily transfer shares of stock issued to the shareholder only to another licensee. No share or shares of any stock of a professional corporation shall be transferred upon the books of the corporation unless the corporation has received a certification of the appropriate licensing board that the transferee is a licensee. Provided, it shall be lawful in the case of professional corporations rendering services as defined in Chapters 83A, 89A, 89C, 89E, and 89F, for nonlicensed employees of the corporation to own not more than one-third of the total issued and outstanding shares of the corporation; and provided further, with respect to a professional corporation rendering services as defined in Chapters 83A, 89A, 89C, and 89E of the General Statutes, an employee retirement plan qualified under section 401 of the Internal Revenue Code of 1986, as amended (or any successor section), is deemed for purposes of this section to be a licensee if the trustee or trustees of the plan are licensees. Provided further, subject to any additional conditions that the appropriate licensing board may by rule or order impose in the public interest, it shall be lawful for individuals who are not licensees but who perform professional services on behalf of a professional corporation in another jurisdiction in which the corporation maintains an office, and who are duly licensed to perform professional services under the laws of the other jurisdiction, to be shareholders of the corporation so long as there is at least one shareholder who is a licensee as defined in G.S. 55B-2, and the corporation renders its professional services in the State only through those shareholders that are licensed in North Carolina. Upon the transfer of any shares of such corporation to a nonlicensed employee of such corporation, the corporation shall inform the appropriate licensing board of the name and address of the transferee and the number of shares issued to the nonprofessional transferee. The issuance or transfer of any share of stock in violation of this section is void. No shareholder of a professional corporation shall enter into a voting trust agreement or any other type of agreement vesting in another person the authority to exercise the voting power of any of the stock of a professional corporation.

154

(a1)   Any person may own up to forty-nine percent of the stock of a professional corporation rendering services under Chapter 93 of the General Statutes as long as:

(1)   Licensees continue to own and control voting stock that represents at least fifty-one percent (51%) of the votes entitled to be cast in the election of directors of the professional corporation; and

(2)   All licensees who perform professional services on behalf of the corporation comply with Chapter 93 of the General Statutes and the rules adopted thereunder.

(b)   A professional corporation formed pursuant to this Chapter may issue one hundred percent (100%) of its capital stock to another professional corporation in order for that corporation (the distributing corporation) to distribute in accordance with section 355 of the Internal Revenue Code of 1986, as amended (or any succeeding section), the stock of the controlled corporation to one or more shareholders of the distributing corporation authorized under this section to hold the shares. The distributing corporation shall distribute the stock of the controlled corporation within 30 days after the stock is issued to the distributing corporation. A share of stock of the controlled corporation that is not transferred in accordance with this subsection within 30 days after the share was issued to the distributing corporation is void. (1969, c. 718, s. 6; 1977, c. 855, s. 1; 1989, c. 258; 1991, c. 179, s. 1; c. 205, s. 3; 1995, c. 351, s. 16; 1999-440, s. 1; 2000-115, s. 5.)

§ 55B-7. Death or disqualification of a stockholder or employee.

(a)   If any officer, shareholder, agent or employee of a corporation organized under this Chapter who is a licensee becomes legally disqualified to render professional services within this State, he shall sever all employment with, and financial interest in, such corporation forthwith. A corporation's failure to comply with this provision shall constitute grounds for the forfeiture of its certificate of incorporation and its dissolution. When a corporation's failure to comply with this provision is brought to the attention of the Secretary of State, the Secretary of State shall forthwith certify that fact to the Attorney General for appropriate action to dissolve the corporation.

(b)   A professional corporation shall report to the appropriate licensing board the death of any of its shareholders within 30 days thereafter. Within one year of the date of such death, all of the shares owned by such deceased shareholder shall be transferred to and acquired by the professional corporation or persons qualified to own such shares. In the absence of an agreement which determines the equitable value of the shares, then the price for such shares shall be the fair market value of the stock, but not less than the book value as of the end of the month immediately preceding the death or disqualification. Notwithstanding any other provisions of this Chapter, the shares of stock owned by such deceased shareholder may be owned and held by the person or persons who may be legally entitled to receive such shares for a period of one year after the death of such deceased shareholder, or in the case of the death of the owner of all the shares of such corporation, for such period of time as may be necessary to liquidate the corporation. (1969, c. 718, s. 7.)

§ 55B-8. Rendition of professional services.

A professional service corporation may render professional services only through its officers, employees and agents who are duly licensed to render such professional services; provided, however, this provision shall not be interpreted to include in the term "employee," as used herein, clerks, secretaries, bookkeepers, technicians and other assistants who are not considered by law to be rendering professional services to the public. (1969, c. 718, s. 8.)

§ 55B-9. Professional relationship and liability.

(a)   Relationship. - Nothing in this Chapter shall be interpreted to abolish, modify, restrict, limit or alter the law in this State applicable to the professional relationship and liabilities between the licensee furnishing the professional services and the person receiving such professional service, or the standards of professional conduct applicable to the rendering therein of such services.

(b)   Liability. - A shareholder, a director, or an officer of a professional corporation is not individually liable, directly or indirectly, including by indemnification, contribution, assessment, or otherwise, for the debts, obligations, and liabilities of, or chargeable to, the professional corporation that arise from errors, omissions, negligence, malpractice, incompetence, or

156

malfeasance committed by another shareholder, director, or officer or by a representative of the professional corporation; provided, however, nothing in this Chapter shall affect the liability of a shareholder, director, or officer of a professional corporation for his or her own errors, omissions, negligence, malpractice, incompetence, or malfeasance committed in the rendering of professional services. (1969, c. 718, s. 9; 1993, c. 354, s. 2; 1999-362, s. 2; 2000-140, s. 101(f).)

§ 55B-10. Registration with licensing board.

No professional corporation shall open, operate, or maintain an establishment for any of the purposes set forth in this Chapter without first having obtained a certificate of registration from the licensing board or boards. Applications for such registration shall be made to the licensing board or boards in writing and shall contain the name and address of the corporation and such other information as may be required by the licensing board or boards. If the board finds that no disciplinary action is pending before the board against any of the licensed incorporators, officers, directors, shareholders or employees of such corporation, and if it appears that such corporation will be conducted in compliance with the law and the regulations of the board, the board shall issue, upon the payment of a registration fee, not to exceed fifty dollars ($50.00), a certificate of registration which shall remain effective until January 1 following the date of such registration or until such other expiration or renewal date as may be established by law or by the regulations of the licensing board. (1969, c. 718, s. 10.)

§ 55B-11. Renewal of certificate of registration.

Upon written application of the holder, accompanied by a fee not to exceed the sum of twenty-five dollars ($25.00), the licensing board shall renew the certificate of registration of a professional corporation as required by law or the regulations of the licensing board if the board finds that the corporation has complied with its regulations and the provisions of this section. If the corporation does not apply for renewal of its certificate of registration within 30 days after the date of the expiration of such certificate, the certificate of registration shall be automatically suspended and may be reinstated within the calendar year upon the payment of the required renewal fee plus a penalty of ten dollars

($10.00), if such corporation is then otherwise qualified and entitled to a renewal of its certificate of registration. (1969, c. 718, s. 11.)

§ 55B-12. Application of regulations of licensing boards.

A professional corporation shall be subject to the applicable rules and regulations adopted by, and all the disciplinary powers of, the licensing board as herein defined. Nothing in this Chapter shall impair the disciplinary powers of any licensing board applicable to a licensee as herein defined. No professional corporation may do any act which its shareholders as licensees are prohibited from doing. (1969, c. 718, s. 12.)

§ 55B-13. Suspension or revocation of certificate of registration.

A licensing board may suspend or revoke a certificate of registration issued by it to a domestic or foreign professional corporation for any of the following reasons:

(1)   Upon the failure of such corporation to promptly remove or discharge an officer, director, shareholder or employee who becomes disqualified by reason of the revocation or suspension of his license to practice; or

(2)   Upon a finding by the licensing board that the professional corporation has failed to comply with the provisions of this Chapter or the regulations of the licensing board.

Upon the suspension or revocation of a certificate of registration issued to a professional corporation, such corporation shall cease forthwith to render professional services, and the Secretary of State shall be notified to the end that the corporation may be removed from active status and remain as such until reinstatement. (1969, c. 718, s. 13; 1995, c. 351, s. 17.)

§ 55B-14. Types of professional services.

(a)   A professional corporation shall render only one specific type professional service, and such services as may be ancillary thereto, and shall not engage in any other business or profession; provided, however, such corporation may own real and personal property necessary or appropriate for rendering the type of professional services it was organized to render and it may invest in real estate, mortgages, stocks, bonds, and any other type of investments.

(b)   Notwithstanding subsection (a) of this section, in the case of architectural, landscape architectural, engineering or land surveying, geological, and soil science services, as defined in Chapters 83A, 89A, 89C, 89E, and 89F respectively, one corporation may be authorized to provide such of these services where such corporation, and at least one corporate officer who is a stockholder thereof, is duly licensed by the licensing board of each such profession.

(c)   A professional corporation may also be formed by and between or among:

(1)   A licensed psychologist and a physician practicing psychiatry to render psychotherapeutic and related services.

(2)   Any combination of a registered nurse, nurse practitioner, certified clinical specialist in psychiatric and mental health nursing, certified nurse midwife, and certified nurse anesthetist, to render nursing and related services that the respective stockholders are licensed, certified, or otherwise approved to provide.

(3)   A physician and a physician assistant who is licensed, registered, or otherwise certified under Chapter 90 of the General Statutes to render medical and related services.

(4)   A physician, a licensed psychologist, a licensed clinical social worker, or each of them and a certified clinical specialist in psychiatric and mental health nursing, a licensed marriage and family therapist, a licensed professional counselor, or each of them, to render psychotherapeutic and related services that the respective stockholders are licensed, certified, or otherwise approved to provide.

(5)   A physician and any combination of a nurse practitioner, certified clinical specialist in psychiatric and mental health nursing, or certified nurse midwife,

registered or otherwise certified under Chapter 90 of the General Statutes, to render medical and related services that the respective stockholders are licensed, certified, or otherwise approved to provide.

(6)   A physician practicing anesthesiology and a certified nurse anesthetist to render anesthesia and related medical services that the respective stockholders are licensed, certified, or otherwise approved to provide.

(7)   A physician and an audiologist who is licensed under Article 22 of Chapter 90 of the General Statutes to render audiological and related medical services that the respective stockholders are licensed, certified, or otherwise approved to provide.

(8)   A physician practicing ophthalmology and an optometrist who is licensed under Article 6 of Chapter 90 of the General Statutes to render either or both of ophthalmic services and optometric and related services that the respective stockholders are licensed, certified, or otherwise approved to provide.

(9)   A physician practicing orthopedics and a podiatrist who is licensed under Article 12A of Chapter 90 of the General Statutes to render either or both of orthopedic services and podiatric and related services that the respective stockholders are licensed, certified, or otherwise approved to provide. (1969, c. 718, s. 14; 1971, c. 196, s. 2; 1973, c. 1446, s. 9; 1985, c. 251; 1991, c. 205, s. 4; 1995, c. 382, s. 1; 1997-421, s. 1; 1997-500, s. 1; 1999-136, s. 1; 2000-115, s. 6; 2001-487, s. 40(e); 2003-117, s. 4; 2006-144, s. 3.1; 2007-451, s. 2(a).)

§ 55B-15. Applicability of Chapter.

(a)   This Chapter shall not apply to the following:

(1)   A corporation which prior to June 5, 1969, was permitted by law to render professional services or the corporate successor of that corporation by merger or otherwise by operation of law, provided there is no substantial change in the direct or indirect beneficial ownership of the shares of that corporation as the result of the merger or other transaction. For purposes of this subdivision, a change of twenty percent (20%) or less shall not be considered substantial.

(2)   A corporation authorized in this State to render primary services governed by Articles 1, 2, 4, or 5 of Chapter 87 of the General Statutes, if the

corporation renders services as defined in Chapter 89C of the General Statutes, that are reasonably necessary and connected with the primary services performed by individuals regularly employed in the ordinary course of business by the corporation. The professional services may not be offered, performed, or rendered independently from the primary services rendered by the corporation. This subdivision does not restrict, limit, or modify the requirement that professional services must be provided by individuals regularly employed in the ordinary course of business by the corporation and duly licensed to render these professional services in this State. Nothing in this subdivision shall be interpreted to abolish, modify, restrict, limit, or alter the law in this State applicable to the professional relationship and liabilities between licensees furnishing the professional service and the person receiving the professional service, or the standards of professional conduct applicable to the rendering of the professional service.

(b)   A corporation or its successor exempt under subsection (a) of this section may be brought within the provisions of this Chapter by the filing of an amendment to its articles of incorporation declaring that its shareholders have elected to bring the corporation within the provisions of this Chapter and to make the same conform to all of the provisions of this Chapter. (1969, c. 718, s. 15; 1991, c. 645, s. 20; 1997-244, s. 1.)

§ 55B-16. Foreign professional corporations.

(a)   A foreign professional corporation may apply for a certificate of authority to transact business in this State pursuant to the provisions of this Chapter and Chapter 55 of the General Statutes provided that:

(1)   The corporation obtains a certificate of registration from the appropriate licensing board or boards in this State;

(2)   With respect to each professional service practiced through the corporation in this State, at least one director and one officer shall be a licensee of the licensing board which regulates the profession in this State;

(3)   Each officer, employee, and agent of the corporation who will provide professional services to persons in this State shall be a licensee of the appropriate licensing board in this State;

161

(4)   The corporation shall be subject to the applicable rules and regulations adopted by, and all the disciplinary powers of, the appropriate licensing board or boards in this State;

(5)   The corporation's activities in this State shall be limited as provided by G.S. 55B-14; and

(6)   The application for certificate of authority, in addition to the requirements of G.S. 55-15-03, shall set forth the personal services to be rendered by the foreign professional corporation and the individual or individuals who will satisfy the requirements of G.S. 55B-16(a)(2) and shall be accompanied by a certification by the appropriate licensing board that each individual is a "licensee" as defined in G.S. 55B-2(2) and by additional certifications as may be required to establish that the corporation is a "foreign professional corporation" as defined in G.S. 55B-16(b).

(b)   For purposes of this section, "foreign professional corporation" means a corporation for profit that:

(1)   Is incorporated under a law other than the law of this State;

(2)   Is incorporated for the purpose of rendering professional services of the type that if rendered in this State would require the obtaining of a license from a licensing board pursuant to the statutory provisions referred to in G.S. 55B-2(6); and

(3)   Has as its shareholders only individuals who:

a.   Qualify to hold shares of a corporation organized under this Chapter;

b.   Are licensed to provide professional services as defined in G.S. 55B-2(6) in a state in which the corporation is incorporated or is authorized to transact business, provided that such professional services are the same as the professional service rendered by the corporation;

c.   Are nonlicensed employees of a corporation rendering services of the type defined in Chapters 83A, 89A, 89C, and 89E of the General Statutes, provided that all such nonlicensed employees own no more than one-third of the total issued and outstanding shares of such corporation in the aggregate; or

162

d.   With respect to a professional corporation rendering services under Chapter 93 of the General Statutes, are persons who own not more than forty-nine percent (49%) of the stock in the professional corporation as long as:

1.   Individuals who meet the requirements of sub-subdivision a. or b. of this subdivision own and control voting stock that represents at least fifty-one percent (51%) of the votes entitled to be cast in the election of directors of the professional corporation; and

2.   All licensees who perform professional services on behalf of the corporation in this State comply with Chapter 93 of the General Statutes and the rules adopted thereunder.

(b1)   With respect to a professional corporation rendering services as defined in Chapters 83A, 89A, 89C, and 89E of the General Statutes, an employee retirement plan qualified under section 401 of the Internal Revenue Code of 1986, as amended (or any successor section), is deemed for purposes of this section to be an individual licensee if at least one trustee of the plan is a licensee and all other trustees are licensees or are individuals who are licensed under the laws of a state in which the corporation maintains an office to perform at least one of the professional services, as defined in Chapter 83A, 89A, 89C, or 89E of the General Statutes, rendered by the corporation.

(c)   A foreign professional corporation with a valid certificate of authority has the same but no greater rights and privileges as, and is subject to the same duties, restrictions, penalties, and liabilities now or later imposed on, a domestic professional corporation of like character, except that the provisions of G.S. 55B-6 and G.S. 55B-7 do not apply. (1995, c. 351, s. 18; 1997-485, s. 23; 1999-440, s. 2.)

Chapter 55C.

Foreign Trade Zones.

§ 55C-1. Public corporations authorized to apply for privilege of establishing a foreign trade zone.

Any public corporation of the State of North Carolina, as that term is hereinafter defined is hereby authorized to make application for the privilege of establishing, operating and maintaining a foreign trade zone in accordance with an act of

Congress approved June 18, 1934, entitled, "An Act to Provide for the Establishment, Operation and Maintenance of Foreign Trade Zones in Ports of Entry of the United States," to expedite and encourage foreign commerce, and for other purposes. (1975, 2nd Sess., c. 983, s. 132.)

§ 55C-2. "Public corporation" defined.

The term "public corporation" for the purposes of this Chapter, means the State of North Carolina or any political subdivision thereof, or any public agency of this State or any political subdivision thereof, or any public board, bureau, commission or authority created by the General Assembly, or a corporate municipal instrumentality of one or more states. (1975, 2nd Sess., c. 983, s. 132; 2013-342, s. 2.)

§ 55C-3. Private corporations authorized to apply for privilege of establishing a foreign trade zone.

Any private corporation hereafter organized under the laws of this State for the specific purpose of establishing, operating and maintaining a foreign trade zone in accordance with the act of Congress referred to in G.S. 55C-1 is likewise authorized to make application for the privilege of establishing, operating and maintaining a foreign trade zone in accordance with the said act of Congress. (1975, 2nd Sess., c. 983, s. 132.)

§ 55C-4. Public or private corporation establishing foreign trade zone to be governed by federal law.

Any public or private corporation authorized by this Chapter to make application for the privilege of establishing, operating, and maintaining said foreign trade zone, whose application is granted pursuant to the terms of the aforementioned act of Congress is hereby authorized to establish such foreign trade zone and to operate and maintain the same subject to the conditions and restrictions of the said act of Congress and any amendments thereto, and under such rules and regulations and for the period of time that may be prescribed by the board established by said act of Congress to carry out the provisions of such act. (1975, 2nd Sess., c. 983, s. 132; 1977, c. 782, s. 1.)

Chapter 55D.

Filings, Names, and Registered Agents for Corporations, Nonprofit Corporations, and Partnerships.

Article 1.

General Provisions.

§ 55D-1. Applicable definitions.

The following definitions apply in this Chapter:

(1)   "Corporation" or "domestic corporation" is defined in G.S. 55-1-40(4).

(2)   "Deliver" is defined in G.S. 55-1-40(5).

(3)   "Entity" is defined in G.S. 55-1-40(9).

(4)   "Foreign corporation" is defined in G.S. 55-1-40(10).

(5)   "Foreign limited liability company" has the same meaning as the term "foreign LLC" in G.S. 57D-1-03.

(5a)   "Foreign limited liability limited partnership" is defined in G.S. 59-102(4c).

(6)   "Foreign limited liability partnership" is defined in G.S. 59-32(4g).

(7)   "Foreign limited partnership" is defined in G.S. 59-102(5).

(8)   "Foreign nonprofit corporation" means a foreign corporation as defined in G.S. 55A-1-40(11).

(9)   "Individual" is defined in G.S. 55-1-40(13).

(10)   "Limited liability company" or "domestic limited liability company" has the same meaning as the term "LLC" in G.S. 57D-1-03.

(11)   "Limited liability limited partnership" is defined in G.S. 59-102(6a).

(12)   "Limited liability partnership" or "registered limited liability partnership" means a registered limited liability partnership as defined in G.S. 59-32(7).

(13)   "Limited partnership" or "domestic limited partnership" is defined in G.S. 59-102(8).

(14)   "Nonprofit corporation" or "domestic nonprofit corporation" means a corporation as defined in G.S. 55A-1-40(5).

(15)   "Person" is defined in G.S. 55-1-40(16). (2001-358, s. 1; 2001-387, ss. 161, 173, 175(a); 2001-413, s. 6; 2013-157, s. 6.)

§§ 55D-2 through 55D-4: Reserved for future codification purposes.

§ 55D-5. Rule-making authority.

The Secretary of State may adopt rules to implement the Secretary of State's responsibilities under this Chapter. (2001-358, s. 1; 2001-387, s. 173; 2001-413, s. 6.)

§§ 55D-6 through 55D-9: Reserved for future codification purposes.

Article 2.

Submission of Documents to the Secretary of State for Filing.

§ 55D-10. Filing requirements.

(a)   To be entitled to filing by the Secretary of State under Chapter 55, 55A, 55B, 57D, or 59 of the General Statutes, a document must satisfy the requirements of this section, and of any other section of the General Statutes that adds to or varies these requirements.

(b)   The document must meet all of the following requirements:

(1)   The document must be one that is required or permitted by Chapter 55, 55A, 55B, 57D, or 59 of the General Statutes to be filed in the office of the Secretary of State.

(2)   The document must contain the information required by Chapter 55, 55A, 55B, 57D, or 59 of the General Statutes for that document. It may contain other information as well.

(3)   The document must be typewritten, printed, or in an electronic form acceptable to the Secretary of State.

(4)   The document must be in the English language. A name need not be in English if written in English letters or Arabic or Roman numerals, and the certificate of existence or a document of similar import required of foreign corporations, foreign nonprofit corporations, foreign limited liability companies, and foreign limited liability partnerships need not be in English if accompanied by a reasonably authenticated English translation.

(5)   A document submitted by an entity must be executed by a person authorized to execute documents (i) under G.S. 55-1-20 if the entity is a domestic or foreign corporation, (ii) under G.S. 55A-1-20 if the entity is a domestic or foreign nonprofit corporation, (iii) under G.S. 57D-1-20 if the entity is a domestic or foreign limited liability company, (iv) under G.S. 59-204 if the entity is a domestic or foreign limited partnership, or (v) under G.S. 59-35.1 if the entity is any other partnership as defined in G.S. 59-36 whether or not formed under the laws of the State.

(6)   The person executing the document must sign it and state beneath or opposite the person's signature, the person's name, and the capacity in which the person signs. Any signature on the document may be a facsimile or an electronic signature in a form acceptable to the Secretary of State. The

167

document may but need not contain a seal, attestation, acknowledgment, verification, or proof.

(7)   If the Secretary of State has prescribed a mandatory form for the document, the document must be in or on the prescribed form.

(8)   The document must be delivered to the office of the Secretary of State for filing and must be accompanied by the applicable fees. (1955, c. 1371, s. 1; 1967, c. 13, s. 1; c. 823, s. 16; 1989, c. 265, s. 1; 1989 (Reg. Sess., 1990), c. 1024, s. 12.1(a); 1991, c. 645, s. 15; 1999-369, s. 1.1; 2001-358, ss. 3(a), 4; 2001-387, ss. 173, 175(a); 2001-413, s. 6; 2013-157, s. 7.)

§ 55D-11. Expedited filings.

A person submitting a document for filing may request an expedited filing only at the time the document is submitted. The Secretary of State shall guarantee the expedited filing of the document if the document is in proper form and accompanied by all applicable fees, including the following fee:

(1)   Two hundred dollars ($200.00) for the filing by the end of the same business day of a document received by 12:00 noon; or

(2)   One hundred dollars ($100.00) for the filing of a document within 24 hours after receipt, excluding weekends and holidays.

The Secretary of State shall not collect the fees allowed in this section unless the person submitting the document for filing is informed by the Secretary of State of the fees prior to the filing of the document. (1995, c. 539, s. 1; 2001-358, ss. 3(b), 4; 2001-387, ss. 173, 175(a); 2001-413, s. 6.)

§ 55D-12. Advisory review of documents.

Upon request, the Secretary of State shall review a document prior to its submission for filing to determine whether it satisfies applicable filing requirements. Submission of a document for review shall be accompanied by a fee of two hundred dollars ($200.00) and shall be in accordance with procedures adopted by rule by the Secretary of State. The advisory review shall be completed within 24 hours after submission, excluding weekends and holidays, unless the person submitting the document is otherwise notified in accordance with procedures adopted by rule by the Secretary of State fixing priority between submissions under this section and filings under G.S. 55D-11. Upon completion of the advisory review, the Secretary of State shall notify the person submitting the document of any deficiencies in the document that would prevent its filing. (1997-485, s. 6; 2001-358, ss. 3(b), 4; 2001-387, ss. 173, 175(a); 2001-413, s. 6.)

§ 55D-13. Effective time and date of document.

(a)   Except as provided in subsection (b) of this section and in G.S. 55D-14, a document accepted for filing is effective:

(1)   At the time of filing on the date it is filed, as evidenced by the Secretary of State's date and time endorsement on the filed document; or

(2)   At the time specified in the document as its effective time on the date it is filed.

(b)   A document may specify a delayed effective time and date, and if it does so the document becomes effective at the time and date specified. If a delayed effective date but no time is specified, the document is effective at 11:59:59 P.M. on that date. A delayed effective date for a document may not be later than the 90th day after the date it is filed.

(c)   Except as provided in G.S. 55-2-03(b), 55A-2-03(b), and 57D-2-20(b), the fact that a document has become effective under this section does not determine its validity or invalidity or the correctness or incorrectness of the information contained in the document. (1955, c. 1371, s. 1; 1967, c. 13, s. 1; c. 823, s. 16; 1989, c. 265, s. 1; 1993, c. 552, s. 1; 2001-358, ss. 3(b), 4; 2001-387, ss. 173, 175(a); 2001-413, s. 6; 2013-157, s. 8.)

§ 55D-14. Correcting filed document.

(a)   A person on whose behalf a document was filed in the Office of the Secretary of State may correct that document if it (i) contains a statement that is incorrect and was incorrect when filed or (ii) was defectively executed, attested, sealed, verified, or acknowledged.

(b)   A document is corrected by delivering to the Secretary of State for filing articles of correction that do all of the following:

(1)   Describe the document (including its filing date) or have attached to them a copy of the document.

(2)   Specify the incorrect statement and the reason it is incorrect or the nature of the defect.

(3)   Correct the incorrect statement or defect.

(c)   Articles of correction are effective as of the effective time and date of the document they correct except as to persons relying on the uncorrected document and adversely affected by the correction. As to those persons, articles of correction are effective when filed. (1989, c. 265, s. 1; 1997-485, s. 14; 2001-358, ss. 3(b), 4; 2001-387, ss. 173, 175(a); 2001-413, s. 6.)

§ 55D-15. Filing duty of Secretary of State.

(a)   If a document delivered to the office of the Secretary of State for filing satisfies the requirements of this Chapter and of Chapter 55, 55A, 55B, 57D, or 59 of the General Statutes, the Secretary of State shall file it. Documents filed with the Secretary of State under this Chapter may be maintained by the Secretary either in their original form or in photographic, microfilm, optical disk media, or other reproduced form. The Secretary may make reproductions of documents filed under this Chapter, or under any predecessor law, by photographic, microfilm, optical disk media, or other means of reproduction, and may destroy the originals of those documents reproduced.

(b)   The Secretary of State files a document by endorsing "Filed", together with the Secretary's name and official title and the date and time of filing, on the document. After filing a document, the Secretary of State shall deliver a document copy to the person submitting the document for filing and as provided in G.S. 55D-32.

(c)   If the Secretary of State refuses to file a document, the Secretary shall return it to the person submitting the document for filing within five days after the document was received, together with a written statement of the date of the refusal and a brief explanation of the reason for refusal. The Secretary of State may correct apparent errors and omissions on a document submitted for filing if authorized to make the corrections by the person submitting the document for filing.

(d)   The Secretary of State's duty is to review and file documents that satisfy the requirements of this Chapter and of Chapter 55, 55A, 55B, 57D, or 59 of the General Statutes. The Secretary of State's filing or refusing to file a document does not do any of the following:

(1)   Except as provided in G.S. 55-2-03(b), 55A-2-03(b), or 57D-2-20(b), affect the validity or invalidity of the document in whole or part.

(2)   Relate to the correctness or incorrectness of information contained in the document.

(3)   Create a presumption that the document is valid or invalid or that information contained in the document is correct or incorrect. (1955, c. 1371, s. 1; 1967, c. 13, s. 1; c. 823, s. 16; 1989, c. 265, s. 1; 1989 (Reg. Sess., 1990), c. 1024, s. 12.2; 1993, c. 552, s. 2; 1995, c. 539, s. 2; 2001-358, ss. 3(b), 4, 46; 2001-387, ss. 173, 175(a); 2001-413, s. 6; 2013-157, s. 9.)

§ 55D-16. Appeal from Secretary of State's refusal to file document.

(a)   If the Secretary of State refuses to file a document delivered to the Secretary of State's office for filing, the person on whose behalf the document was submitted for filing may, within 30 days after the date of the refusal, appeal the refusal to the Superior Court of Wake County. The appeal is commenced by filing a petition with the court and with the Secretary of State requesting the court to compel the Secretary of State to file the document. The petition must have attached to it the document to be filed and the Secretary of State's explanation for the refusal to file. No service of process on the Secretary of State is required except for the filing of the petition as set forth in this subsection. The appeal to the superior court is not governed by Chapter 150B of the General Statutes, the Administrative Procedure Act, and shall be determined by a judge of the superior court upon such further notice and opportunity to be heard, if any, as the court may deem appropriate under the circumstances.

(b)   Upon consideration of the petition and any response made by the Secretary of State, the court may, prior to entering final judgment, order the Secretary of State to file the document or take other action the court considers appropriate.

(c)   The court's final decision may be appealed as in other civil proceedings. (1989, c. 265, s. 1; 1989 (Reg. Sess., 1990), c. 1024, s. 12.3; 2001-358, ss. 3(b), 4; 2001-387, ss. 173, 175(a); 2001-413, s. 6.)

§ 55D-17. Evidentiary effect of copy of filed document.

A certificate attached to a copy of a document filed by the Secretary of State, bearing the Secretary of State's signature and the seal of office (both of which may be in facsimile or in any electronic form approved by the Secretary of State) and certifying that the copy is a true copy of the document, is conclusive evidence that the original document is on file with the Secretary of State. A photographic, microfilm, optical disk media, or other reproduced copy of a document filed under this Chapter, Chapter 55, 55A, 55B, 57D, or 59 of the General Statutes, or any predecessor law, when certified by the Secretary, shall be considered an original for all purposes and is admissible in evidence in like manner as an original. (1955, c. 1371, s. 1; 1989, c. 265, s. 1; 1995, c. 539, s. 3; 2001-358, ss. 3(b), 4; 2001-387, ss. 173, 175(a); 2001-413, s. 6; 2013-157, s. 10.)

§ 55D-18. Penalty for signing false document.

(a)   A person commits an offense if the person signs a document the person knows is false in any material respect with intent that the document be delivered to the Secretary of State for filing.

(b)   An offense under this section is a Class 1 misdemeanor. (1989, c. 265, s. 1; 1993, c. 539, s. 439; 1994, Ex. Sess., c. 24, s. 14(c); 2001-358, ss. 3(b), 4; 2001-387, ss. 173, 175(a); 2001-413, s. 6.)

§ 55D-19: Reserved for future codification purposes.

Article 3.

Names.

§ 55D-20. Name requirements.

(a)   In addition to the requirements of any other applicable section of the General Statutes:

(1)   The name of a corporation must contain the word "corporation", "incorporated", "company", or "limited", or the abbreviation "corp.", "inc.", "co.", or "ltd.".

(2)   The name of a limited liability company must contain the words "limited liability company" or the abbreviation "L.L.C." or "LLC", or the combination "ltd. liability co.", "limited liability co.", or "ltd. liability company". Notwithstanding the prior sentence, any limited liability company whose name contained the words "low-profit limited liability company" or the abbreviation "L3C" pursuant to subdivision (6) of this subsection prior to its repeal on January 1, 2014, may continue to use that name unless the limited liability company amends its articles of organization to change its name.

(3)   The name of a limited partnership that is not a limited liability limited partnership must contain the words "limited partnership", the abbreviation "L.P." or "LP", or the combination "ltd. partnership".

(4)   The name of a limited liability limited partnership must contain the words "registered limited liability limited partnership" or "limited liability limited partnership" or the abbreviation "L.L.L.P.", "R.L.L.L.P.", "LLLP", or "RLLLP".

(5)   A registered limited liability partnership's name must contain the words "registered limited liability partnership" or "limited liability partnership" or the abbreviation "L.L.P.", "R.L.L.P.", "LLP" or "RLLP".

173

(6)   Repealed by Session Laws 2013-157, s. 11, effective January 1, 2014.

(b)   In addition to the requirements of subsection (a) of this section, the name of a limited partnership shall not contain the name of a limited partner unless (i) it is also the name of a general partner or the corporate name of a corporate general partner, or (ii) the business of the limited partnership has been carried on under that name before the admission of that limited partner.

(c)   The name of a corporation, nonprofit corporation, or limited liability company shall not contain language stating or implying that the entity is organized for a purpose other than that permitted by G.S. 55-3-01, 55A-3-01, or 57D-2-01 and by its articles of incorporation or organization.

(d)   The use of assumed names or fictitious names, as provided for in Chapter 66, is not affected by this Chapter or by Chapter 55, 55A, 57D, or 59 of the General Statutes.

(e)   The filing of any document, the reservation or registration of any name under this Chapter or under Chapter 55, 55A, 55B, 57D, or 59 of the General Statutes, or the issuance of a certificate of authority to transact business or conduct affairs or a statement of foreign registration does not authorize the use in this State of a name in violation of the rights of any third party under the federal trademark act, the trademark act of this State, or other statutory or common law, and is not a defense to an action for violation of any of those rights. (1901, c. 2, s. 8; 1903, c. 453; Rev., s. 1137; 1913, c. 5, s. 1; C.S., s. 1114; 1935, cc. 166, 320; 1939, c. 222; G.S., s. 55-2; 1955, c. 1371, s. 1; 1959, c. 1316, s. 28; 1969, c. 751, ss. 4-6; 1973, c. 469, s. 45.3; 1989, c. 265, s. 1; 1989 (Reg. Sess., 1990), c. 1024, s. 12.5; 1995, c. 539, ss. 4, 5; 2001-358, ss. 14(a), 15; 2001-387, ss. 162, 173, 175(a); 2001-413, s. 6; 2010-187, s. 3; 2013-157, s. 11.)

§ 55D-21. Entity names on the records of the Secretary of State; availability.

(a)   The following entities are subject to this section:

(1)   Domestic corporations, nonprofit corporations, limited liability companies, limited partnerships, and registered limited liability partnerships.

(2)   Foreign corporations, foreign nonprofit corporations, foreign limited liability companies, and foreign limited partnerships applying for or maintaining a certificate of authority to transact business or conduct affairs in this State.

(3)   Foreign limited liability partnerships applying for or maintaining a statement of foreign registration.

(b)   Except as authorized by subsection (c) of this section, the name of an entity subject to this section, including a fictitious name for a foreign entity, must be distinguishable upon the records of the Secretary of State from:

(1)   The name of a domestic corporation, nonprofit corporation, limited liability company, limited partnership, or registered limited liability partnership, or of a foreign corporation, foreign nonprofit corporation, foreign limited liability company, or foreign limited partnership authorized to transact business or conduct affairs in this State, or a foreign limited liability partnership maintaining a statement of foreign registration in this State;

(2)   A name reserved or registered under G.S. 55D-23 or registered under G.S. 55D-24; and

(3)   The fictitious name adopted by a foreign corporation, foreign nonprofit corporation, foreign limited liability company, or foreign limited partnership authorized to transact business or conduct affairs, or a foreign limited liability partnership maintaining a statement of foreign registration in this State because its real name is unavailable.

(c)   A person may apply to the Secretary of State for authorization to use a name that is not distinguishable upon the Secretary of State's records from one or more of the names described in subsection (b) of this section. The Secretary of State shall authorize use of the name applied for if:

(1)   The other person who has or uses the name or who has reserved or registered the name consents in writing to the use and submits an undertaking in form satisfactory to the Secretary of State to change its name to a name that is distinguishable upon the records of the Secretary of State from the name of the applicant; or

(2)   The applicant delivers to the Secretary of State a certified copy of the final judgment of a court of competent jurisdiction establishing the applicant's right to use the name applied for in this State.

175

(d)   Except as otherwise provided in this subsection, the name of a corporation dissolved under Article 14 of Chapter 55 of the General Statutes, of a nonprofit corporation dissolved under Article 14 of Chapter 55A of the General Statutes, of a limited liability company dissolved under Article 6 of Chapter 57D of the General Statutes, of a limited partnership dissolved under Part 8 of Article 5 of Chapter 59 of the General Statutes, or of a limited liability partnership whose registration as a limited liability partnership has been cancelled under G.S. 59-84.2 or revoked under G.S. 59-84.4, may not be used by another entity until one of the following occurs:

(1)   In the case of a nonjudicial dissolution other than an administrative dissolution or cancellation of registration as a limited liability partnership, 120 days after the effective date of the dissolution or cancellation.

(2)   In the case of an administrative dissolution or revocation of registration as a limited liability partnership, the expiration of five years after the effective date of the administrative dissolution or revocation.

(3)   In the case of a judicial dissolution, 120 days after the later of the date the judgment has become final or the effective date of the dissolution. The person applying for the name must certify to the Secretary of State that no appeal or other judicial review of the judgment directing dissolution is pending.

(4)   The dissolved entity changes its name to a name that is distinguishable upon the records of the Secretary of State from the names of other domestic corporations, nonprofit corporations, limited liability companies, limited partnerships, or registered limited liability partnerships or foreign corporations, foreign nonprofit corporations, foreign limited liability companies, or foreign limited partnerships authorized to transact business or conduct affairs in this State, or foreign limited liability partnerships maintaining a statement of foreign registration in this State. (1901, c. 2, s. 8; 1903, c. 453; Rev., s. 1137; 1913, c. 5, s. 1; C.S., s. 1114; 1935, cc. 166, 320; 1939, c. 222; G.S., s. 55-2; 1955, c. 1371, s. 1; 1959, c. 1316, s. 28; 1969, c. 751, ss. 4-6; 1973, c. 469, s. 45.3; 1989, c. 265, s. 1; 1989 (Reg. Sess., 1990), c. 1024, s. 12.5; 1995, c. 539, ss. 4, 5; 2001-358, ss. 14(a), 15; 2001-387, ss. 163, 173, 175(a); 2001-390, s. 15; 2001-413, s. 6; 2001-487, s. 62(h); 2002-159, s. 23; 2013-157, s. 12.)

§ 55D-22. Names of foreign entities.

(a)   If the name of a foreign corporation, foreign nonprofit corporation, foreign limited liability company, foreign limited partnership, or foreign limited liability partnership does not satisfy the requirements of G.S. 55D-20 and G.S. 55D-21, then to obtain or maintain a certificate of authority to transact business or conduct affairs in this State or a statement of foreign registration in this State, the entity may:

(1)   If a foreign corporation or foreign nonprofit corporation, add the word "corporation", "incorporated", "company", or "limited", or the abbreviation "corp.", "inc.", "co.", or "ltd." to its corporate name for use in this State;

(2)   If a foreign limited liability company, add the words "limited liability company", or the abbreviation "L.L.C.", or "LLC", or the combination "ltd. liability co.", "limited liability co.", or "ltd. liability company" to its name for use in this State if the addition will cause the name to satisfy the requirements of G.S. 55D-20 and G.S. 55D-21;

(3)   If a foreign limited partnership that is not a foreign limited liability limited partnership, add the words "limited partnership" or the abbreviation "L.P." or "LP", or the combination "ltd. partnership";

(4)   If a foreign limited partnership that is a foreign limited liability limited partnership, add the words "registered limited liability limited partnership" or "limited liability limited partnership" or the abbreviation "L.L.L.P.", "R.L.L.L.P.", "LLLP", or "RLLLP";

(5)   If a foreign limited liability partnership, add the words "registered limited liability partnership", or "limited liability partnership" or the abbreviation "L.L.P.", "R.L.L.P.", "LLP", or "RLLP"; or

(6)   Use a fictitious name, which includes one or more of the words, abbreviations, or combinations in subdivisions (1) through (5) of this subsection if applicable, to transact business or conduct affairs in this State if its real name is unavailable and it delivers to the Secretary of State for filing a copy of the resolution adopting the fictitious name.

(b)   If a foreign corporation, foreign nonprofit corporation, foreign limited liability company, or foreign limited partnership authorized to transact business or conduct affairs in this State, or a foreign limited liability partnership maintaining a statement of foreign registration, changes its name to one that

177

does not satisfy the requirements of this Article, it may not transact business or conduct affairs in this State under the changed name until it adopts a name satisfying the requirements of this Article and obtains an amended certificate of authority or statement of foreign registration under G.S. 55-15-04, 55A-15-04, 57D-7-04, 59-91, or 59-905, as applicable. (2001-358, s. 15; 2001-387, ss. 164, 173, 175(a); 2001-413, s. 6; 2013-157, s. 13.)

§ 55D-23. Reserved name.

(a)   A person may reserve the exclusive use of a name for an entity, including a fictitious name for a foreign corporation, foreign nonprofit corporation, foreign limited liability company, foreign limited partnership, or foreign limited liability partnership whose name is not available, by filing an application with the Secretary of State. The application must set forth the name and address of the applicant and the name proposed to be reserved. If the Secretary of State finds that the name applied for is available, the Secretary of State shall reserve the name for the applicant's exclusive use for a nonrenewable 120-day period.

(b)   The owner of a reserved name may transfer the reservation to another person by filing with the Secretary of State a signed notice of the transfer that states the name and address of the transferee.

(c)   Any person acquiring the goodwill of a domestic corporation, nonprofit corporation, limited liability company, limited partnership, or registered limited liability partnership, or of a foreign corporation, foreign nonprofit corporation, foreign limited liability company, or foreign limited partnership authorized to transact business or conduct affairs in this State, or of a foreign limited liability partnership maintaining a statement of foreign registration in this State may, on furnishing the Secretary of State satisfactory evidence of such acquisition, reserve for 10 years the exclusive right to any name that became available as a result of the acquisition. (1901, c. 2, s. 8; 1903, c. 453; Rev., s. 1137; 1913, c. 5, s. 1; C.S., s. 1114; 1935, cc. 166, 320; 1939, c. 222; G.S., s. 55-2; 1955, c. 1371, s. 1; 1959, c. 1316, s. 28; 1969, c. 751, ss. 4-6; 1973, c. 469, s. 45.3; 1989, c. 265, s. 1; 2001-358, ss. 14(b), 15; 2001-387, ss. 173, 175(a); 2001-413, s. 6.)

§ 55D-24. Registered name.

(a)   A foreign corporation, foreign nonprofit corporation, foreign limited liability company, foreign limited partnership, or foreign limited liability partnership may register its name, or its name with any addition required by G.S. 55D-22, if the name to be registered is distinguishable upon the records of the Secretary of State from the names that are not available under G.S. 55D-21(b).

(b)   An entity described in subsection (a) of this section registers its name, or its name with any addition required by G.S. 55D-22, by filing with the Secretary of State an application:

(1)   Setting forth its name, or its name with any addition required by G.S. 55D-22, the state or country and date of its incorporation or formation, and a brief description of the nature of the business or activities in which it is engaged; and

(2)   Accompanied by a certificate of existence (or a document of a similar import) from the state or country of incorporation or formation.

(c)   The name is registered for the applicant's exclusive use upon the effective date of the application and until the end of the calendar year in which it became effective.

(d)   An entity whose registration is effective may renew it for successive years by filing with the Secretary of State a renewal application, which complies with the requirements of subsection (b) of this section, between October 1 and December 31 of the preceding year. The renewal application renews the registration for the following calendar year. Any renewal application filed after the expiration of the registration shall be treated as a new application for registration.

(e)   An entity whose registration is effective may thereafter become authorized to transact business or conduct affairs under that name or consent in writing to the use of that name by:

(1)   A domestic corporation, nonprofit corporation, limited liability company, limited partnership, or registered limited liability partnership thereafter incorporated, formed, or registered in this State under that name;

179

(2)   A domestic corporation, nonprofit corporation, limited liability company, limited partnership, or registered limited liability partnership that changes its name to that name; or

(3)   Another foreign corporation, foreign nonprofit corporation, foreign limited liability company, foreign limited partnership, or foreign limited liability partnership that becomes authorized to transact business or conduct affairs in this State under that name.

The registration terminates when the domestic corporation, nonprofit corporation, limited liability company, limited partnership, or registered limited liability partnership is incorporated, formed, registered, or changes its name or the foreign corporation, foreign nonprofit corporation, foreign limited liability company, foreign limited partnership, or foreign limited liability partnership qualifies or registers or consents to the qualification or registration of another entity under the registered name. (1901, c. 2, s. 8; 1903, c. 453; Rev., s. 1137; 1913, c. 5, s. 1; C.S., s. 1114; 1935, cc. 166, 320; 1939, c. 222; G.S., s. 55-2; 1955, c. 1371, s. 1; 1959, c. 1316, s. 28; 1969, c. 751, ss. 4-6; 1973, c. 469, s. 45.3; 1989, c. 265, s. 1; 2001-358, ss. 14(b), 15; 2001-387, ss. 165(a), 165(b), 173, 175(a); 2001-413, s. 6.)

§ 55D-25. Reserved and registered names; powers of the Secretary of State.

The Secretary of State may revoke any reservation or registration of a name if the Secretary of State:

(1)   Gives written notice by registered or certified mail, return receipt requested, to the person who made the reservation or registration of the date and time of a hearing;

(2)   Conducts a hearing not less that 15 days after receipt of the notice as shown by the return receipt; and

(3)   Finds that the application therefor or any transfer thereof was not made in good faith or that any statement contained in the application for reservation or registration was false when such application was filed or has thereafter become false. (1901, c. 2, s. 8; 1903, c. 453; Rev., s. 1137; 1913, c. 5, s. 1; C.S., s. 1114; 1935, cc. 166, 320; 1939, c. 222; G.S., s. 55-2; 1955, c. 1371, s. 1; 1959, c. 1316, s. 28; 1969, c. 751, ss. 4-6; 1973, c. 469, s. 45.3; 1989, c. 265, s. 1;

1993, c. 552, s. 7; 2001-358, ss. 14(b), 15; 2001-387, ss. 173, 175(a); 2001-413, s. 6.)

§ 55D-26. Real property records.

(a)   A certificate issued by the Secretary of State as described in subsection (b) of this section must be recorded when:

(1)   The name of any domestic corporation, nonprofit corporation, limited liability company, limited partnership, or registered limited liability partnership or foreign corporation, foreign nonprofit corporation, foreign limited liability company, foreign limited partnership, or foreign limited liability partnership that holds title to real property in this State is changed upon amendment to its articles of incorporation or organization, its certificate of limited partnership, or its registration as a limited liability partnership or foreign limited liability partnership; or

(2)   Title to real property in this State held by any entity listed in subdivision (1) of this subsection is vested by operation of law in another entity upon merger, consolidation, or conversion of the entity.

The certificate must recite the name change, merger, consolidation, or conversion and must be recorded in the office of the register of deeds of the county where the property lies or, if the property is located in more than one county in each county where any portion of the property lies.

(b)   The Secretary of State shall issue uniform certificates for recordation in accordance with this section. In the case of a foreign corporation, foreign nonprofit corporation, foreign limited liability company, foreign limited partnership, or foreign limited liability partnership, a similar certificate by any competent authority of the jurisdiction of incorporation may be recorded in accordance with this section.

(c)   The certificate required by this section must be recorded by the register of deeds in the same manner as deeds, and for the same fees, but no formalities as to acknowledgement, probate, or approval by any other officer shall be required. The former name of the entity holding title to the real property before the name change, merger, consolidation, or conversion shall appear in the "Grantor" index, and the new name of the corporation or the name of the

181

other entity holding title to the real property by virtue of the merger, consolidation, or conversion shall appear in the "Grantee" index. (1989, c. 265, s. 1; 1991, c. 645, s. 2(a); 1999-369, s. 1.4; 2001-358, ss. 14(b), 15; 2001-387, ss. 166, 173, 175(a); 2001-413, s. 6.)

§§ 55D-27 through 55D-29: Reserved for future codification purposes.

Article 4.

Registered Office and Registered Agent.

§ 55D-30. Registered office and registered agent required.

(a)   Each domestic corporation, nonprofit corporation, limited liability company, limited partnership, and limited liability partnership, each foreign limited liability partnership maintaining a statement of foreign registration, and each foreign corporation, nonprofit corporation, limited liability company, and limited partnership authorized to transact business or conduct affairs in this State must continuously maintain in this State:

(1)   A registered office that may be the same as any of its places of business or any place where it conducts affairs; and

(2)   A registered agent, who must be:

a.   An individual who resides in this State and whose business office is identical with the registered office;

b.   A domestic corporation, nonprofit corporation, or limited liability company whose business office is identical with the registered office; or

c.   A foreign corporation, foreign nonprofit corporation, or foreign limited liability company authorized to transact business or conduct affairs in this State whose business office is identical with the registered office.

(b)   The sole duty of the registered agent to the entity is to forward to the entity at its last known address any notice, process, or demand that is served on the registered agent. (1901, c. 5; Rev., s. 1243; C.S., s. 1137; 1937, c. 133, ss. 1-3; G.S., ss. 55-38, 55-39; 1955, c. 1371, s. 1; 1957, c. 979, s. 17; 1989, c. 265, s. 1; 2000-140, s. 101(a); 2001-358, ss. 44, 45; 2001-387, ss. 173, 175(a); 2001-413, s. 6.)

§ 55D-31. Change of registered office or registered agent.

(a)   An entity required to maintain a registered office and registered agent under G.S. 55D-30 may change its registered office or registered agent by delivering to the Secretary of State for filing a statement of change that sets forth all of the following:

(1)   The name of the entity.

(2)   The street address, and the mailing address if different from the street address, of its current registered office, and the county in which it is located.

(3)   If the address of the entity's registered office is to be changed, the street address, and the mailing address if different from the street address, of the new registered office, and the county in which it is located.

(4)   The name of its current registered agent.

(5)   If the current registered agent is to be changed, the name of the new registered agent and the new agent's written consent (either on the statement or attached to it) to the appointment.

(6)   That after the change or changes are made, the addresses of its registered office and the business office of its registered agent will be identical.

(b)   If a registered agent changes the address of the agent's business office, the agent may change the address of the registered office of any entity for which the agent is the registered agent in this State by notifying the entity in writing of the change and signing and delivering to the Secretary of State for filing a statement that complies with the requirements of subsection (a) of this section and recites that the entity has been notified of the change.

(c)   A domestic corporation, limited liability company, limited liability limited partnership, registered limited liability partnership, foreign corporation, foreign limited liability company, or foreign limited liability partnership may change its registered office or registered agent by including in its annual report required by G.S. 55-16-22, 57D-2-24, 59-84.4, or 59-210 the information and any written consent required by subsection (a) of this section. (1901, c. 2, s. 31; Rev., s. 1176; C.S., s. 1133; G.S., s. 55-34; 1955, c. 1371, s. 1; 1957, c. 979, ss. 6, 7; 1965, c. 298, s. 1; 1967, c. 823, s. 17; 1973, c. 262; c. 469, s. 3; 1989, c. 265, s. 1; 1991, c. 645, s. 3; 2001-358, ss. 44, 45; 2001-387, ss. 167, 173, 175(a); 2001-413, s. 6; 2013-157, s. 14.)

§ 55D-32. Resignation of registered agent.

(a)   The registered agent of an entity may resign by signing and filing with the Secretary of State a statement of resignation which may include a statement that the registered office is also discontinued. The statement must include or be accompanied by a certification from the registered agent that the agent has mailed or delivered to the entity at its last known address written notice of this resignation. This certification shall include the name and title of the individual notified, if any, and the address to which the notice was mailed or delivered.

(b)   After filing the statement the Secretary of State shall mail a copy to the registered office (if not discontinued) and a copy to the entity at its principal office address on file with the Secretary of State or, if none is on file, at the address contained in the certification included in or accompanying the statement of resignation.

(c)   The agency appointment is terminated, and, if applicable, the registered office discontinued on the 31st day after the date on which the statement was filed. (1901, c. 2, s. 31; Rev., s. 1176; C.S., s. 1133; G.S., s. 55-34; 1955, c. 1371, s. 1; 1957, c. 979, ss. 6, 7; 1965, c. 298, s. 1; 1967, c. 823, s. 17; 1973, c. 262; c. 469, s. 3; 1989, c. 265, s. 1; 1989 (Reg. Sess., 1990), c. 1024, s. 12.6; 2001-358, ss. 44, 45; 2001-387, ss. 168, 173, 175(a); 2001-413, s. 6.)

§ 55D-33. Service on entities.

184

(a)   Service of process, notice or demand required or permitted by law to be served on an entity may be served on the registered agent required by G.S. 55D-30.

(b)   When an entity required to maintain a registered office and registered agent under G.S. 55D-30 fails to appoint or maintain a registered agent in this State, or when its registered agent cannot with due diligence be found at the registered office, or when the Secretary of State revokes a certificate of authority or a statement of foreign registration of a foreign entity authorized to transact business or conduct affairs in this State, the Secretary of State becomes an agent of the entity upon whom any such process, notice or demand may be served. Service on the Secretary of State of any such process, notice or demand is made by delivering to and leaving with the Secretary of State or any clerk authorized by the Secretary of State to accept service of process, duplicate copies of the process, notice or demand and the applicable fee. In the event any such process, notice or demand is served on the Secretary of State in the manner provided by this subsection, the Secretary of State shall immediately mail one of the copies thereof, by registered or certified mail, return receipt requested, to the entity at its principal office or, if there is no mailing address for the principal office on file, to the entity at its registered office. Service on an entity under this subsection is effective for all purposes from and after the date of the service on the Secretary of State.

(c)   The Secretary of State shall keep a record of all processes, notices and demands served upon the Secretary of State under this section and shall record therein the date of service and the Secretary of State's action with reference thereto.

(d)   Nothing in this section affects the right to serve any process, notice or demand required or permitted by law to be served upon an entity in any other manner now or hereafter permitted by law. (1937, c. 133, ss. 1-3; G.S., s. 55-39; 1955, c. 1371, s. 1; 1977, 2nd Sess., c. 1219, s. 33; 1989, c. 265, s. 1; 2000-140, s. 43; 2001-358, ss. 44, 45; 2001-387, ss. 173, 175(a); 2001-413, s. 6.)

Chapter 56.

Electric, Telegraph and Power Companies.

§§ 56-1 through 56-11. Repealed by Session Laws 1963, c. 1165, s. 1.

Chapter 57.

Hospital, Medical and Dental Service Corporations.

§§ 57-1 through 57-38: Recodified as Articles 65 and 66 of Chapter 58.

Chapter 57A.

Health Maintenance Organization Act.

§§ 57A-1 through 57A-29. Recodified as §§ 57B-1 to 57B-25.

Chapter 57B.

Health Maintenance Organization Act.

§§ 57B-1 through 57B-25: Recodified as Article 67 of Chapter 58.

Chapter 57C.

North Carolina Limited Liability Company Act

§§ 57C-1-01 through 57C-10-07: Repealed by Session Laws 2013-157, s. 1, effective January 1, 2014.

§§ 57C-7-08 through 57C-7-10: Repealed by Session Laws 2001-358, s. 49, effective January 1, 2002.

§§ 57C-1-01 through 57C-10-07: Repealed by Session Laws 2013-157, s. 1, effective January 1, 2014.

Chapter 57D.

North Carolina Limited Liability Company Act.

Article 1.

General Provisions.

Part 1. Short Title; Reservation of Power; Definitions.

§ 57D-1-01. Short title.

This Chapter is the "North Carolina Limited Liability Company Act" and may be cited by that name. (2013-157, s. 2.)

§ 57D-1-02. Governing law; jurisdiction of the superior courts; intent; reservation of power to amend or repeal.

(a)   This Chapter and any other applicable laws of this State govern (i) the internal affairs of every LLC, including the interpretation, construction, and enforcement of operating agreements and determining the rights and duties of interest owners, managers, and other company officials and (ii) any liability that interest owners or managers or other company officials may have for the liabilities of the LLC.

(b)   The superior courts of this State have jurisdiction to enforce the provisions of this Chapter.

(c)   The General Assembly may amend or repeal all or any part of this Chapter at any time, and all LLCs and the rights and duties of interest owners, managers, and other company officials subject to this Chapter will be subject to any such amendment or repeal. Except as otherwise provided in this Chapter, all amendments of this Chapter apply to all LLCs, foreign LLCs, interest owners, and managers and other company officials, including those LLCs and foreign LLCs in existence or person having such interests and status, at the time of the enactment of any such amendment.

(d)   Each provision of this Chapter is severable, such that if any provision, including any clause of any provision, of this Chapter or application thereof to any person or in a particular context is held to be invalid, such invalidity will not affect other provisions or applications of this Chapter that can be given effect without the invalid provision or application. (2013-157, s. 2.)

187

§ 57D-1-03. Definitions.

Unless otherwise specifically provided, the following definitions apply in this Chapter:

(1)   Approve. - With respect to a manager or other company official, member, or organizer and a decision or other action to be taken by the managers or other applicable company officials, members, or organizers, as the case may be, (i) the affirmative vote of that person at a meeting of the managers or other applicable company officials, members, or organizers, as applicable, or (ii) any other expression of assent to the action to be taken that is made in the manner or form required to establish the assent of the members to amendments of the operating agreement.

(2)   Articles of organization. - The document filed under G.S. 57D-2-20 (or former G.S. 57C-2-20 for LLCs formed before January 1, 2014), for the purpose of forming an LLC, as amended or restated.

(3)   Business. - Any lawful trade, investment, or other purpose or activity, whether or not conducted or undertaken for profit, except that the term "business," as used in Article 7 of this Chapter, or to which reference is otherwise made in this Chapter to a foreign LLC "transacting business" (or is authorized or required to be authorized to "transact business") in this State, has the same meaning in that context as applied in Article 15 of Chapter 55 of the General Statutes.

(4)   Capital interest. - An interest owner's interest in or share of the owners' equity of the LLC which may be based on the method of accounting consistently applied under which the LLC maintains its financial records to be made available to the members under G.S. 57D-3-04(a)(2).

(5)   Company official. - Any person exercising any management authority over the limited liability company whether the person is a manager or referred to as a manager, director, or officer or given any other title.

(6)   Contribution amount. - The fair market value, net of liabilities assumed (or to which any property contributed to the LLC is subject, but not in excess of the fair market value of the property that is subject to the liability), or other consideration paid by the LLC, of contributions in any form described in G.S.

188

57D-4-01 made in respect of an economic interest, determined as of the time the contribution is made, reduced by any money or other property or services promised to be transferred or rendered to or on behalf of the LLC in respect of the economic interest that are discharged without performance.

(7)   Corporation. - A domestic corporation or a foreign corporation as those terms are defined in G.S. 55-1-40.

(8)   Debtor in bankruptcy. - A person who is the subject of either of the following:

a.   An order for relief under Title 11 of the United States Code or a successor statute of general application.

b.   A comparable order under federal, State, or foreign law governing insolvency.

(9)   Distribution. - Except as provided in the last sentence of this definition of distribution with respect to G.S. 57D-4-05, 57D-4-06, and 57D-6-12, the direct or indirect transfer of money or other property to, or incurrence of indebtedness by, an LLC for the benefit of an interest owner in respect of the interest owner's ownership interest. The amount of a distribution is the fair market value of the property distributed, net of liabilities assumed, or other consideration paid by the interest owner (or to which any property distributed to the interest owner is subject, but not in excess of the fair market value of the property that is subject to the liability), determined as of the time the distribution is made. As used in G.S. 57D-4-05, 57D-4-06, and 57D-6-12, "distribution" does not include payments made to, or an account of, an interest owner that constitute compensation for services and does not include payments made in the ordinary course of business under a bona fide retirement plan or other benefits program.

(10)   Economic interest. - The proprietary interest of an interest owner in the capital, income, losses, credits, and other economic rights and interests of a limited liability company, including the right of the owner of the interest to receive distributions from the limited liability company.

(11)   Economic interest owner. - A person who owns an economic interest but is not a member.

189

(12) Entity. - A corporation, limited liability company, partnership (including a limited partnership), unincorporated association, trust, estate, government or governmental agency, instrumentality, or other entity.

(13) Foreign LLC. - An unincorporated entity organized under the law of (i) a state other than this State that is denominated thereunder as a limited liability company or (ii) a foreign jurisdiction other than a state, and the statute under which it is organized is substantially similar to the limited liability company statute of any state and is not more appropriately characterized as a corporation, partnership, or trust.

(14) Individual. - A human being.

(15) Interest owner. - A member or an economic interest owner.

(16) Liabilities, debts, and obligations. - Have the same meaning and are used interchangeably throughout this Chapter. Reference to "liabilities," "debts," or "obligations," whether individually or in any combination, means all liabilities, debts, and obligations, whether arising in contract, tort, or other applicable law.

(17) Limited liability company. - An LLC or foreign LLC.

(18) Limited partnership. - A domestic limited partnership or a foreign limited partnership as those terms are defined in G.S. 59-102.

(19) LLC. - An entity formed under this Chapter (or former Chapter 57C of the General Statutes) that has not become another entity or form of entity by merger, conversion, or other means.

(20) Manager. - Has the following meanings: (i) with respect to an LLC, any person designated as a manager as provided in the operating agreement or, if applicable, in G.S. 57D-3-20(d) and (ii) with respect to a foreign LLC, any person designated as a manager under the law of the jurisdiction in which the foreign LLC is organized.

(21) Member. - A person who has been admitted as a member of the LLC as provided in the operating agreement or G.S. 57D-3-01, who was a member of the LLC immediately before the repeal of Chapter 57C of the General Statutes until the person ceases to be a member as provided in the operating agreement or G.S. 57D-3-02, or, with respect to a foreign LLC, a person who has been admitted as a member of the foreign LLC under the law of the jurisdiction in

which the foreign LLC is organized until the person ceases to be a member under that law.

(22)   Nonprofit corporation. - A domestic corporation or a foreign corporation as those terms are defined in G.S. 55A-1-40.

(23)   Operating agreement. - Any agreement concerning the LLC or any ownership interest in the LLC to which each interest owner is a party or is otherwise bound as an interest owner. Subject to other controlling law, the operating agreement may be in any form, including written, oral, or implied, or any combination thereof. The operating agreement may specify the form that the operating agreement must take, in which case any purported amendment to the operating agreement or other agreement expressed in a nonconforming manner will not be deemed to be part of the operating agreement and will not be enforceable to the extent it would be part of the operating agreement if it were in proper form. Subject to G.S. 57D-2-21 and the other provisions of this Chapter governing articles of organization, the articles of organization are to be deemed to be, or be part of, the operating agreement. If the LLC has only one interest owner and no operating agreement to which another person is a party, then any document or record intended by the interest owner to serve as the operating agreement will be the operating agreement.

(24)   Organizer. - A person who executes the articles of organization in the capacity of an organizer.

(25)   Ownership interest. - All of an interest owner's rights and obligations as an interest owner in an LLC, including (i) any economic interest, (ii) any right to participate in the management or approve actions proposed by persons responsible for the management of the LLC, (iii) any right to bring a derivative action, and (iv) any right to inspect the books and records of or receive information from the LLC.

(26)   Person. - An individual or an entity.

(27)   Principal office. - The principal executive office of the limited liability company as stated in its most recent annual report filed by the Secretary of State or, if the limited liability company has never filed an annual report, in its articles of organization or application for a certificate of authority.

191

(28)   Proceeding. - Any civil or criminal proceeding or other action pending before any court of law or other governmental body or agency or any arbitration proceeding.

(29)   Professional service. - Has the meaning provided in G.S. 55B-2.

(30)   Professional limited liability company. - A limited liability company subject to G.S. 57D-2-02.

(31)   Record. - When used as a noun, information that is inscribed on a tangible medium or that is stated in an electronic or other medium and is retrievable in readable form.

(32)   Secretary of State. - The Secretary of State of North Carolina.

(33)   State. - A state, territory, or possession of the United States, the District of Columbia, or the Commonwealth of Puerto Rico, and "this State" refers to the State of North Carolina.

(34)   Transfer. - As a noun, the transfer of legal, equitable, or beneficial ownership by sale, exchange, assignment, gift, donation, grant, or other conveyance or disposition of any kind, whether voluntary or involuntary, including transfers by operation of law or legal process and includes, with respect to the ownership interest of an interest owner for purposes of G.S. 57D-3-02(a)(3), any (i) appointment of a receiver, trustee, liquidator, custodian, or other similar official for that interest owner or all or any part of the property of that interest owner under any law of bankruptcy or insolvency; (ii) gift, donation, transfer by will or intestacy, or other similar type of transfer or disposition, whether during one's life or because of death; (iii) appointment of a personal or other legal representative or other person serving in a similar capacity of a deceased interest owner; (iv) appointment of a guardian or other person serving in a similar capacity of an interest owner who has been adjudicated to be incompetent by a court of competent jurisdiction; and (v) other transfer or disposition to a spouse or former spouse (including by reason of a separation agreement or divorce, equitable, community or marital property distribution, judicial decree, or other court order concerning the division or partition of property between spouses, former spouses, or other persons); and, as a verb, the act of making any transfer. (2013-157, s. 2.)

§ 57D-1-04: Reserved for future codification purposes.

§ 57D-1-05: Reserved for future codification purposes.

§ 57D-1-06: Reserved for future codification purposes.

§ 57D-1-07: Reserved for future codification purposes.

§ 57D-1-08: Reserved for future codification purposes.

§ 57D-1-09: Reserved for future codification purposes.

§ 57D-1-10: Reserved for future codification purposes.

§ 57D-1-11: Reserved for future codification purposes.

§ 57D-1-12: Reserved for future codification purposes.

§ 57D-1-13: Reserved for future codification purposes.

§ 57D-1-14: Reserved for future codification purposes.

§ 57D-1-15: Reserved for future codification purposes.

§ 57D-1-16: Reserved for future codification purposes.

§ 57D-1-17: Reserved for future codification purposes.

§ 57D-1-18: Reserved for future codification purposes.

§ 57D-1-19: Reserved for future codification purposes.

Part 2. Filing Documents.

§ 57D-1-20. Filing requirements.

(a)   A document required or permitted by this Chapter to be filed by the Secretary of State must be filed as provided in Chapter 55D of the General Statutes.

(b)   A document submitted on behalf of a limited liability company must be executed by one of the following:

(1)   A manager or other company official.

(2)   If the document is the articles of organization, a person acting in the capacity of an organizer or a member as provided in G.S. 57D-2-21(a)(2).

(3)   If the LLC has never had any members, an organizer.

(4)   If the LLC is in the hands of a receiver, trustee, or other court-appointed fiduciary, by that fiduciary. (2013-157, s. 2)

§ 57D-1-21. Forms.

(a)   The Secretary of State may promulgate and furnish on request forms for the following:

(1)   An application for a certificate of existence.

(2)   A foreign LLC's application for a certificate of authority to transact business in this State.

(3)   A foreign LLC's application for a certificate of withdrawal.

(b)   If the Secretary of State so requires, use of the forms listed in subsection (a) of this section is mandatory.

(c)   The Secretary of State may promulgate and furnish on request forms for other documents required or permitted to be filed by this Chapter, but their use is not mandatory. (2013-157, s. 2.)

§ 57D-1-22. Filing, service, and copying fees.

(a)   The Secretary of State shall collect the following fees when the documents described in this subsection are delivered to the Secretary of State for filing:

Document	Fee
(1) Articles of organization	$125.00
(2) Application for reserved name	10.00

(3) Notice of transfer of reserved name
10.00

(4) Application for registered name
10.00

(5) Application for renewal of registered name
10.00

(6) Limited liability company's statement of change of registered agent or
5.00

registered office or both

(7) Agent's statement of change of registered office for each affected
5.00

limited liability company

(8) Agent's statement of resignation
No fee

(9) Designation of registered agent or registered office or both
5.00

(10) Amendment of articles of organization
50.00

(11) Restated articles of organization without amendment of articles
10.00

(12) Restated articles of organization with amendment of articles
50.00

(13) Articles of conversion (other than articles of conversion included as
50.00

part of another document)

(14) Articles of merger
50.00

(15) Articles of dissolution
30.00

(16) Cancellation of articles of dissolution
10.00

(17) Certificate of administrative dissolution
No fee

(18) Application for reinstatement following administrative dissolution
100.00

(19) Certificate of reinstatement
No fee

(20) Certificate of judicial dissolution
No fee

(21) Application for certificate of authority
250.00

(22) Application for amended certificate of authority
50.00

(23) Application for certificate of withdrawal
10.00

(24) Certificate of revocation of authority to transact business
No fee

(25) Articles of correction
10.00

(26) Application for certificate of existence or authorization (paper)
15.00

(27) Application for certificate of existence or authorization (electronic)
10.00

(28) Annual report
200.00

(29) Any other document required or permitted to be filed by this Chapter
10.00

(b)   The Secretary of State shall collect a fee of ten dollars ($10.00) each time process is served on the Secretary of State under this Chapter. The party to a proceeding causing service of process is entitled to recover this fee as costs if the party prevails in the proceeding.

(c)   The Secretary of State shall collect the following fees for copying and certifying a copy of any filed document relating to a limited liability company:

(1)   One dollar ($1.00) a page for copying.

(2)   Fifteen dollars ($15.00) for a paper certificate.

(3)   Ten dollars ($10.00) for an electronic certificate. (2013-157, s. 2.)

§ 57D-1-23. Execution by judicial act.

Any person who is adversely affected by the failure or refusal of any person to execute and deliver to the Secretary of State for filing any document to be filed under this Chapter may petition the superior court in the county where the limited liability company's principal office or, if none in this State, its registered office is or was last located or, if there is no such office, in the County of Wake to direct the execution and delivery to the Secretary of State for filing of the document. If the court finds that it is proper for the document to be executed and delivered to the Secretary of State for filing and there has been failure or refusal by the applicable company officials to do so, it shall order the Secretary of State to make the filing. (2013-157, s. 2.)

§ 57D-1-24. Certificate of existence; certificate of authorization.

(a)   Anyone may apply to the Secretary of State for a certificate of existence for an LLC or a certificate of authorization for a foreign LLC.

(b)   A certificate of existence or authorization sets forth the following:

(1)   The limited liability company's name and, in the case of a foreign LLC, any different name that the foreign LLC is authorized under Article 3 of Chapter 55D of the General Statutes to use to transact business in this State, as provided in the foreign LLC's certificate of authority.

(2)   That (i) the articles of organization for the LLC have been filed and are in effect and the date on which the filed articles of organization became effective or (ii) a certificate of authority has been issued to the foreign LLC and is in effect and the date on which the certificate of authority became effective.

(3)   That the articles of organization of an LLC or the certificate of authority of a foreign LLC are not suspended under G.S. 57D-1-32(a)(or for limited liability companies formed before January 1, 2014, former G.S. 57C-1-32(a)) for failure to answer interrogatories propounded by the Secretary of State or under G.S. 105-230 for failure to pay a tax or fee or file a report or return.

(4)   That the LLC has not been administratively dissolved under G.S. 57D-6-06 (or for limited liability companies formed before January 1, 2014, former G.S. 57C-6-03) and no decree of judicial dissolution has been filed under G.S. 57D-6-05 (or, for limited liability companies formed before January 1, 2014, former G.S. 57C-6-02) or, with respect to a foreign LLC, no application for a certificate of withdrawal or a certificate of revocation has been filed under Article 7 of this Chapter (or, for limited liability companies formed before January 1, 2014, former Article 7 of Chapter 57C of the General Statutes).

(5)   That, in the case of an LLC, articles of dissolution have not been filed nor have articles of merger or conversion been filed causing it to merge or convert into another entity or form of entity.

(6)   Other facts of record in the Office of the Secretary of State pertaining to the limited liability company that may be requested by the applicant.

(c)   A certificate of existence or authorization issued by the Secretary of State may be relied upon as conclusive evidence as to the accuracy of its contents. (2013-157, s. 2.)

§ 57D-1-25: Reserved for future codification purposes.

§ 57D-1-26: Reserved for future codification purposes.

§ 57D-1-27: Reserved for future codification purposes.

§ 57D-1-28: Reserved for future codification purposes.

§ 57D-1-29: Reserved for future codification purposes.

Part 3. Secretary of State.

§ 57D-1-30. Powers of the Secretary of State.

The Secretary of State has the power necessary to perform the duties required by this Chapter. (2013-157, s. 2.)

§ 57D-1-31. Interrogatories by Secretary of State.

The Secretary of State may propound to any limited liability company that the Secretary of State has reason to believe is subject to the provisions of this Chapter, and to any manager or other company official thereof, such written interrogatories as may be necessary and proper to enable the Secretary of State to ascertain whether the limited liability company has complied with all of the provisions of this Chapter applicable to it. Subject to applicable jurisdictional requirements, the interrogatories must be answered within 30 days after the mailing thereof, or within such additional time as the Secretary of State may fix, and the answers thereto must be full and complete and made in writing and under oath. If the interrogatories are directed to an individual, they must be answered by the individual, and if directed to a limited liability company, they must be answered by a manager or other company official thereof. The Secretary of State shall certify to the Attorney General for such action all interrogatories and answers thereto that disclose a violation of any of the provisions of this Chapter requiring or permitting action by the Attorney General. (2013-157, s. 2.)

§ 57D-1-32. Penalties imposed on limited liability companies for failure to answer interrogatories.

(a)   In addition to the recourse that the Secretary of State may have under G.S. 57D-6-06 and Part 3 of Article 7 of this Chapter to administratively dissolve an LLC or revoke the certificate of authority of the foreign LLC, if a limited liability company knowingly fails or refuses to answer truthfully and fully within the time prescribed in this Chapter interrogatories propounded by the Secretary of State in accordance with the provisions of this Chapter, the Secretary of State may suspend its articles of organization or its certificate of authority to do business in this State. The Secretary of State shall immediately notify by mail the limited liability company of its suspension. The powers, privileges, and franchises conferred on the limited liability company by the articles of organization or the certificate of authority terminate upon their suspension. Any act performed or attempted to be performed during the period of suspension is invalid and of no effect unless and to the extent the Secretary of State reinstates the limited liability company.

(b)   The Secretary of State shall reinstate a limited liability company upon the limited liability company fully complying with its obligations under G.S. 57D-1-31, paying all State taxes, fees, and penalties due from it (which total amount due may be computed, for years before and after the suspension, in the same manner as if the suspension had not taken place) and paying to the Secretary of State twenty-five dollars ($25.00) to cover the cost of reinstatement. Upon reinstatement of an LLC's articles of organization or a foreign LLC's certificate of authority by the Secretary of State, (i) the limited liability company may again exercise its rights, privileges, and franchises in this State, and (ii) the Secretary of State shall make the appropriate entry thereof on the records of the Secretary of State. The entry of reinstatement in the records of the Secretary of State relates back to and takes effect as of the date of the suspension by the Secretary of State, and the limited liability company may resume conducting its business as if the suspension had never occurred, subject to the rights of any person who relied, to that person's prejudice, on the suspension. The Secretary of State shall immediately notify by mail the limited liability company of the reinstatement.

(c)   When the articles of organization or certificate of authority of a limited liability company have or has been suspended by the Secretary of State under subsection (a) of this section and the limited liability company has ceased to operate as a going concern, if there remains property held in the name of the limited liability company that is not disposed at the time of the suspension, or there remain future interests that may accrue to the limited liability company, its successor, or its interest owners, then any interested party may apply to the superior court for the appointment of a receiver. Application for the receiver may be made in a civil action to which all interest owners are made parties. The applicant may serve persons whom the applicant either is unable to locate or are unknown by publication made in the same manner as the publication of notice under G.S. 57D-6-11. A guardian ad litem may be appointed for any interest owners who are infants or incompetent. The receiver shall enter into a bond if the court requires one and shall give notice to creditors by publication or otherwise as the court may prescribe. Any creditor who fails to file a claim with the receiver within the time set will be barred of the right to participate in the distribution of the assets. The receiver may (i) sell the property interests of the limited liability company on such terms and in such manner as the court may order, (ii) apply the proceeds to the payments of any debt of the limited liability company, and (iii) distribute the remainder among the interest owners in accordance with the manner in which liquidating distributions are to be made by the limited liability company. Amounts due to any interest owner who is unknown or whose whereabouts are unknown are to be paid to the office of the clerk of the superior court and disbursed according to law. If the records of the limited liability company are lost or do not reflect the owners of the property interests, the court shall determine the owners from the best evidence available, and the receiver will be protected in acting in accordance with the court's finding. This proceeding is authorized for the sole purpose of providing a procedure for disposing of the assets of the limited liability company by payment of its debts and by the transfer to its interest owners, or their representatives, of their shares of the limited liability company's remaining assets.

(d)   Each manager or other company official of a limited liability company who fails or refuses within the time prescribed by this Chapter to answer truthfully and fully interrogatories propounded to the manager or other company official by the Secretary of State in accordance with the provisions of this Chapter shall be guilty of a Class 1 misdemeanor. (2013-157, s. 2.)

202

§ 57D-1-33. Information disclosed by interrogatories.

Interrogatories propounded by the Secretary of State and the answers thereto will not be open to public inspection nor shall the Secretary of State disclose any facts or information obtained therefrom, except to the extent applicable law requires the Secretary of State to make the information public or the interrogatories or the answers thereto are required for evidence in any proceedings by this State. (2013-157, s. 2.)

Article 2.

Purposes, Powers, Formation, Annual Report, Name, Registered Office, and Agent.

Part 1. Purposes and Powers.

§ 57D-2-01. Nature, purposes, duration, existence.

(a)   An LLC is an entity distinct from its interest owners.

(b)   An LLC has perpetual duration.

(c)   Subject to subsection (d) of this section, an LLC may engage in any lawful business.

(d)   A limited liability company engaging in a business that is subject to regulation under another statute of this State may be formed or authorized to transact business under this Chapter if not precluded by the other statute and is otherwise subject to the application of the other statute, which in the case of a limited liability company rendering a professional service requires giving effect to G.S. 57D-2-02.

(e)   After the dissolution of an LLC, the LLC continues its existence but shall wind up pursuant to G.S. 57D-6-07. (2013-157, s. 2.)

§ 57D-2-02. Professional limited liability companies.

(a)   Except as set forth in this subsection, a limited liability company may engage in rendering professional services only to the extent that it would be able to render those services were it a corporation, including, as applicable, complying with Chapter 55B of the General Statutes and the statutes referenced in the definition of "professional service" in G.S. 55B-2(6). Chapter 55B of the General Statutes and each statute referenced therein are deemed amended and to apply with such changes as are necessary to cause them to be applicable to limited liability companies in the same degree as for corporations but subject to any provisions contained herein pursuant to which limited liability companies, or their members, managers, and other company officials, are treated differently from corporations, or their shareholders, directors, and officers.

For purposes of applying the provisions, conditions, and limitations of Chapter 55B of the General Statutes and the statutes referenced therein to limited liability companies that engage in rendering professional services, unless the context specifically requires otherwise, the following rules of construction shall apply:

(1)   References to Chapter 55 of the General Statutes are treated as references to this Chapter, and references to a "corporation" or "foreign corporation" are treated as references to an LLC or foreign LLC, respectively.

(2)   References to "articles of incorporation" are treated as references to articles of organization.

(3)   The persons executing the articles of organization of an LLC are treated in the same manner as the incorporators of a professional corporation.

(4)   References to "directors" are treated as references to company officials having equal or greater authority in the management of a limited liability company as directors of a domestic corporation or foreign corporation, as the case may be.

(5)   References to "officers" are treated as references to company officials whose authority to manage the limited liability company is equal to or greater than that exercised by officers of a domestic corporation.

(6)   A professional limited liability company is not required to have more than one company official who would be treated as a director, officer, or both under Chapter 55B of the General Statutes.

(7)   A manager or other company official who has the authority of both a director and an officer if the limited liability were a company or a corporation is to be treated as holding both positions for purposes of applying Chapter 55B of the General Statutes to the limited liability company.

(8)   References to "shares" of a shareholder are treated as references to the ownership interest of an interest owner and, where the context so indicates or requires, a portion of an interest owner's ownership interest.

(9)   References to "shareholders" are treated as references to interest owners.

(10)   The name of a limited liability company that is to render a professional service and is subject to this section shall comply with Article 3 of Chapter 55D of the General Statutes and, in addition, shall contain the word "Professional" or the abbreviation "P.L.L.C." or "PLLC."

(b)   Nothing in this Chapter abolishes, modifies, restricts, limits, or alters the law in this State applicable to the professional relationship and liabilities between the individual furnishing the professional services and the person receiving the professional services, the standards of professional conduct applicable to the rendering of the services, or any responsibilities, obligations, or sanctions imposed under applicable licensing statutes. A member, manager, or other company official of a professional limited liability company is not individually liable, directly or indirectly, including by indemnification, contribution, assessment, or otherwise, for debts, obligations, and liabilities of, or chargeable to, the professional limited liability company that arise from errors, omissions, negligence, malpractice, incompetence, or malfeasance committed by another member, manager, or other company official, employee, agent, or other representative of the professional limited liability company, except nothing in this Chapter affects the liability of a member, manager, or other company official of a professional limited liability company for his or her own errors, omissions,

205

negligence, malpractice, incompetence, or malfeasance committed in the rendering of professional services. (2013-157, s. 2.)

§ 57D-2-03. Powers of the LLC.

Unless this Chapter provides otherwise or the powers of the LLC are limited under the operating agreement, an LLC has the same powers as an individual or a domestic corporation to do all things necessary or convenient to carry out its business. (2013-157, s. 2.)

§ 57D-2-04: Reserved for future codification purposes.

§ 57D-2-05: Reserved for future codification purposes.

§ 57D-2-06: Reserved for future codification purposes.

§ 57D-2-07: Reserved for future codification purposes.

§ 57D-2-08: Reserved for future codification purposes.

§ 57D-2-09: Reserved for future codification purposes.

§ 57D-2-10: Reserved for future codification purposes.

§ 57D-2-11: Reserved for future codification purposes.

§ 57D-2-12: Reserved for future codification purposes.

§ 57D-2-13: Reserved for future codification purposes.

§ 57D-2-14: Reserved for future codification purposes.

§ 57D-2-15: Reserved for future codification purposes.

§ 57D-2-16: Reserved for future codification purposes.

§ 57D-2-17: Reserved for future codification purposes.

§ 57D-2-18: Reserved for future codification purposes.

§ 57D-2-19: Reserved for future codification purposes.

Part 2. Formation; Articles of Organization; Amendment of Articles; Annual Report.

§ 57D-2-20. Formation.

(a)	One or more persons may cause an LLC to be formed by delivering executed articles of organization to the Secretary of State for filing in accordance with this Chapter and Chapter 55D of the General Statutes. An LLC may also be formed through the conversion of another eligible entity into an LLC pursuant to Part 2 of Article 9 of this Chapter.

(b)	An LLC is formed at the time the articles of organization filed by the Secretary of State become effective. Filing of the articles of organization by the Secretary of State is conclusive proof that all conditions to the formation of the LLC have been satisfied except in a proceeding by the State to cancel or revoke the articles of organization or involuntarily dissolve the LLC.

(c)	If initial members are not identified in the articles of organization of an LLC in the manner provided in G.S. 57D-3-01(a)(1), the organizer or organizers shall either identify the initial members of the LLC or dissolve the LLC. Unless otherwise provided in the articles of organization, all decisions to be made by the organizers require the approval of a majority of the organizers. (2013-157, s. 2.)

§ 57D-2-21. Articles of organization.

(a)	The articles of organization must include the following information:

(1)	A name of the LLC that satisfies the provisions of G.S. 55D-20 and G.S. 55D-21.

(2)	The name and address of each person executing the articles of organization and whether the person is executing the articles of organization in the capacity of a member or an organizer.

(3)	The street address, and the mailing address if different from the street address, of the LLC's initial registered office, the county in which the initial registered office is located, and the name of the LLC's initial registered agent at that address.

(4)	The street address, and the mailing address if different from the street address, of the LLC's principal office, if any, and the county in which the principal office, if any, is located.

(5)   If the LLC is to render professional services and is subject to G.S. 57D-2-02 as a professional limited liability company, the professional services to be rendered by the LLC.

(b)   The articles of organization may include any other provision that is or may be included in an operating agreement. (2013-157, s. 2.)

§ 57D-2-22. Amendment of articles of organization.

(a)   An LLC may amend its articles of organization to add or change a provision that is required or permitted in the articles of organization or to delete a provision that is not required to be included in the articles of organization. Whether a provision is required or permitted in the articles of organization is determined as of the effective date of the amendment. The LLC shall amend or otherwise correct its articles of organization when (i) there is a change in the name of the LLC or (ii) they contain an inaccurate statement.

(b)   Any amendment to the articles of organization must be approved by either of the following:

(1)   All of the members.

(2)   If no member of the LLC has been identified in the manner provided in this Chapter, a majority of the organizers. (2013-157, s. 2.)

§ 57D-2-23. Restated articles of organization.

(a)   An LLC may restate its articles of organization at any time.

(b)   The restated articles of organization may include one or more amendments to the articles of organization. The restated articles of organization shall include a statement of the address of the current registered office and the name of the current registered agent of the LLC.

(c)   An LLC restating its articles of organization must deliver to the Secretary of State for filing articles of restatement that include the following:

209

(1)   The name of the LLC.

(2)   Attached as an exhibit thereto, the text of the restated articles of organization.

(3)   A statement that the restated articles of organization do not contain an amendment or, if the articles of organization do contain an amendment, a statement that there is an amendment that was duly adopted by the LLC.

(d)   Restated articles of organization supersede the original articles of organization as theretofore amended.

(e)   The Secretary of State may certify restated articles of organization as the articles of organization currently in effect without including the other information required by subsection (c) of this section. (2013-157, s. 2.)

§ 57D-2-24. Annual report for Secretary of State.

(a)   Excluding professional limited liability companies governed by G.S. 57D-2-02, each LLC and each foreign LLC authorized to transact business in this State must deliver to the Secretary of State for filing annual reports on a form prescribed by, and in the manner required by, the Secretary of State and as otherwise provided in subsection (b) of this section. Each annual report must specify the year for which the report applies and provide the information required by this subsection. The information must be current as of the date the limited liability company completes the report. If the information in the limited liability company's most recent annual report has not changed, the limited liability company may certify in its annual report that the information has not changed in lieu of restating the information.

The following information must be included in each annual report:

(1)   The name of the limited liability company and, in the case of a foreign LLC, any different name that the foreign LLC is authorized under Article 3 of Chapter 55D of the General Statutes to use to transact business in this State, as provided in the foreign LLC's certificate of authority.

(2)　　In the case of a foreign LLC, the name of the jurisdiction under whose law the foreign LLC is organized.

(3)　　The street address, and the mailing address if different from the street address, of the limited liability company's registered office in the State, the county in which the registered office is located, the name of its registered agent at that office, and a statement of any change of the registered office or registered agent.

(4)　　The address and telephone number of its principal office.

(5)　　The names, titles, and business addresses of the limited liability company's principal company officials.

(6)　　A brief description of the nature of its business.

(b)　　The Secretary of State must notify limited liability companies of the annual report filing requirement. The first annual report of a limited liability company is due to be delivered to the Secretary of State by April 15 of the year following (i) in the case of an LLC, the calendar year in which the LLC's articles of organization or articles of organization and conversion filed by the Secretary of State become effective or (ii) in the case of a foreign LLC, the calendar year in which the Secretary of State issues to the foreign LLC a certificate of authority to transact business in this State.

The limited liability company shall deliver an annual report by April 15 of each subsequent year until (i) in the case of an LLC, the effective date of its articles of dissolution filed by the Secretary of State or the effective date of either a certificate of dissolution for an LLC that is not reinstated under G.S. 57D-6-06(c) or a decree of dissolution that is filed by the Secretary of State as provided in G.S. 57D-6-05; (ii) in the case of a foreign LLC, the foreign LLC receives a certificate of withdrawal from the Secretary of State or the Secretary of State revokes the foreign LLC's certificate of authority under Part 3 of Article 7 of this Chapter; or (iii) in the case of either an LLC or foreign LLC, the effective date of a merger or conversion under Article 9 of this Chapter in which the limited liability company is a merging entity or a converting entity but not the surviving entity.

(c)　　If an annual report does not contain the information required by this section, the Secretary of State shall promptly notify the reporting limited liability company in writing and return the report to it for correction. If the report is

211

corrected to contain the information required by this section and delivered to the Secretary of State within 30 days after the effective date of notice, it is deemed to be timely delivered.

(d)   Amendments to any previously filed annual report may be delivered for filing by the Secretary of State at any time for the purpose of correcting, updating, or augmenting the information contained in the annual report. (2013-157, s. 2.)

§ 57D-2-25: Reserved for future codification purposes.

§ 57D-2-26: Reserved for future codification purposes.

§ 57D-2-27: Reserved for future codification purposes.

§ 57D-2-28: Reserved for future codification purposes.

§ 57D-2-29: Reserved for future codification purposes.

Part 3. Operating Agreement.

§ 57D-2-30. Scope, function, and limitations of operating agreements.

(a)   The operating agreement governs the internal affairs of an LLC and the rights, duties, and obligations of (i) the interest owners, and the rights of any other persons to become interest owners, in relation to each other, the LLC, and their ownership interests or rights to acquire ownership interests and (ii) the company officials in relation to each other, the LLC, and the interest owners. Subject to the limitations set forth in subsections (b), (c), (d), and (e) of this section, the provisions of this Chapter and common law will apply only to the extent contrary or inconsistent provisions are not made in, or are not otherwise supplanted, varied, disclaimed, or nullified by, the operating agreement. The provisions of the operating agreement are severable and each will apply to the extent it is valid and enforceable.

(b) The operating agreement may not supplant, vary, disclaim, or nullify the provisions of this Chapter or their application to the extent the provisions do any of the following:

(1) Concern the functions of, including the filings and payments to be made, and the manner in which they are to be made by or to the Secretary of State, the Attorney General, the courts, or any other governmental official, agency, or authority, including Article 1 of this Chapter, G.S. 57D-2-21(a), 57D-2-22(a), 57D-2-23, 57D-2-24, 57D-2-40, 57D-6-02(1), 57D-6-03(a) through (c), 57D-6-04, 57D-6-05, 57D-6-06, the last sentence of G.S. 57D-6-07(c), 57D-6-09, and 57D-10-01; except, the operating agreement may provide the forum in which disputes concerning the LLC or the rights and duties of interest owners and other parties to the operating agreement are to be resolved.

(2) Apply to persons who are not parties to or otherwise bound by the operating agreement, including the extent to which G.S. 57D-5-03 may be applicable to such persons or for which they may be entitled to recovery or other relief thereunder, or the extent to which G.S. 57D-1-02, 57D-6-08(1), 57D-6-10, 57D-6-11, 57D-6-12, and 57D-6-13 are applicable to creditors or such persons.

(3) Diminish the rights and protections of the LLC under G.S. 57D-4-05 and G.S. 57D-4-06.

(4) Diminish the rights and protections of members under G.S. 57D-3-04(a), except as permitted by and otherwise subject to subsections (b) through (f) of G.S. 57D-3-04.

(5) Eliminate the right of a member to bring a derivative action under Article 8 of this Chapter unless the operating agreement provides an alternative remedy, which may include the right to bring a direct action in lieu of a derivative action or modifying the procedures provided in Article 8 of this Chapter governing derivative actions.

(6)   Eliminate the right of a member to bring an action to have the LLC judicially dissolved under clause (i) in G.S. 57D-6-02(2), unless the operating agreement provides an alternative remedy.

(7)   Are set forth in this section, G.S. 57D-1-01, 57D-2-01(d), 57D-2-02, 57D-2-03, 57D-2-20, 57D-3-23, 57D-5-01, 57D-6-01, clause (ii) of 57D-6-02(2), 57D-6-07(b) and (f), and all sections and subsections of Article 9 of this Chapter other than G.S. 57D-9-21(b), (c), and (e), 57D-9-22(b), 57D-9-23(b), 57D-9-31(b) through (e), 57D-9-41(b), (d), and (f), and 57D-9-42(b).

(c)   Oral or implied provisions in the operating agreement may not supplant, vary, disclaim, or nullify any contrary or inconsistent written provisions in the operating agreement to the detriment of the rights of persons who are not parties to the operating agreement to the extent that they reasonably rely on those written provisions in the operating agreement.

(d)   In the event of a conflict between the operating agreement and a provision in any document of an LLC filed by the Secretary of State:

(1)   The operating agreement shall prevail as to parties to the operating agreement and company officials.

(2)   The document filed by the Secretary of State shall prevail as to persons who are not parties to the operating agreement and are not company officials to the extent that they reasonably rely on the document filed by the Secretary of State.

(e)   Except as provided in or permitted by this Chapter or other applicable law, the laws of agency and contract, including the implied contractual covenant of good faith and fair dealing and the requirement that the terms of an operating agreement not be unconscionable at the time they are made, govern the administration and enforcement of operating agreements. (2013-157, s. 2.)

§ 57D-2-31. Parties to, and other persons subject to or having rights under, the operating agreement.

(a)   The LLC is deemed to be a party to the operating agreement and, therefore, is bound by and may enforce the provisions thereunder applicable to the LLC.

(b)   A person who becomes an interest owner is deemed to assent to, and is bound by, and, subject to Article 5 of this Chapter, is entitled to the rights applicable to the interest owner's ownership interest provided under, and is otherwise deemed to be a party to, the operating agreement.

(c)   A person need not be an interest owner to be a party to the operating agreement.

(d)   An operating agreement may require amendments to the operating agreement be approved by persons who are not interest owners and may provide rights to persons who are not interest owners and not otherwise parties to the operating agreement.

(e)   Any person bound by the operating agreement is bound by any amendment adopted, as provided in the operating agreement. (2013-157, s. 2.)

§ 57D-2-32. Remedies for breach of operating agreement or occurrence of identified events; reliance on operating agreement.

(a)   An operating agreement may subject interest owners and other persons who are parties to or otherwise bound by the operating agreement to specified remedies for breach of the operating agreement or the occurrence of a specified event. Such remedies may include the recovery of reasonable attorneys' fees, the assessment of interest without the assessment being subject to the laws of usury, and the imposition of penalties that would otherwise be unenforceable as stipulated or liquidated damages.

(b)   Unless otherwise provided in the operating agreement, an interest owner or other person who is a party to or bound by the operating agreement will not be liable to the LLC or an interest owner or other person who is a party to the operating agreement for that person's reliance on the provisions of the operating agreement. (2013-157, s. 2.)

§ 57D-2-33: Reserved for future codification purposes.

§ 57D-2-34: Reserved for future codification purposes.

§ 57D-2-35: Reserved for future codification purposes.

§ 57D-2-36: Reserved for future codification purposes.

§ 57D-2-37: Reserved for future codification purposes.

§ 57D-2-38: Reserved for future codification purposes.

§ 57D-2-39: Reserved for future codification purposes.

Part 4. Registered Office and Registered Agent.

§ 57D-2-40. Registered office and registered agent.

Each LLC must maintain a registered office and registered agent as required by Article 4 of Chapter 55D of the General Statutes and is subject to service on the Secretary of State under that Article. (2013-157, s. 2.)

§ 57D-2-41: Reserved for future codification purposes.

§ 57D-2-42: Reserved for future codification purposes.

§ 57D-2-43: Reserved for future codification purposes.

§ 57D-2-44: Reserved for future codification purposes.

§ 57D-2-45: Reserved for future codification purposes.

§ 57D-2-46: Reserved for future codification purposes.

§ 57D-2-47: Reserved for future codification purposes.

§ 57D-2-48: Reserved for future codification purposes.

§ 57D-2-49: Reserved for future codification purposes.

Article 3.

Membership and Management.

Part 1. Membership.

§ 57D-3-01. Admission of members; economic interest owners.

(a)   A person becomes a member through the following:

217

(1)   In the case of a person executing the articles of organization in the capacity of a member as provided in G.S. 57D-2-21(a)(2), or otherwise being named in the articles of organization as a member, at the time the articles of organization become effective under G.S. 55D-13.

(2)   In the case of a person acquiring an ownership interest from the LLC, (i) upon being identified as a member by the organizers as provided in G.S. 57D-2-20(c) or (ii) upon the unanimous approval of the members as provided in G.S. 57D-3-03(2).

(3)   In the case of an economic interest owner, in the manner provided in G.S. 57D-5-04(a) or G.S. 57D-6-01(3).

(4)   In the case of an eligible entity converting or merging into the LLC, as provided in the plan of conversion or plan of merger upon such plan becoming effective as provided in G.S. 57D-9-23(a)(5) or G.S. 57D-9-43(a)(6).

(b)   A person becomes an economic interest owner through the following:

(1)   In the case of a person acquiring an economic interest from the LLC, upon the unanimous approval of the members.

(2)   In the case of a person acquiring an economic interest or portion thereof from an interest owner, as provided in G.S. 57D-5-02.

(3)   In the case of an eligible entity converting or merging into the LLC, as provided in the plan of conversion or plan of merger upon such plan becoming effective as provided in G.S. 57D-9-23(a)(5) or G.S. 57D-9-43(a)(6).

(c)   To be a member a person need not make or have the obligation to make any contributions to the LLC or share in any profits or losses of, or distributions from, the LLC or otherwise own an economic interest in the LLC. (2013-157, s. 2.)

§ 57D-3-02. Cessation of membership.

(a)   A person ceases to be a member upon the occurrence of any of the following events:

218

(1)   The person does any of the following:

a.   Becomes a debtor in bankruptcy.

b.   Executes an assignment for the benefit of creditors, including the execution of a deed of trust or deed of assignment for the benefit of creditors causing all debts of the person to become due and payable under G.S. 23-1.

c.   Petitions for, consents to, or acquiesces in the appointment of a trustee, receiver, or liquidator of the person or all or substantially all of the person's property.

(2)   In the case of an individual, the person's death or being adjudicated by a court of competent jurisdiction as incompetent to manage his or her person or property.

(3)   In the case of a member with an economic interest, the transfer or abandonment of the person's entire economic interest, excluding the liquidation of a member's economic interest in connection with the dissolution and winding up of the LLC under G.S. 57D-6-08(2), regardless of whether the transferee is or becomes a member.

(4)   The person abandoning all of the rights of his ownership interest except his economic interest, or any portion thereof.

(b)   Upon the occurrence of any of the events described in subdivisions (1) and (2) of subsection (a) of this section with respect to a member, that person or that person's estate, as applicable, will automatically become an economic interest owner entitled only to the economic interest attributable to the person's ownership interest, but that person or that person's estate, as applicable, and any other person who ceases to be a member shall remain liable to the LLC for any obligation the person may have under G.S. 57D-4-02, 57D-4-06, and 57D-6-12(a)(2). (2013-157, s. 2.)

§ 57D-3-03. Approval of members.

The approval of all members is required to do any of the following:

(1)   Adopt or amend an operating agreement.

(2)   Admit any person as a member.

(3)   Other than in the ordinary course of business, transfer in one transaction or a series of related transactions all or substantially all of the assets of the LLC prior to the dissolution of the LLC.

(4)   Dissolve the LLC under circumstances other than those for which the LLC may be dissolved under Article 6 of this Chapter.

(5)   Convert the LLC into a different eligible entity under Article 9 of this Chapter.

(6)   Merge the LLC with or into another eligible entity under Article 9 of this Chapter. (2013-157, s. 2.)

§ 57D-3-04. Information rights.

(a)   Subject to the other provisions of this section, each member may inspect and copy or otherwise obtain from the LLC any of the following:

(1)   A copy of the articles of organization and any other writing constituting all or part of the operating agreement, including any executed power of attorney under which all or any part of the operating agreement was adopted, that are in effect or were in effect at any time during any of the LLC's preceding four fiscal years.

(2)   Either, as the LLC may elect, (i) a copy of any federal, state, or local income tax returns of the LLC, including any amendments and supplements made to those returns, filed with taxing authorities that pertain to any of the LLC's preceding four fiscal years or (ii) financial statements of the LLC of the type described in subsections (a) and (b) of G.S. 55-16-20 that pertain to any of the LLC's preceding four fiscal years.

(3)   A list of the names and last known business, residence, or mailing addresses of the LLC's current interest owners, their status as members or economic interest owners, the date on which each became an interest owner, and, if applicable, the dates on which a person's status as a member changed to

220

that of an economic interest owner or the person's status as an economic interest owner changed to that of a member.

(4)   Information, the type and detail of which may be prescribed by the operating agreement, from which (i) the member's capital interest may be ascertained and (ii) unless and to the extent the operating agreement does not provide otherwise, each of the other interest owners' capital interests may be ascertained, including the amount of money and a description and statement of the agreed value of any other property or services that each person who has been an interest owner has paid or otherwise transferred or has agreed to pay or otherwise transfer, and the extent to which that agreement by the interest owner has been fulfilled, to or for the benefit of the LLC in exchange for a capital interest.

(5)   Information from which the status of the business and the financial condition of the LLC may be ascertained.

(b)   Inspection rights and rights to copy LLC records may be exercised through a member's agent.

(c)   In connection with any member, manager, or other company official exercising management or other control rights or performing that person's duties to the LLC or the members, the LLC shall provide that person with, or access to, all information related to the applicable matter that is known by the LLC and is material to the proper exercise and performance of those rights and duties.

(d)   To exercise inspection and other information rights, a member must sign and deliver written notice of exercise to the LLC at least seven days before the date on which the inspection is to take place. That notice must state (i) the records or other information to be inspected and copied or otherwise provided by the LLC and (ii) the purpose for, and intended use of, the information. Within the period provided in the exercise notice, the LLC shall either comply with the member's demand or deliver written notice to the member of the extent to which the LLC declines to make available any of the demanded information and the reasons for that decision.

(e)   The exercise of a member's rights to inspect and copy the LLC's records is to take place at the LLC's principal office, or other location or locations selected by the LLC, during the LLC's regular hours of operation unless the LLC directs otherwise. The LLC may require a member to pay the labor, material,

221

and other costs it incurs or would otherwise incur to comply with the member's demand to inspect and copy the LLC's records.

(f)   The LLC (i) need not disclose to any member or any agent or representative of a member any information related to any other interest owner, except to the extent required by subdivision (3) of subsection (a) of this section, but subject to the restrictions that may be imposed under clauses (ii) and (iii) of this subsection, or is not otherwise related to the member's ownership interest; (ii) may impose conditions, restrictions, limitations, and standards on the exercise of a member's inspection and other information rights, including redacting names and other confidential information, providing summaries of documents, or requiring the member to enter an agreement to not disclose and otherwise maintain the confidentiality of the information provided; and (iii) need not disclose or otherwise make available to a member, manager, or other company official trade secrets or other confidential information of a nature that its disclosure could adversely affect the LLC, to the extent that the managers or other applicable company officials determine the information cannot be adequately safeguarded by other means, until either there no longer is a risk that its disclosure will adversely affect the LLC or the LLC becomes able to protect itself in some other way. (2013-157, s. 2.)

§ 57D-3-05: Reserved for future codification purposes.

§ 57D-3-06: Reserved for future codification purposes.

§ 57D-3-07: Reserved for future codification purposes.

§ 57D-3-08: Reserved for future codification purposes.

§ 57D-3-09: Reserved for future codification purposes.

§ 57D-3-10: Reserved for future codification purposes.

§ 57D-3-11: Reserved for future codification purposes.

§ 57D-3-12: Reserved for future codification purposes.

§ 57D-3-13: Reserved for future codification purposes.

§ 57D-3-14: Reserved for future codification purposes.

§ 57D-3-15: Reserved for future codification purposes.

§ 57D-3-16: Reserved for future codification purposes.

§ 57D-3-17: Reserved for future codification purposes.

§ 57D-3-18: Reserved for future codification purposes.

§ 57D-3-19: Reserved for future codification purposes.

Part 2. Managers.

§ 57D-3-20. Management; managers.

(a)   The management of an LLC and its business is vested in the managers.

(b)   Each manager has equal rights to participate in the management of the LLC and its business. Management decisions approved by a majority of the managers are controlling. The managers may make management decisions without a meeting and without notice.

(c)   Subject to the direction and control of a majority of the managers as provided in G.S. 57D-3-20(b), each manager may act on behalf of the LLC in the ordinary course of the LLC's business.

(d)   All members by virtue of their status as members are managers of the LLC, together with any other person or persons who may be designated as a manager in, or in the manner provided in, the operating agreement. If the operating agreement provides or otherwise contemplates that members are not necessarily managers by virtue of their status as members, then those persons designated as managers in, or in the manner provided in, the operating agreement will be managers. The operating agreement may provide that the LLC is to be managed by one or more company officials who are not designated as managers. All members will be managers for any period during which the LLC would otherwise not have any managers or other company officials.

(e)   A person shall continue to serve as a manager until the earliest of the following occurs: (i) the person's resignation as a manager; (ii) any event described in G.S. 57D-3-02(a) with respect to the person, substituting therein the term "manager" in lieu of the term "member" for purposes of this subsection; or (iii) that person, or the member or all of a class or group of less than all of the members who appointed the person to be a manager, ceases to be a member. (2013-157, s. 2.)

§ 57D-3-21. Duties of company officials; standards of conduct.

(a)   The managers shall manage the LLC and conduct the LLC's business in accordance with the operating agreement.

224

(b)   Each manager shall discharge that person's duties (i) in good faith, (ii) with the care an ordinary prudent person in a like position would exercise under similar circumstances, and (iii) subject to the operating agreement, in a manner the manager believes to be in the best interests of the LLC. In discharging such duties, a manager is entitled to rely on information, opinions, reports, or statements, including financial statements or other financial data, if prepared or presented by any person or group of persons the manager believes to be reliable and competent in such matters and the manager does not have actual knowledge concerning the matter in question that makes such reliance unwarranted.

(c)   A manager is not liable to the LLC for any act or omission as a manager if the manager acts in compliance with this section. (2013-157, s. 2.)

§ 57D-3-22. Delegation of authority of managers and other company officials.

The managers having general power to manage the LLC may delegate authority to act on behalf of the LLC to persons other than managers. The delegation of authority may be general or limited to specific matters. No such delegation of authority will cause any manager to cease to be a manager or cause the person to whom authority is so delegated to be a manager. Any duties of the managers will apply with respect to their delegation to, and direction and control of, any person to whom they delegate any of their responsibilities. (2013-157, s. 2.)

§ 57D-3-23. Application to company officials.

G.S. 57D-3-20(e), 57D-3-21, and 57D-3-22 shall apply to company officials who are not managers by substituting the term "company official" in lieu of the term "manager" in each place where the term appears in those provisions. (2013-157, s. 2.)

§ 57D-3-24: Reserved for future codification purposes.

§ 57D-3-25: Reserved for future codification purposes.

§ 57D-3-26: Reserved for future codification purposes.

§ 57D-3-27: Reserved for future codification purposes.

§ 57D-3-28: Reserved for future codification purposes.

§ 57D-3-29: Reserved for future codification purposes.

Part 3. Liability.

§ 57D-3-30. Liability of members, managers, and other company officials to third parties.

A person who is an interest owner, manager, or other company official is not liable for the obligations of the LLC solely by reason of being an interest owner, manager, or other company official. (2013-157, s. 2.)

§ 57D-3-31. Indemnification.

(a)   An LLC shall indemnify a person who is wholly successful on the merits or otherwise in the defense of any proceeding to which the person was a party because the person is or was a member, a manager, or other company official if the person also is or was an interest owner at the time to which the claim relates, acting within the person's scope of authority as a manager, member, or other company official against expenses incurred by the person in connection with the proceeding.

(b)   An LLC shall reimburse a person who is or was a member for any payment made and indemnify the person for any obligation, including any judgment, settlement, penalty, fine, or other cost, incurred or borne in the authorized conduct of the LLC's business or preservation of the LLC's business or property, whether acting in the capacity of a manager, member, or other company official if, in making the payment or incurring the obligation, the person complied with the duties and standards of conduct (i) under G.S. 57D-3-21, as modified or eliminated by the operating agreement or (ii) otherwise imposed by this Chapter or other applicable law. (2013-157, s. 2.)

Article 4.

Contributions and Distributions.

§ 57D-4-01. Form of contributions.

An interest owner may make contributions to the LLC in any form, including (i) money or other property, services rendered, or any other direct or indirect benefit to the LLC and (ii) promissory notes or other obligations to transfer money or other property, perform services, or provide any other direct or indirect benefits to the LLC. (2013-157, s. 2.)

§ 57D-4-02. Liability for contributions.

If an interest owner has contributed a promissory note or other obligation to transfer money or other property, to perform services, or to provide other benefits to the LLC and the interest owner would but for this section be excused from the performance of that obligation by reason of the interest owner's death or disability or other supervening impossibility or impracticability of performance under contract or other applicable law, the LLC may require the interest owner to pay to the LLC an amount of money equal to the value of the unperformed portion of the promised performance or exercise remedies available under other applicable law. (2013-157, s. 2.)

§ 57D-4-03. Interim distributions.

Distributions to interest owners before the dissolution and winding up of the LLC or, as provided in G.S. 57D-6-08(2), after the dissolution of the LLC, may be made at such times and in such amounts as determined by the LLC in proportion to the ratios that the aggregate contribution amounts of the interest owners bear to one another, determined immediately before the time that the distributions are to be made. (2013-157, s. 2.)

§ 57D-4-04. Distribution in kind.

An LLC may distribute property other than money if the interest owners receive interests of identical character in, or units of identical character of, such property in the same proportions as if the distribution were being made in money equal to the net value of the property being distributed. (2013-157, s. 2.)

§ 57D-4-05. Restrictions on making distributions.

(a)   No distribution may be made by an LLC if, after giving effect to the distribution, either of the following would occur:

(1)   The LLC would not be able to pay its debts as they become due in the ordinary course of business.

(2)   The LLC's total liabilities would exceed the value of the LLC's assets.

(b)   For purposes of subsection (a) of this section, the following apply:

(1)   An LLC may determine the value of its assets, the amount of its liabilities, and the time payments of its liabilities are to be made using accounting practices and principles that are reasonable under the circumstances.

(2)   The amount of a liability for which the creditor's recourse is limited to specific collateral will not exceed the value of the collateral.

(c)   Except as provided in subsection (e) of this section, the effect of a distribution under subsection (a) of this section is measured (i) in the case of any distribution of indebtedness as of the date the indebtedness is distributed and (ii) in all other cases, either as of the date the distribution is authorized if the distribution occurs within 120 days after the date authorization is made or as of the date the distribution is made if payment occurs more than 120 days after the date authorization is made.

(d)   Except as provided in subsection (e) of this section, an LLC's indebtedness issued as a distribution made in accordance with this section is a liability of the LLC to be paid under the law applicable to debtors and creditors.

(e)   An LLC's indebtedness issued as a distribution is not a liability of the LLC for purposes of subsection (a) of this section if its terms provide that payment of principal and interest are to be made only to the extent that at the time of such payment a distribution to interest owners could then be made under this section. Subsection (a) of this section applies to each payment of principal or interest made under any indebtedness described in the preceding sentence and not to the issuance of the indebtedness. (2013-157, s. 2.)

§ 57D-4-06. Liability for wrongful distributions.

(a)   If a distribution is made in violation of G.S. 57D-4-05, then each manager or other company official who alone or with other company officials had the authority to and did approve the distribution is personally liable to the LLC but not any other person for the amount of the distribution that exceeds the amount that could have been distributed without violating G.S. 57D-4-05 only if it is established that the company official did not act in compliance with G.S. 57D-3-21, without regard to any modification or elimination of such duties and standards of conduct under the operating agreement. Except as otherwise provided in G.S. 57D-11-03(d), a proceeding under this subsection is barred unless it is commenced within two years after the distribution.

(b)   Each manager or other company official held liable under subsection (a) of this section for a wrongful distribution is entitled to the following:

229

(1)   Contribution from each other manager or other company official who could be held liable under subsection (a) of this section for the wrongful distribution.

(2)   Reimbursement from each interest owner for the amount the interest owner received knowing that the distribution was made in violation of G.S. 57D-4-05. (2013-157, s. 2.)

§ 57D-4-07. Right to distribution.

An interest owner who is entitled to receive a distribution has the status of and is entitled to all remedies available to a creditor of the LLC with respect to the distribution. (2013-157, s. 2.)

Article 5.

Transfer of Ownership Interests; Withdrawal.

§ 57D-5-01. Nature of ownership interest.

An ownership interest is personal property. (2013-157, s. 2.)

§ 57D-5-02. Transfer of economic interests.

An economic interest is transferable in whole or in part. The transfer of an economic interest or portion thereof does not entitle the transferee to become or exercise any rights of a member other than to receive the economic interest or the portion thereof assigned to the transferee. (2013-157, s. 2.)

§ 57D-5-03. Rights of judgment creditor.

(a)   On application to a court of competent jurisdiction by any judgment creditor of an interest owner, the court may charge the economic interest of an interest owner with the payment of the unsatisfied amount of the judgment with interest. To the extent so charged, the judgment creditor has only the right to receive the distributions that otherwise would be paid to the interest owner with respect to the economic interest.

(b)   A charging order is a lien on the judgment debtor's economic interest to the extent provided in this section from the time that such charging order is served upon the LLC in accordance with Rule 4(j)(8) of the Rules of Civil Procedure. If more than one charging order is properly served upon the LLC with respect to an economic interest, the liens shall have priority in the order in which the charging orders were served, except that a charging order in favor of a judgment creditor that has previously delivered to the LLC garnishment process relating to an economic interest pursuant to G.S. 1-440.25 shall relate back to the date of service of the garnishment process.

(c)   This Chapter does not deprive any interest owner of a right, including any benefit of any exemption law applicable to the interest owner's ownership interest.

(d)   The entry of a charging order is the exclusive remedy by which a judgment creditor of an interest owner may satisfy the judgment from or with the judgment debtor's ownership interest. (2013-157, s. 2.)

§ 57D-5-04. Certain rights and liabilities of economic interest owners and transferors of ownership interests.

(a)   An economic interest owner may become a member only with that person's approval and through any of the following:

(1)   As provided in the operating agreement.

(2)   By the approval of the members as provided in G.S. 57D-3-03(2).

(3)   In the manner permitted under G.S. 57D-6-01(3) if the LLC ceases to have any members.

231

(b)   Except as provided in the following sentence of this subsection, a transferee of an ownership interest or portion thereof who is or becomes a member has to the extent transferred to the transferee (i) the rights and powers and is subject to the restrictions and liabilities of a member under the operating agreement and this Chapter with respect to the transferred ownership interest and (ii) is liable for any obligations of the transferor to make contributions under G.S. 57D-4-02 with respect to the transferred ownership interest. A transferee of an ownership interest or portion thereof is not liable for obligations of the transferor under G.S. 57D-4-06 or obligations that are unknown to the transferee at the time the transferee became a member.

(c)   Whether or not a transferee of an ownership interest or portion thereof is or becomes a member, (i) the transferor is not released from liability that the transferor may have under G.S. 57D-4-02, G.S. 57D-4-06, or under the operating agreement and (ii) the transferee takes the ownership interest subject to those liabilities. (2013-157, s. 2.)

§ 57D-5-05. No right to voluntarily withdraw capital or terminate obligations.

Except as otherwise required by this Chapter or other applicable law, an interest owner may not (i) withdraw or compel the company to purchase or otherwise liquidate all or any portion of the equity owner's capital interest or (ii) extinguish, abandon, or otherwise diminish the interest owner's obligations in respect of the interest owner's ownership interest. (2013-157, s. 2.)

Article 6.

Dissolution.

§ 57D-6-01. Dissolution.

An LLC is dissolved upon the occurrence of any of the following:

(1)   An event causing the LLC to dissolve under the operating agreement.

232

(2)   If the LLC never had a member, as approved by the organizers under G.S. 57D-2-20(c).

(3)   If the LLC ever had a member, the 90th day after the day on which the LLC ceases to have any members, unless within that 90-day period one or more persons are admitted as a member or members by the person, including the former member, owning or otherwise controlling the ownership interest of the last member.

(4)   Entry of a decree of judicial dissolution under G.S. 57D-6-05.

(5)   Subject to G.S. 57D-6-06(c), the filing by the Secretary of State of a certificate of dissolution under G.S. 57D-6-06. (2013-157, s. 2.)

§ 57D-6-02. Grounds for judicial dissolution.

The superior court may dissolve an LLC in a proceeding brought by either of the following:

(1)   The Attorney General, if it is established that (i) the LLC obtained its articles of organization through fraud or (ii) the LLC continued to exceed or abuse the authority conferred on it by law 20 or more days after the date the Attorney General delivered to the LLC written notice of the LLC's unauthorized acts.

(2)   A member, if it is established that (i) it is not practicable to conduct the LLC's business in conformance with the operating agreement and this Chapter or (ii) liquidation of the LLC is necessary to protect the rights and interests of the member. (2013-157, s. 2.)

§ 57D-6-03. Procedure for judicial dissolution.

(a)   A proceeding under G.S. 57D-6-02 to dissolve an LLC is to be brought against the LLC. The party bringing the dissolution proceeding may not join an interest owner or company official as a party to the proceeding unless and to the extent relief is sought against the interest owner or company official for that person's own actions.

233

(b)   Venue for a proceeding brought under G.S. 57D-6-02 to dissolve an LLC lies in (i) the county in this State where the LLC's principal office is located, which the party bringing the dissolution proceeding may assume to be the principal place of business disclosed in the LLC's most recent annual report or, if no annual report for the LLC has ever been filed by the Secretary of State, as provided in the LLC's articles of organization or (ii) if the LLC has no principal office in this State, and the most recent filings of the Secretary of State do not state that the LLC's principal office is located in this State, the county in this State where those filings state the LLC's registered office is or was last located.

(c)   In connection with a proceeding brought under G.S. 57D-6-02 to dissolve an LLC, the court may issue injunctions, appoint one or more persons to serve as receiver with powers and duties the court may grant under G.S. 57D-6-04, or take other action required to manage the LLC and its assets.

(d)   In any proceeding brought by a member under clause (ii) of G.S. 57D-6-02(2) in which the court determines that dissolution is necessary, the court will not order dissolution if after the court's decision the LLC or one or more other members elect to purchase the ownership interest of the complaining member at its fair value in accordance with any procedures the court may provide. (2013-157, s. 2.)

§ 57D-6-04. Receivership.

(a)   The court in a proceeding brought under G.S. 57D-6-02 to dissolve an LLC, or in a proceeding brought under G.S. 57D-6-07(c), may appoint one or more persons to serve as a receiver to manage the business of the LLC pending the court's decision on dissolution and if dissolution is decreed by the court to wind up the LLC. Before appointing a person to serve as a receiver of an LLC, the court shall hold a hearing on the subject after delivering notice, or causing the party who brought the dissolution proceeding to deliver notice, of the hearing to all parties and any other interested persons designated by the court.

(b)   The court may require the receiver to post bond with or without sureties in an amount the court directs.

(c)   The court shall describe the powers and duties of the receiver in its appointing order, which the court from time to time may amend. The powers may include the authority to do any of the following:

(1)   Dispose of all or any portion of the assets of the LLC wherever located, at a public or private sale.

(2)   Sue and defend in the receiver's own name as receiver of the LLC.

(3)   Exercise all of the powers of the LLC to the extent necessary to manage the business of the LLC or wind up the LLC following dissolution.

(d)   The court may order the LLC to compensate the receiver and reimburse the receiver's expenses, including the fees and expenses of attorneys and other professionals retained by the receiver. (2013-157, s. 2.)

§ 57D-6-05. Decree of judicial dissolution.

(a)   If after a hearing the court determines that one or more grounds for judicial dissolution described in G.S. 57D-6-02 exist and the alternative to judicial dissolution under G.S. 57D-6-03(d) is not applicable, it may enter a decree dissolving the LLC and the clerk of the court shall deliver a certified copy of the decree to the Secretary of State for filing.

(b)   After entering the decree of dissolution, the court shall direct the winding up of the LLC in accordance with G.S. 57D-6-07 and G.S. 57D-6-08 and may direct notification of claimants in accordance with G.S. 57D-6-10, 57D-6-11, and 57D-6-13. (2013-157, s. 2.)

§ 57D-6-06. Administrative dissolution.

(a)   The Secretary of State may administratively dissolve an LLC if the Secretary of State determines that the LLC has done any of the following:

(1)   The LLC has not paid within 60 days after they are due any penalties, fees, or other payments due under this Chapter.

(2)   The LLC does not deliver its annual report to the Secretary of State on or before the 60th day after it is due.

(3)   The LLC has been without a registered agent or registered office in this State for 60 days or more.

(4)   The LLC has not notified the Secretary of State within 60 days that its registered agent or registered office has been changed, that its registered agent has resigned, or that its registered office has been discontinued.

(5)   The LLC knowingly fails or refuses to answer completely and accurately within the time prescribed in this Chapter interrogatories propounded by the Secretary of State in accordance with the provisions of this Chapter.

(b)   If the Secretary of State determines that one or more grounds exist under subsection (a) of this section for dissolving an LLC, the Secretary of State shall mail the LLC notice of that determination. If, within 60 days after the notice is mailed, the LLC does not correct each ground for dissolution or demonstrate to the satisfaction of the Secretary of State that each ground does not exist, the Secretary of State shall administratively dissolve the LLC by signing a certificate of dissolution that recites the ground or grounds for dissolution and the effective date of the dissolution. The Secretary of State shall file the original certificate of dissolution and mail a copy to the LLC.

(c)   An LLC administratively dissolved under this section may apply to the Secretary of State for reinstatement. The procedures for reinstatement and for the appeal of any denial of the LLC's application for reinstatement are the same as those applicable to a domestic corporation under G.S. 55-14-22, 55-14-23, and 55-14-24. If, at the time the LLC applies for reinstatement, the name of the LLC is not distinguishable from the name of another entity authorized to be used under G.S. 55D-21, then the LLC must change its name to a name that is distinguishable on the records of the Secretary of State from the name of the other entity before the Secretary of State may prepare a certificate of reinstatement. The effect of reinstatement of an LLC is the same as for a domestic corporation under G.S. 55-14-22. (2013-157, s. 2.)

§ 57D-6-07. Winding up.

(a)   After its dissolution, an LLC shall wind up. The winding up may include continuing the business of the LLC for a period of time.

(b)   Subject to subsection (c) of this section, the managers or other applicable company officials shall wind up the LLC after its dissolution. If the dissolved LLC has no managers or other applicable company officials, the person, including a former member, owning or otherwise controlling the ownership interest of the person who was the last member of the LLC may serve or appoint one or more persons to serve as manager to wind up the LLC.

(c)   On application of the person, including a former member, owning or otherwise controlling the ownership interest of the last member, the superior court may wind up the LLC or appoint a receiver under G.S. 57D-6-04 to wind up the LLC. Venue for a proceeding on such application lies in (i) the county in this State where the LLC's principal office is located, which the person bringing the dissolution proceeding may assume to be the principal place of business disclosed in the LLC's most recent annual report or, if no annual report has ever been filed for the LLC by the Secretary of State, as provided in the LLC's articles of organization or (ii) if the LLC has no principal office in this State and the most recent filings of the Secretary of State do not state that the LLC's principal office is located in this State, the county in this State where those filings state the LLC's registered office is or was last located. The court shall order notice of the proceeding be given by the person making the application to all interested persons designated by the court.

(d)   The person or persons charged with winding up the LLC shall collect the LLC's assets, dispose of the LLC's properties that will not be distributed in kind, discharge or make provision for discharging the LLC's liabilities, and distribute the LLC's remaining assets as provided in G.S. 57D-6-08(2).

(e)   The dissolution of the LLC does not transfer title to the LLC's assets, prevent transfer of ownership interests, or subject its managers or other company officials to standards of conduct different from those prescribed in Article 3 of this Chapter.

(f)   The dissolution of the LLC does not prevent commencement of a proceeding by or against the LLC in its own name, abate or suspend a proceeding by or against the LLC, or terminate the authority of the registered agent of the LLC. (2013-157, s. 2.)

§ 57D-6-08. Marshaling of assets.

During the winding up of an LLC, the LLC's assets are to be applied as follows:

(1)   First to creditors, including interest owners, managers, and other company officials who are creditors in satisfaction, whether by payment or making provision for payment of all liabilities of the LLC.

(2)   The balance to the interest owners as distributions made in the manner provided in G.S. 57D-4-03. (2013-157, s. 2.)

§ 57D-6-09. Articles of dissolution.

Upon dissolution of an LLC, the LLC shall deliver articles of dissolution to the Secretary of State for filing. The articles of dissolution must provide the following information:

(1)   The name of the LLC.

(2)   The effective date of the dissolution.

(3)   Any other information the LLC elects to provide. (2013-157, s. 2.)

§ 57D-6-10. Known claims against dissolved LLC.

(a)   A dissolved LLC for which articles of dissolution, a certificate of dissolution, or a decree of dissolution filed by the Secretary of State has become effective may dispose of known claims against it by notifying claimants in writing of the dissolution. The notice must do the following:

(1)   Describe information that must be included in a claim.

(2)   Provide an address where claims may be sent.

(3)   State the deadline, which may not be fewer than 120 days from the date of the notice, by which the dissolved LLC must receive the claim.

(4)   State that the claim will be barred if not received by the deadline.

(b)   A claim against the dissolved LLC is barred if either of the following occurs:

(1)   The LLC does not receive the claim by the deadline from a claimant who received notice under subsection (a) of this section.

(2)   A claimant whose claim was rejected by written notice from the dissolved LLC does not commence a proceeding in a proper forum to enforce the claim within 90 days from the date of receipt of the rejection notice.

(c)   For purposes of this section, "claim" does not include a contingent liability or a claim based on an event occurring after dissolution. (2013-157, s. 2.)

§ 57D-6-11. Unknown and certain other claims against dissolved LLC.

(a)   A dissolved LLC for which articles of dissolution, a certificate of dissolution, or a decree of dissolution filed by the Secretary of State has become effective may publish notice of its dissolution and request that persons with claims against the LLC present them in accordance with the notice. The notice must meet the following requirements:

(1)   Be published one time in a newspaper of general circulation in the county in this State where the LLC's principal office is or was last located, or, if the LLC never had a principal office in this State, the county in this State where the LLC's registered office is or was last located.

(2)   Describe the information that must be included in a claim and provide an address where the claim may be sent.

(3)   State that a claim against the LLC will be barred unless a proceeding to enforce the claim is commenced in a proper forum within five years after the publication of the notice.

(b)   If the dissolved LLC publishes a newspaper notice in accordance with subsection (a) of this section, the claim of each of the following claimants is barred unless the claimant commences a proceeding in a proper forum to enforce the claim against the dissolved LLC within five years after the publication date of the newspaper notice:

(1)   A claimant who did not receive written notice under G.S. 57D-6-10.

(2)   A claimant whose claim was timely sent to the dissolved LLC but not acted on.

(3)   A claimant whose claim is contingent or based on an event occurring after the effective date of the filing by the Secretary of State of the articles of dissolution. (2013-157, s. 2.)

§ 57D-6-12. Enforcement of claims.

(a)   A claim against a dissolved LLC under G.S. 57D-6-10 or G.S. 57D-6-11 may be enforced against either of the following:

(1)   Against the dissolved LLC to the extent of its undistributed assets, including coverage under any insurance policy.

(2)   Except as provided in G.S. 57D-6-13(d), against the interest owners of the dissolved LLC in proportion to but not in excess of the distributions, if any, made to each interest owner following the LLC's dissolution.

(b)   G.S. 57D-6-10 and G.S. 57D-6-11 do not extend any applicable period of limitation. (2013-157, s. 2.)

§ 57D-6-13. Court proceedings for contingent claims.

(a)   A dissolved LLC that has published a notice under G.S. 57D-6-11 may file an application with the superior court of the county in this State where the LLC's principal office is or was last located or, if the LLC never had a principal office in this State, the county in this State where the LLC's registered office is or was last located for a determination of the amount and form of security to be provided for payment of claims that are contingent or have not been made known to the dissolved LLC or that are based on an event occurring after

240

dissolution but that, based on the facts known to the dissolved LLC, are estimated to arise after dissolution. Provisions need not be made for any claim that is or is anticipated to be barred under G.S. 57D-6-11(b).

(b)   Within 10 days after the filing of the application, the dissolved LLC shall deliver notice of the proceeding to each claimant holding a claim described in subsection (a) of this section whose contingent claim is shown on the records of the dissolved LLC.

(c)   The court may appoint a guardian ad litem to represent all claimants whose identities are unknown in any proceeding brought under this section. The dissolved LLC shall pay the fees and expenses of the guardian, including expert witness fees.

(d)   Provision by the dissolved LLC for security in the amount and the form ordered by the court under subsection (a) of this section satisfies the dissolved LLC's obligations with respect to claims described in subsection (a) of this section, and the claims may not be enforced against an interest owner who receives assets in liquidation of the LLC. (2013-157, s. 2.)

Article 7.

Foreign LLCs.

Part 1. Certificate of Authority.

§ 57D-7-01. Authority to transact business.

(a)   A foreign LLC may not transact business in this State until it obtains a certificate of authority from the Secretary of State.

(b)   Without excluding other activities that may not constitute transacting business in this State, a foreign LLC is not considered to be transacting business in this State for the purposes of this Chapter by reason of conducting in this State any one or more of the following activities:

(1)   Maintaining or defending any proceeding or effecting the settlement thereof or the settlement of claims or disputes.

(2)   Holding meetings of its members, managers, or other company officials or carrying on other activities concerning its internal affairs.

(3)   Maintaining bank accounts or borrowing money in this State, with or without providing security for repayment or other performance and without regard to the frequency of such transactions.

(4)   Maintaining offices or agencies for the exchange or other transfer and registration of all or any class or portion of its membership or other equity or beneficial ownership interests or securities, or appointing and maintaining trustees or depositories with relation to its membership or other equity or beneficial ownership interests or securities.

(5)   Soliciting or procuring orders, whether by mail or through employees or agents or otherwise, where the orders require acceptance to be made outside of the territory of this State to become binding contracts.

(6)   Making or investing in loans with or without security, including servicing of mortgages or deeds of trust through independent agencies within the territory of this State, conducting foreclosure proceedings and selling or acquiring property in foreclosure sales, and managing or renting property acquired in foreclosure sales in connection with and in furtherance of efforts to sell and otherwise liquidate such property, provided no office or agency of the foreign LLC is maintained in this State.

(7)   Taking security for or collecting debts due the foreign LLC or enforcing any rights the foreign LLC may have in property subject to or otherwise providing security with respect to the repayment or other performance of the debt obligations.

(8)   Transacting business in interstate commerce.

(9)   Conducting an isolated transaction completed within a period of six months but not repeated transactions of a similar nature.

(10)   Selling property or services through independent contractors.

(11)   Owning real or personal property. (2013-157, s. 2.)

§ 57D-7-02. Consequences of transacting business without authority.

(a)   No foreign LLC transacting business in this State without permission obtained through a certificate of authority may maintain any proceeding in any court of this State unless the foreign LLC has obtained a certificate of authority prior to trial. An issue arising under this subsection must be raised by motion and determined by the trial judge prior to trial.

(b)   A foreign LLC failing to obtain a certificate of authority as required by this Chapter is liable to this State for the years, including any partial year, during which it transacted business in this State without a certificate of authority in an amount equal to all fees and taxes that would have been imposed by law on the foreign LLC had it duly applied for and received such permission, plus interest and all penalties imposed by law for failure to pay such fees and taxes. In addition, the foreign LLC is liable for a civil penalty of ten dollars ($10.00) for each day, but not to exceed a total of one thousand dollars ($1,000) for each year, including any partial year it transacts business in this State without a certificate of authority. The Attorney General may bring actions to recover all amounts due this State under the provisions of this subsection. The clear proceeds of civil penalties provided for in this subsection shall be remitted to the Civil Penalty and Forfeiture Fund in accordance with G.S. 115C-457.2.

(c)   Notwithstanding subsection (a) of this section, the failure of a foreign LLC to obtain a certificate of authority does not impair the validity of its acts or prevent it from defending any proceeding in this State.

(d)   The Secretary of State shall require every foreign LLC transacting business in this State to comply with the provisions of this Chapter. The Secretary of State may conduct such investigations as may be necessary to ascertain compliance by foreign LLCs with this Chapter. (2013-157, s. 2.)

§ 57D-7-03. Application for certificate of authority.

(a)   A foreign LLC may apply for a certificate of authority to transact business in this State by delivering an application to the Secretary of State for filing. The application must provide the following information:

(1)   The name of the foreign LLC and, if different, a name that satisfies the requirements of Article 3 of Chapter 55D of the General Statutes.

(2)   The name of the jurisdiction under whose law it is organized.

(3)   The street address, and the mailing address if different from the street address, of its principal office, if any, and the county in which the principal office, if any, is located.

(4)   The street address, and the mailing address if different from the street address, of its registered office in this State and the name of its registered agent at that office.

(5)   The names, titles, and business addresses of the foreign LLC's principal company officials.

(b)   A foreign LLC shall deliver with the completed application for the certificate of authority a certificate of existence or a document of similar import duly authenticated by the Secretary of State or other official having custody of limited liability company records in the jurisdiction under whose law it is organized.

(c)   If the Secretary of State finds that the application conforms to law, the Secretary of State when all taxes, fees, and other payments have been tendered as prescribed in this Chapter, shall do the following:

(1)   File the application and the certificate of existence or a document of similar import as described in subsection (b) of this section, as provided in G.S. 55D-15.

(2)   Issue a certificate of authority to transact business in this State to which the Secretary of State shall affix the exact or conformed copy of the application.

(3)   Send to the foreign LLC or its representative the certificate of authority, together with the exact or conformed copy of the application affixed thereto. (2013-157, s. 2.)

§ 57D-7-04. Amended certificate of authority.

244

(a)   A foreign LLC authorized to transact business in this State shall obtain an amended certificate of authority from the Secretary of State if it changes either of the following:

(1)   Its name.

(2)   The jurisdiction of its organization.

(b)   A foreign LLC may apply for an amended certificate of authority by delivering an application to the Secretary of State for filing that sets forth the following:

(1)   The name of the foreign LLC and if different the name provided in the foreign LLC's certificate of authority that the foreign LLC is authorized to use to transact business in this State.

(2)   The name of the jurisdiction under whose law it is organized.

(3)   The date it was originally authorized to transact business in this State.

(4)   A statement of the change or changes being made.

(c)   Except for the content of the application, the requirements of G.S. 57D-7-03 for obtaining an original certificate of authority apply to obtaining an amended certificate under this section. (2013-157, s. 2.)

§ 57D-7-05. Effect of certificate of authority.

(a)   A certificate of authority authorizes the foreign LLC to which it is issued to transact business in this State subject to the right of the State to revoke the certificate as provided in this Chapter. A foreign LLC may qualify in this State as executor, administrator, or guardian, or as trustee under the will of any person domiciled in this State at the time of that person's death only in accordance with applicable provisions of Article 24 of Chapter 53 of the General Statutes.

(b)   A foreign LLC qualifying as testamentary trustee or executor under the provisions of this section shall appoint a process agent and file such appointment with the court as required by G.S. 28A-4-2(4).

(c)   Except as otherwise provided by this Chapter, a foreign LLC with a valid certificate of authority has the same but no greater rights and has the same but no greater privileges as, and is subject to the same duties, restrictions, penalties, and liabilities now or later imposed on, an LLC of like character. (2013-157, s. 2.)

§ 57D-7-06. Registered office and registered agent of foreign LLC.

Each foreign LLC authorized to transact business in this State must maintain a registered office and registered agent as required by Article 4 of Chapter 55D of the General Statutes and is subject to service on the Secretary of State under that Article. (2013-157, s. 2.)

§ 57D-7-07: Reserved for future codification purposes.

§ 57D-7-08: Reserved for future codification purposes.

§ 57D-7-09: Reserved for future codification purposes.

§ 57D-7-10: Reserved for future codification purposes.

§ 57D-7-11: Reserved for future codification purposes.

§ 57D-7-12: Reserved for future codification purposes.

§ 57D-7-13: Reserved for future codification purposes.

§ 57D-7-14: Reserved for future codification purposes.

§ 57D-7-15: Reserved for future codification purposes.

§ 57D-7-16: Reserved for future codification purposes.

§ 57D-7-17: Reserved for future codification purposes.

§ 57D-7-18: Reserved for future codification purposes.

§ 57D-7-19: Reserved for future codification purposes.

Part 2. Withdrawal.

§ 57D-7-20. Withdrawal of foreign LLC.

(a)   A foreign LLC authorized to transact business in this State may not withdraw from this State until it obtains a certificate of withdrawal from the Secretary of State.

(b)   A foreign LLC authorized to transact business in this State may apply for a certificate of withdrawal by delivering an application to the Secretary of State for filing. The application must state the following:

(1)   The name of the foreign LLC and if different the name provided in the foreign LLC's certificate of authority that the foreign LLC is authorized to use to transact business in this State.

(2)   The name of the jurisdiction under whose law it is organized.

(3)   That the foreign LLC is not transacting business in this State and that it surrenders its authority to transact business in this State.

(4)   That the foreign LLC revokes the authority of its registered agent to accept service of process and consents to service of process in any proceeding based on any cause of action arising in this State, or arising out of business transacted in this State, during the time the foreign LLC was authorized to transact business in this State, being made on such foreign LLC by service thereof on the Secretary of State.

(5)   A mailing address to which the Secretary of State may mail a copy of any process served on the Secretary of State under subdivision (4) of this subsection.

(6)   A commitment to deliver to the Secretary of State for filing a statement of any subsequent change in its mailing address.

(c)   If the Secretary of State finds that the application conforms to law, the Secretary of State shall do the following:

(1)   File the application for the certificate of withdrawal as provided in G.S. 55D-15.

(2)   Issue a certificate of withdrawal to which the Secretary of State shall affix the exact or conformed copy of the application.

(3)   Send to the foreign LLC or its representative the certificate of withdrawal together with the exact or conformed copy of the application affixed thereto.

(d)   After the withdrawal of the foreign LLC is effective, service of process on the Secretary of State in accordance with subsection (b) of this section may be made by delivering to the Secretary of State, or to any clerk authorized by the Secretary of State to accept service of process, duplicate copies of that process and the fee required by G.S. 57D-1-22(b). Upon receipt of process in the manner provided in this subsection, the Secretary of State shall mail a copy of the process by registered or certified mail, return receipt requested, to the foreign LLC at the mailing address designated pursuant to subsection (b) of this section. (2013-157, s. 2.)

§ 57D-7-21. Withdrawal of foreign LLC by reason of a merger, consolidation, or conversion; qualification of successor.

(a)   Whenever a foreign LLC authorized to transact business in this State ceases its separate existence as a result of a statutory merger, consolidation, or other reorganization permitted by the law of the jurisdiction under which it is organized, or converts into another type of entity as permitted by that law, the surviving or resulting entity shall apply for a certificate of withdrawal for the foreign LLC by delivering to the Secretary of State for filing a copy of the articles of merger, consolidation, or other reorganization or conversion or a certificate reciting the facts of the merger, consolidation, or other reorganization or conversion, duly authenticated by the Secretary of State or other official having custody of limited liability company records in the jurisdiction under the law of which the foreign LLC was organized. If the surviving or resulting entity is not authorized to transact business in this State, the application for the certificate of withdrawal must state, and therefore modify the information described below that otherwise is required to be provided under G.S. 57D-7-20(b) to the extent of conflict, the following:

(1)   The name of the foreign LLC and, if different, the name provided in the foreign LLC's certificate of authority that the foreign LLC is authorized to use to transact business in this State.

(2)   The name of the jurisdiction under whose law it is organized.

(3)   The type of entity and name of the surviving or resulting entity.

(4)   That the surviving or resulting entity is not transacting business in this State and the foreign LLC surrenders its authority to transact business in this State.

(5)   That the surviving or resulting entity revokes the authority of the foreign LLC's registered agent to accept service of process and consents to service of process in any proceeding based on any cause of action arising in this State, or arising out of business transacted in this State, during the time the foreign LLC

249

was authorized to transact business in this State, being made on the surviving or resulting entity by service thereof on the Secretary of State.

(6)   A mailing address to which the Secretary of State may mail a copy of any process served on the Secretary of State under subdivision (5) of this subsection.

(7)   A commitment to deliver to the Secretary of State for filing a statement of any subsequent change in the surviving or resulting entity's mailing address.

(b)   If the Secretary of State finds that the articles or certificate described in subsection (a) of this section relating to the merger, consolidation, or other reorganization or conversion and the application for the certificate of withdrawal conform to law, the Secretary of State shall do the following:

(1)   File the articles or certificate and the application for the certificate of withdrawal as provided in G.S. 55D-15.

(2)   Issue a certificate of withdrawal.

(3)   Send to the surviving or resulting entity or its representative the certificate of withdrawal, together with the exact or conformed copy of the application, if required, affixed thereto.

(c)   After the withdrawal of the foreign LLC is effective, service of process on the Secretary of State in accordance with subsection (a) of this section is to be made by delivering to the Secretary of State or to any clerk authorized by the Secretary of State to accept service of process duplicate copies of process and the fee required by G.S. 57D-1-22(b). Upon receipt of process in the manner provided in this subsection, the Secretary of State shall immediately mail a copy of the process by registered or certified mail, return receipt requested, to the surviving or resulting entity at the mailing address designated pursuant to subsection (a) of this section. (2013-157, s. 2.)

§ 57D-7-22. Authority of Attorney General.

The Attorney General may maintain an action to restrain a foreign LLC from transacting business in this State in violation of this Article. (2013-157, s. 2.)

§ 57D-7-23: Reserved for future codification purposes.

§ 57D-7-24: Reserved for future codification purposes.

§ 57D-7-25: Reserved for future codification purposes.

§ 57D-7-26: Reserved for future codification purposes.

§ 57D-7-27: Reserved for future codification purposes.

§ 57D-7-28: Reserved for future codification purposes.

§ 57D-7-29: Reserved for future codification purposes.

Part 3. Revocation of Certificate of Authority.

§ 57D-7-30. Grounds for revocation.

(a)   The Secretary of State may commence a proceeding under G.S. 57D-7-31 to revoke the certificate of authority of a foreign LLC authorized to transact business in this State if any of the following occurs:

(1)   The foreign LLC is delinquent in delivering its annual report.

(2)   The foreign LLC does not pay within 60 days after they are due any penalties, fees, or other payments due under this Chapter.

(3)   The foreign LLC is without a registered agent or registered office in this State for 60 days or more.

(4)   The foreign LLC does not inform the Secretary of State under G.S. 55D-31 or G.S. 55D-32 that its registered agent or registered office has changed, that its registered agent has resigned, or that its registered office has been discontinued within 60 days of the change, resignation, or discontinuance.

(5)   A company official or agent of the foreign LLC signed a document that the company official or agent knew was false in any material respect with intent that the document be delivered to the Secretary of State for filing.

(6)   The Secretary of State receives a duly authenticated certificate from the Secretary of State or other official having custody of the records of the limited liability companies in the state or country under whose law the foreign LLC is organized stating that it has been dissolved or merged into another entity.

(7)   The foreign LLC is exceeding the authority conferred upon it by this Chapter.

(8)   The foreign LLC knowingly fails or refuses to answer truthfully and fully within the time prescribed in this Chapter interrogatories propounded by the Secretary of State in accordance with the provisions of this Chapter.

(b)   Nothing herein repeals or modifies any provision of the Revenue Act relating to the suspension of the certificate of authority of foreign LLCs for failure to comply with the provisions thereof. (2013-157, s. 2.)

§ 57D-7-31. Procedure for and effect of revocation.

(a)   If the Secretary of State determines that one or more grounds exist under G.S. 57D-7-30 for revocation of a certificate of authority, the Secretary of State shall mail to the foreign LLC written notice of that determination.

(b)   If the foreign LLC does not correct each ground for revocation or demonstrate to the satisfaction of the Secretary of State that each ground determined by the Secretary of State does not exist within 60 days after notice is mailed, the Secretary of State may revoke the foreign LLC's certificate of authority by signing a certificate of revocation that recites the ground or grounds for revocation and its effective date. The Secretary of State shall file the original of the certificate and mail a copy to the foreign LLC.

(c)   The authority of a foreign LLC to transact business in this State ceases on the date shown on the certificate revoking its certificate of authority.

(d)   The Secretary of State's revocation of a foreign LLC's certificate of authority appoints the Secretary of State as the foreign LLC's agent for service of process in any proceeding based on a cause of action arising in this State or arising out of business transacted in this State during the time the foreign LLC was authorized to transact business in this State. The Secretary of State shall then proceed in accordance with G.S. 55D-33.

(e)   Revocation of a foreign LLC's certificate of authority does not terminate the authority of the registered agent of the foreign LLC.

(f)   The foreign LLC will not be granted a new certificate of authority until each ground for revocation has been substantially corrected to the satisfaction of the Secretary of State. (2013-157, s. 2.)

§ 57D-7-32. Appeal from revocation.

(a)   A foreign LLC may appeal the Secretary of State's revocation of its certificate of authority to the Superior Court of Wake County within 30 days after the certificate of revocation is mailed to the foreign LLC by the Secretary of State. The appeal is commenced by filing a petition with the court and with the Secretary of State requesting the court to set aside the revocation. Copies of the foreign LLC's certificate of authority and the Secretary of State's certificate of revocation are to be attached to the petition. No service of process on the Secretary of State is required except for the filing of the petition as set forth in this subsection. The appeal to the superior court will be determined by a judge of the superior court upon such further evidence, notice, and opportunity to be heard, if any, as the court may deem appropriate under the circumstances. The foreign LLC will have the burden of establishing that it is entitled to have the revocation set aside.

253

(b)   Upon consideration of the petition and any response made by the Secretary of State, the court may prior to entering final judgment order the Secretary of State to set aside the revocation or may take any other action the court considers appropriate.

(c)   The court's final decision may be appealed as in other civil proceedings. (2013-157, s. 2.)

§ 57D-7-33. Inapplicability of Administrative Procedure Act.

The Administrative Procedure Act shall not apply to any proceeding or appeal provided for in G.S. 57D-7-30 through G.S. 57D-7-32. (2013-157, s. 2.)

Article 8.

Derivative Actions.

§ 57D-8-01. Member derivative actions.

(a)   Subject to the provisions of G.S. 57D-8-02 and G.S. 57D-8-03, a member may bring a derivative action if the following conditions are met:

(1)   Either (i) the member was a member of the LLC at the time of the act or omission for which the proceeding is brought or (ii) all or any portion of the member's ownership interest devolves by operation of law from an ownership interest that was owned by a member at that time.

(2)   The member made written demand on the LLC to take suitable action, and either (i) the LLC notified the member that the member's demand was rejected, (ii) 90 days have expired from the date the demand was made, or (iii) irreparable injury to the LLC would result by waiting for the expiration of the 90-day period.

(b)   For purposes of this Article, a "derivative action" or a "derivative proceeding" is a proceeding brought in the superior court of this State in the right of an LLC or, to the extent provided in G.S. 57D-8-06, in the right of a foreign LLC, to recover a judgment in favor of the LLC or, if applicable, the foreign LLC. (2013-157, s. 2.)

§ 57D-8-02. Stay of proceedings.

If the LLC commences an inquiry into the allegations set forth in the demand or complaint, the court may stay a derivative proceeding. (2013-157, s. 2.)

§ 57D-8-03. Dismissal.

(a)   The court shall dismiss a derivative proceeding on motion of the LLC if one of the groups specified in subsection (b) or (f) of this section determines after conducting an inquiry upon which its conclusions are based that the maintenance of the derivative proceeding is not in the best interest of the LLC.

(b)   The inquiry and determination with respect to the demanded action is to be made either (i) pursuant to subsection (f) of this section or (ii) by either of the following:

(1)   A majority vote or other approval of those persons who have the authority individually or collectively to cause the LLC to bring an action in the superior court of this State for the recovery or other remedy sought in the derivative action and are independent.

(2)   A majority vote of a committee composed of two or more independent persons appointed by a majority vote or other approval of those persons described in subdivision (b)(1) of this section.

(c)   For purposes of this section, none of the following factors by itself will necessarily preclude a person from being considered to be independent:

(1)   The nomination or election of the person by persons who are defendants in the derivative proceeding or against whom action is demanded.

(2)   The naming of the person as a defendant in the derivative proceeding or as a person against whom action is demanded.

255

(3)   The approval by the person of the act being challenged in the derivative proceeding or demand if the act resulted in no personal benefit to the person.

(d)   If a derivative proceeding is commenced after a determination has been made rejecting a demand by a member, the complaint must allege particular facts that if proved would preclude the court from dismissing the derivative proceeding under subsection (a) of this section. Defendants may make a motion to dismiss a complaint under subsection (a) of this section for failure to comply with this subsection. Prior to the court's ruling on such a motion to dismiss, the plaintiff may engage in discovery only to the extent it is germane and necessary to develop facts that establish that the dismissal of the derivative proceeding under subsection (a) of this section is unwarranted.

(e)   If a majority of the persons having the authority to cause the LLC to bring a proceeding in the superior court of this State for the recovery or other remedy sought in the derivative action are independent, then the plaintiff will have the burden of proving that the requirements of subsection (a) of this section have not been met, but if a majority of such persons are not independent, then the LLC has the burden of proving that the requirements of subsection (a) of this section have been met.

(f)   The court may appoint a panel composed of one or more independent persons on motion of the LLC to make a determination whether the maintenance of the derivative proceeding is in the best interest of the LLC. The plaintiff has the burden of proving that the requirements of subsection (a) of this section have not been met. (2013-157, s. 2.)

§ 57D-8-04. Discontinuance or settlement.

(a)   A derivative proceeding may not be discontinued or settled without the court's approval. If the court determines that a proposed discontinuance or settlement will substantially affect the interests of the LLC's members, the court shall direct that notice be given to the members who would be affected.

(b)   The court shall determine the manner and form of the notice and the manner in which costs of the notice will be borne. (2013-157, s. 2.)

256

§ 57D-8-05. Payment of expenses.

On termination of the derivative proceeding, the court may do any of the following:

(1)   Order the LLC to pay the plaintiff's expenses, including attorneys' fees, incurred in the proceeding if it finds that the proceeding has resulted in a substantial benefit to the LLC.

(2)   Order the plaintiff to pay any defendant's expenses, including attorneys' fees, incurred in defending the proceeding if it finds that the proceeding was commenced or maintained without cause or for an improper purpose.

(3)   Order a party to pay an opposing party's expenses, including attorneys' fees, incurred as a result of the filing of a pleading, motion, or other paper, if the court after inquiry finds that the pleading, motion, or other paper was not well grounded in fact or was not warranted by existing law or a good-faith argument for the extension, modification, or reversal of existing law and that it was interposed for an improper purpose, such as to harass or to cause unnecessary delay or needless increase in the cost of litigation. (2013-157, s. 2.)

§ 57D-8-06. Applicability to foreign LLCs.

In any derivative proceeding in the right of a foreign LLC, the matters covered by this Article will be governed by the law of the jurisdiction of the foreign LLC's organization except for the matters governed by G.S. 57D-8-02, 57D-8-04, and 57D-8-05. (2013-157, s. 2.)

§ 57D-8-07. Privileged communications.

In any derivative proceeding, no member is entitled to obtain or have access to any communication within the scope of the LLC's attorney-client privilege that could not be obtained by, or would not be accessible to, a party in a proceeding other than on behalf of the LLC. (2013-157, s. 2.)

Article 9.

Conversion and Merger.

Part 1. Definitions.

§ 57D-9-01. Definitions.

Unless otherwise specifically provided, the following definitions apply in this Article:

(1)   Articles of organization and conversion. - The document filed by the Secretary of State under G.S. 57D-9-22 for the purpose of converting an eligible entity into an LLC.

(2)   Converting entity. - An eligible entity that converts into another eligible entity pursuant to Part 2 or Part 3 of this Article 9.

(3)   Converting LLC. - A converting entity that is an LLC.

(4)   Eligible entity. - A corporation, including a professional corporation as defined in G.S. 55B-2 and a foreign professional corporation defined in G.S. 55B-16, a domestic or foreign nonprofit corporation, a limited liability company, a domestic or foreign limited partnership, a registered limited liability partnership or foreign limited liability partnership as defined in G.S. 59-32, or any other partnership as defined in G.S. 59-36, whether or not formed under the laws of this State.

(5)   Merging entity. - An eligible entity that is a party to a merger.

(6)   Merging LLC. - A merging entity that is an LLC.

(7)   Surviving entity. - The eligible entity into which a converting entity converts or into which an eligible entity is merged. (2013-157, s. 2.)

§ 57D-9-02: Reserved for future codification purposes.

§ 57D-9-03: Reserved for future codification purposes.

§ 57D-9-04: Reserved for future codification purposes.

§ 57D-9-05: Reserved for future codification purposes.

§ 57D-9-06: Reserved for future codification purposes.

§ 57D-9-07: Reserved for future codification purposes.

§ 57D-9-08: Reserved for future codification purposes.

§ 57D-9-09: Reserved for future codification purposes.

§ 57D-9-10: Reserved for future codification purposes.

§ 57D-9-11: Reserved for future codification purposes.

§ 57D-9-12: Reserved for future codification purposes.

§ 57D-9-13: Reserved for future codification purposes.

§ 57D-9-14: Reserved for future codification purposes.

§ 57D-9-15: Reserved for future codification purposes.

§ 57D-9-16: Reserved for future codification purposes.

§ 57D-9-17: Reserved for future codification purposes.

§ 57D-9-18: Reserved for future codification purposes.

§ 57D-9-19: Reserved for future codification purposes.

Part 2. Conversion to an LLC.

§ 57D-9-20. Conversion.

An eligible entity other than an LLC may convert to an LLC if both of the following requirements are met:

(1)   The conversion is permitted by the law governing the organization and internal affairs of the converting entity.

(2)   The converting entity complies with the requirements of this Part and, to the extent applicable, the law governing its organization and internal affairs immediately before the conversion. (2013-157, s. 2.)

§ 57D-9-21. Plan of conversion.

(a)   The converting entity must approve a written plan of conversion containing the following:

(1)   The name, type of entity, and jurisdiction whose law governs the organization and internal affairs of the converting entity immediately before the conversion.

(2)   A statement that the converting entity will deliver to the Secretary of State for filing articles of organization and conversion for the purpose of converting the eligible entity into an LLC.

(3)   The name the entity will have when the conversion becomes effective.

(4)   The terms and conditions of the conversion.

(5)   The manner and basis for converting the interests in the converting entity into ownership interests, obligations, or securities of the surviving entity or into cash or other property or any combination thereof.

(b)   The plan of conversion may contain other provisions relating to the conversion.

(c)   The provisions of the plan of conversion, other than the provisions required by subdivisions (1) and (2) of subsection (a) of this section, may be made dependent on facts objectively ascertainable outside the plan of conversion if the plan of conversion provides the manner in which the facts will operate on the affected provisions. The facts may include, for example, any of the following:

(1)   Statistical or market indices, market prices of any security or group of securities, interest rates, currency exchange rates, or similar economic or financial data.

261

(2)   A determination or action by the converting entity or by any other person, group, or body.

(3)   The terms of, or actions taken under, an agreement to which the converting entity is a party or any other agreement or document.

(d)   The plan of conversion must be approved in accordance with the law governing the organization and internal affairs of the converting entity immediately before the conversion.

(e)   After a plan of conversion has been approved as provided in subsection (d) of this section, but before articles of conversion become effective, the plan of conversion may be amended or abandoned to the extent permitted by the law that governs the organization and internal affairs of the converting entity. (2013-157, s. 2.)

§ 57D-9-22. Filing of articles of organization and conversion by the converting entity.

(a)   After a plan of conversion has been approved by the converting entity as provided in G.S. 57D-9-21, the converting entity shall deliver articles of organization and conversion to the Secretary of State for filing. The articles of organization and conversion must contain (i) the information required by G.S. 57D-2-21 and (ii) the following information:

(1)   The name, type of entity, and jurisdiction whose law governs the organization and internal affairs of the converting entity immediately before the conversion.

(2)   A statement that the articles of organization and conversion are being submitted for the purpose of converting the eligible entity into an LLC.

(3)   The name the entity will have when the conversion becomes effective.

(4)   The mailing address of the converting entity immediately before the conversion and, if different, the mailing address it will have when the conversion becomes effective.

(5)   A statement that a plan of conversion has been approved by the converting entity as required by law.

(b)   If the plan of conversion is abandoned after the articles of organization and conversion have been delivered to the Secretary of State but before the articles of organization and conversion become effective, the converting entity must deliver to the Secretary of State for filing prior to the time the articles of organization and conversion become effective an amendment withdrawing such articles.

(c)   Certificates of conversion must be registered as provided in G.S. 47-18.1. (2013-157, s. 2.)

§ 57D-9-23. Effective date; effects of conversion.

(a)   The conversion takes effect when the articles of organization and conversion of the converting entity filed by the Secretary of State become effective, at which time the following shall occur:

(1)   The converting entity ceases its prior form of organization and continues in existence as the surviving entity.

(2)   The title to all real estate and other property owned by the converting entity continues to be vested in the surviving entity without reversion or impairment.

(3)   All liabilities of the converting entity continue as liabilities of the surviving entity.

(4)   A proceeding pending by or against the converting entity remains pending by or against the surviving entity as if the conversion did not occur.

(5)   The equity or beneficial ownership interests in the converting entity that are to be converted into ownership interests, obligations, or securities of the surviving entity or into the right to receive cash or other property are thereupon so converted, and the former holders of equity or beneficial ownership interests in the converting entity are entitled only to the rights provided, including by reference, in the plan of conversion and the surviving entity's operating agreement.

(b)   The conversion does not affect the liability or absence of liability of an equity or beneficial owner of the converting entity for any acts, omissions, or obligations of the converting entity made or incurred prior to the effectiveness of the conversion. A conversion under this Part does not constitute a dissolution or termination of the converting entity. (2013-157, s. 2.)

§ 57D-9-24: Reserved for future codification purposes.

§ 57D-9-25: Reserved for future codification purposes.

§ 57D-9-26: Reserved for future codification purposes.

§ 57D-9-27: Reserved for future codification purposes.

§ 57D-9-28: Reserved for future codification purposes.

§ 57D-9-29: Reserved for future codification purposes.

Part 3. Conversion of an LLC.

§ 57D-9-30. Conversion.

An LLC may convert to a different eligible entity if both of the following requirements are met:

(1)   The conversion is permitted by the law that will govern the organization and internal affairs of the surviving entity.

(2)   The converting LLC complies with the requirements of this Part and to the extent applicable the law that will govern the organization and internal affairs of the surviving entity. (2013-157, s. 2.)

§ 57D-9-31. Plan of conversion.

(a)   The converting LLC must approve a written plan of conversion containing the following:

(1)   The name of the converting LLC immediately before the conversion.

(2)   The name the surviving entity will have, the type of entity it will be, and the jurisdiction whose law will govern its organization and internal affairs when the conversion becomes effective.

(3)   The terms and conditions of the conversion.

(4)   The manner and basis for converting the ownership interests in the converting LLC into interests, obligations, or securities of the surviving entity or into cash or other property or any combination thereof.

(b)   The plan of conversion may contain other provisions pertaining to the conversion.

(c)   The provisions of the plan of conversion, other than the provisions required by subdivisions (1) and (2) of subsection (a) of this section, may be made dependent on facts objectively ascertainable outside the plan of conversion if the plan of conversion provides the manner in which the facts will operate on the affected provisions. The facts may include, for example, any of the following:

(1)   Statistical or market indices, market prices of any security or group of securities, interest rates, currency exchange rates, or similar economic or financial data.

(2)   A determination or action by the converting LLC or by any other person, group, or body.

(3)   The terms of, or actions taken under, an agreement to which the converting LLC is a party or any other agreement or document.

(d)   The converting LLC shall provide a copy of the plan of conversion to each member of the converting LLC prior to its approval. Under G.S. 57D-3-03(5), all of the members of the converting LLC must approve the plan of conversion. In addition, any economic interest owner of the converting LLC who because of the conversion will become personally liable upon the conversion for liabilities of the surviving entity, whether arising before or after the conversion, must approve the plan of conversion.

(e)   After a plan of conversion has been approved by the converting LLC as provided in subsection (d) of this section, but before the articles of conversion become effective, the plan of conversion may be amended or abandoned as follows:

(1)   The plan of conversion may be amended as provided in the plan of conversion or, if not so provided, as approved by the converting LLC in the manner provided in subsection (d) of this section.

(2)   The plan of conversion may be abandoned, subject to any contractual rights, as provided in the plan of conversion or if not so provided as approved by the converting LLC in the manner provided in subsection (d) of this section. (2013-157, s. 2.)

§ 57D-9-32. Articles of conversion.

(a)   After a plan of conversion has been approved by the converting LLC as provided in G.S. 57D-9-31, the converting LLC shall deliver articles of conversion to the Secretary of State for filing. The articles of conversion must contain the following information:

(1)   The name of the converting LLC immediately before the conversion.

(2)   The name the surviving entity will have, the type of entity it will be, and the jurisdiction whose law will govern its organization and internal affairs upon the conversion becoming effective.

(3)   The mailing address of the converting LLC immediately before the conversion and, if different, the mailing address the surviving entity will have when the conversion becomes effective.

(4)   A statement that a plan of conversion has been approved by the converting LLC as required by law.

(5)   If the surviving entity is not authorized to transact business in this State, a statement that the surviving entity (i) consents to service of process in any proceeding based on any cause of action arising in respect of the converting LLC being made on the surviving entity by service on the Secretary of State and (ii) commits to deliver to the Secretary of State for filing a statement of any change in the surviving entity's mailing address to which the Secretary of State may mail a copy of process served on the Secretary of State.

(b)   If the converting LLC is converting to an eligible entity whose formation, or whose status as a registered limited liability partnership as defined in G.S. 59-32, requires the filing of a document by the Secretary of State, then notwithstanding subsection (a) of this section, that document must be delivered to and filed by the Secretary of State with the articles of conversion.

(c)   If the plan of conversion is abandoned after the articles of conversion have been filed by the Secretary of State, but before the articles of conversion become effective, the converting LLC must deliver to the Secretary of State for filing prior to the time the articles of conversion become effective an amendment of the articles of conversion withdrawing the articles of conversion.

(d)   The conversion takes effect in accordance with the law that will govern the organization and internal affairs of the surviving entity.

(e)   Certificates of conversion must be registered as provided in G.S. 47-18.1. (2013-157, s. 2.)

§ 57D-9-33. Effects of conversion.

(a)   When the conversion takes effect, the following shall occur:

(1)   The converting LLC ceases its prior form of organization and continues in existence as the surviving entity.

(2)   The title to all real estate and other property owned by the converting LLC continues to be vested in the surviving entity without reversion or impairment.

(3)   All liabilities of the converting LLC continue as liabilities of the surviving entity.

(4)   A proceeding pending by or against the converting LLC remains pending by or against the surviving entity as if the conversion did not occur.

(5)   The ownership interests in the converting LLC that are to be converted into equity or beneficial ownership interests, obligations, or securities of the surviving entity or into the right to receive cash or other property are thereupon so converted, and the former holders of ownership interests in the converting LLC are entitled only to the rights provided, including by reference, in the plan of conversion.

(b)   The conversion does not affect the liability or absence of liability of any interest owner of the converting LLC for any acts, omissions, or obligations of the converting LLC made or incurred prior to the effectiveness of the conversion. A conversion under this Part does not constitute a dissolution or termination of the converting LLC.

(c)   If the surviving entity is not a domestic corporation or a domestic limited partnership at the time the conversion takes effect, the surviving entity is deemed to consent to each of the following:

(1)   That it may be served with process in this State in any proceeding to enforce any obligation of (i) the converting LLC, if before the conversion the converting LLC was subject to suit in this State on the obligation or (ii) the surviving entity arising from the conversion.

(2)   That it has appointed the Secretary of State as its agent for service of process in any such proceeding. Service of process on the Secretary of State must be made by delivering to the Secretary of State or to any clerk authorized by the Secretary of State to accept service of process duplicate copies of the

process and the fee required by G.S. 57D-1-22(b). Upon receipt of service of process on behalf of a surviving entity in the manner provided for in this section, the Secretary of State shall immediately mail a copy of the process by registered or certified mail, return receipt requested, to the surviving entity. If the surviving entity is authorized to transact business in this State, the address for mailing will be its principal office designated in the latest document filed by the Secretary of State that is authorized by law to designate the principal office or, if there is no principal office on file, its registered office. If the surviving entity is not authorized to transact business in this State, the address for mailing will be the mailing address of the surviving entity provided under G.S. 57D-9-32(a)(3). (2013-157, s. 2.)

§ 57D-9-34: Reserved for future codification purposes.

§ 57D-9-35: Reserved for future codification purposes.

§ 57D-9-36: Reserved for future codification purposes.

§ 57D-9-37: Reserved for future codification purposes.

§ 57D-9-38: Reserved for future codification purposes.

§ 57D-9-39: Reserved for future codification purposes.

Part 4. Merger.

§ 57D-9-40. Merger.

An LLC may merge with one or more other eligible entities if both of the following requirements are met:

(1)   The merger is permitted by the law governing the organization and internal affairs of each other merging entity.

(2)   Each merging entity complies with the requirements of this Part and to the extent applicable the law other than this Part governing the organization and internal affairs of each merging entity. (2013-157, s. 2.)

§ 57D-9-41. Plan of merger.

(a)   Each merging entity must approve a written plan of merger containing the following:

(1)   The name, type of entity, and jurisdiction whose law governs the organization and internal affairs of each merging entity immediately before the merger.

(2)   The name of the surviving entity.

(3)   The terms and conditions of the merger.

(4)   The manner and basis for converting the interests in each merging entity into interests, obligations, or securities of the surviving entity or into cash or other property or any combination thereof.

(5)   If the surviving entity is an LLC, any amendments to its articles of organization that are to be made in connection with the merger.

(b)   The plan of merger may contain other provisions pertaining to the merger.

(c)   The provisions of the plan of merger, other than the provisions referred to in subdivisions (1), (2), and (5) of subsection (a) of this section, may be made dependent on facts objectively ascertainable outside the plan of merger if the plan of merger provides the manner in which the facts will operate on the affected provisions. The facts may include, for example, any of the following:

270

(1)   Statistical or market indices, market prices of any security or group of securities, interest rates, currency exchange rates, or similar economic or financial data.

(2)   A determination or action by the merging LLC or by any other person, group, or body.

(3)   The terms of or actions taken under an agreement to which the merging LLC is a party, or any other agreement or document.

(d)   A merging LLC shall provide a copy of the plan of merger to each member of the merging LLC prior to its approval. Under G.S. 57D-3-03(6), all of the members of the merging LLC must approve the plan of merger. In addition, any economic interest owner of the merging LLC who because of the merger will become personally liable upon the merger for liabilities of the merging LLC, any other merging entity, or the surviving entity, whether arising before or after the merger, must approve the plan of merger.

(e)   The plan of merger must be approved in accordance with the law governing the organization and internal affairs of each merging entity.

(f)   After a plan of merger has been approved, but before the articles of merger become effective, the plan of merger may be amended or abandoned as follows:

(1)   The plan of merger may be amended as provided in the plan of merger or if not so provided in the manner provided in subsections (d) and (e) of this section.

(2)   The plan of merger may be abandoned, subject to any contractual rights, as provided in the plan of merger or if not so provided in the manner provided in subsections (d) and (e) of this section. (2013-157, s. 2.)

§ 57D-9-42. Articles of merger.

(a)   After a plan of merger has been approved by each merging entity as provided in G.S. 57D-9-41, the surviving entity shall deliver articles of merger to the Secretary of State for filing. The articles of merger shall state the following:

271

(1)   The name, type of entity, and jurisdiction whose law governs the organization and internal affairs of each merging entity immediately before the merger.

(2)   The name of the surviving entity.

(3)   The mailing address of each merging entity immediately before the merger and the mailing address the surviving entity will have when the merger becomes effective.

(4)   If the surviving entity is an LLC, any amendment to its articles of organization as provided in the plan of merger.

(5)   A statement that the plan of merger has been approved by each merging entity in the manner required by law.

(6)   If the surviving entity is not authorized to transact business in this State, a statement that the surviving entity (i) consents to service of process in any proceeding based on any cause of action arising in respect of a merging LLC being made on the surviving entity by service on the Secretary of State and (ii) commits to deliver to the Secretary of State for filing a statement of any change in the surviving entity's mailing address to which the Secretary of State may mail a copy of process served on the Secretary of State.

(b)   If the plan of merger is amended after the articles of merger have been filed, but before the articles of merger become effective, and any statement in the articles of merger becomes incorrect as a result of the amendment, the surviving entity shall deliver to the Secretary of State for filing prior to the time the articles of merger become effective an amendment to the articles of merger correcting the incorrect statement. If the articles of merger are abandoned after the articles of merger are filed but before the articles of merger become effective, the surviving entity shall deliver to the Secretary of State for filing prior to the time the articles of merger become effective an amendment to the articles of merger stating that they have been abandoned.

(c)   A merger takes effect when the articles of merger become effective, which in the case of a merging LLC is when the articles of merger filed by the Secretary of State become effective.

272

(d)   Certificates of merger must be registered as provided in G.S. 47-18.1. (2013-157, s. 2.)

§ 57D-9-43. Effects of merger.

(a)   When the merger takes effect, the following shall occur:

(1)   Each merging entity other than the surviving entity merges into the surviving entity, and the separate existence of each merging entity other than the surviving entity ceases.

(2)   The title to all real estate and other property owned by each merging entity is vested in the surviving entity without reversion or impairment.

(3)   The surviving entity has all liabilities of each merging entity.

(4)   A proceeding pending by or against any merging entity remains pending by or against such merging entity as if the merger did not occur, or the surviving entity may be substituted in the proceeding for a merging entity whose separate existence ceases in the merger.

(5)   If an LLC is the surviving entity, its articles of organization will be amended to the extent provided in the articles of merger.

(6)   The equity or beneficial ownership interests in, and the obligations and securities of, each merging entity that are to be converted into interests, obligations, or securities of the surviving entity or into the right to receive cash or other property are thereupon so converted, and the former holders of the equity and beneficial ownership interests are entitled only to the rights provided to them in the plan of merger or, in the case of former holders of shares in a domestic corporation, any rights they may have under Article 13 of Chapter 55 of the General Statutes.

(7)   If the surviving entity is not a domestic corporation, the surviving entity is deemed to agree that it will promptly pay to the dissenting shareholders of any merging entity that is a domestic corporation the amount, if any, to which they are entitled under Article 13 of Chapter 55 of the General Statutes and otherwise to comply with the requirements of Article 13 of Chapter 55 of the General Statutes as if it were a domestic corporation.

273

(b)   The merger does not affect the liability or absence of liability of any holder of an interest in a merging entity for any acts, omissions, or obligations of any merging entity made or incurred prior to the effectiveness of the merger. The cessation of the separate existence of a merging entity in the merger does not constitute a dissolution or termination of the merging entity.

(c)   If the surviving entity is not a domestic eligible entity when the merger takes effect, the surviving entity is deemed to consent to each of the following:

(1)   That it may be served with process in this State in any proceeding to enforce (i) any obligation of a domestic merging entity if before the merger the domestic merging entity was subject to suit in this State on the obligation, (ii) the rights of dissenting shareholders of any merging domestic corporation under Article 13 of Chapter 55 of the General Statutes, and (iii) any obligation of the surviving entity arising from the merger.

(2)   That it has appointed the Secretary of State as its agent for service of process in any such proceeding. Service of process on the Secretary of State is made by delivering to the Secretary of State or to any clerk authorized by the Secretary of State to accept service of process duplicate copies of such process and the fee required by G.S. 57D-1-22(b). Upon receipt of service of process on behalf of a surviving entity in the manner provided for in this section, the Secretary of State shall immediately mail a copy of the process by registered or certified mail, return receipt requested, to the surviving entity. If the surviving entity is authorized to transact business in this State, the address for mailing will be its principal office designated in the latest document filed by the Secretary of State that is authorized by law to designate the principal office or, if there is no principal office on file, its registered office. If the surviving entity is not authorized to transact business in this State, the address for mailing will be the mailing address of the surviving entity provided under G.S. 57D-9-42(a). (2013-157, s. 2.)

§ 57D-9-44: Reserved for future codification purposes.

§ 57D-9-45: Reserved for future codification purposes.

§ 57D-9-46: Reserved for future codification purposes.

§ 57D-9-47: Reserved for future codification purposes.

§ 57D-9-48: Reserved for future codification purposes.

§ 57D-9-49: Reserved for future codification purposes.

Article 10.

Miscellaneous.

§ 57D-10-01. Purpose; public policy.

(a)   This Chapter is to be applied to promote its purposes and policies.

(b)   The purpose of this Chapter is to provide a flexible framework under which one or more persons may organize and manage one or more businesses as they determine to be appropriate with minimum prescribed formalities or constraints.

(c)   It is the policy of this Chapter to give the maximum effect to the principle of freedom of contract and the enforceability of operating agreements. (2013-157, s. 2.)

§ 57D-10-02. Rules of construction; coordination with other law.

275

(a)   Unless displaced by this Chapter, the rules of law and equity supplement this Chapter.

(b)   The rule that statutes in derogation of the common law are to be strictly construed does not apply to this Chapter.

(c)   This Chapter modifies, limits, and supersedes the federal Electronic Signatures in Global and National Commerce Act, 15 U.S.C. § 7001 et seq., but does not modify, limit, or supersede section 101(c) of that act, 15 U.S.C. § 7001(c), or authorize electronic delivery of any of the notices described in section 103(b) of that act, 15 U.S.C. § 7003(b).

(d)   G.S. 25-9-406 and G.S. 25-9-408 do not apply to any ownership interest or any portion thereof, including any economic interest. To the extent of any conflict or inconsistency between this subsection and G.S. 25-9-406 and G.S. 25-9-408, this subsection prevails. Accordingly, neither G.S. 25-9-406 nor G.S. 25-9-408 will render invalid, unenforceable, or ineffective any contrary or inconsistent provision contained in an operating agreement.

(e)   In this Chapter, unless otherwise specified or indicated by the context, including as may otherwise be provided in the operating agreement under Part 3 of Article 2 of this Chapter, without the need for repetitious use of qualifiers, further statement, or clarification in the text of any provision of this Chapter, the following rules of construction shall apply:

(1)   The provisions of this Chapter are to be applied in a manner that is reasonable under the circumstances.

(2)   References to "members," "interest owners," "managers," "company officials," "operating agreement," "articles of organization," and other terms that relate to limited liability companies are deemed to refer to an LLC or foreign LLC as the context indicates.

(3)   The words "this Chapter," "hereof," "hereby," "hereunder," "herein," and words of similar impact are to be read to refer to Chapter 57D of the General Statutes as a whole and not to any particular provision of this Chapter.

(4)   The word "including" is to be read as if it is followed by the words "without limitation" and, therefore, denotes examples that are only illustrative and does not narrow or limit the scope of the standard, concept, or other applicable subject being described or illustrated.

276

(5)   The words "or" and "any" are not exclusive.

(6)   The captions and headings of provisions of this Chapter are for convenience of reference only and are not to be construed as part of this Chapter or serve to limit or expand the scope of the provisions.

(f)   Action validly taken pursuant to one provision of this Chapter is not rendered invalid solely because it is substantively the same or similar to an action that could be taken pursuant to some other provision of this Chapter but fails to satisfy one or more requirements prescribed by that other provision.

(g)   An operating agreement that provides for the application of the law of this State is governed by and will be construed under the laws of this State in accordance with its terms. (2013-157, s. 2.)

§ 57D-10-03: Reserved for future codification purposes.

§ 57D-10-04: Reserved for future codification purposes.

§ 57D-10-05: Reserved for future codification purposes.

§ 57D-10-06: Reserved for future codification purposes.

§ 57D-10-07: Reserved for future codification purposes.

§ 57D-10-08: Reserved for future codification purposes.

§ 57D-10-09: Reserved for future codification purposes.

Article 11.

Transition Provisions.

§ 57D-11-01. Applicability of act.

The provisions of this Chapter apply to every LLC, whether formed on, before, or after January 1, 2014, and the interest owners of every LLC, except to the extent expressly excepted by this Chapter. (2013-157, s. 2.)

§ 57D-11-02. Application to qualified foreign LLCs.

A foreign LLC authorized to transact business in this State immediately before the repeal of Chapter 57C of the General Statutes is subject to this Chapter but is not required to obtain a new certificate of authority to transact business under this Chapter. The certificate of authority of such a foreign LLC issued under former Chapter 57C of the General Statutes before its repeal is to be deemed to have been issued under this Chapter. (2013-157, s. 2.)

§ 57D-11-03. Saving provisions.

(a)   The existence of LLCs formed before January 1, 2014, shall not be impaired by the repeal of Chapter 57C of the General Statutes or the enactment of this Chapter, by any change made by this Chapter in the requirements for the formation of LLCs, nor by any amendment or repeal by this Chapter of the laws under which they were formed or created, and, except as otherwise expressly provided in this Chapter, the repeal of former Chapter 57C of the General Statutes shall not affect any liability or penalty incurred under the provisions of that Chapter prior to its repeal.

278

(b)   Any proceeding commenced before January 1, 2014, may be completed in accordance with the law then in effect.

(c)   An LLC dissolved before January 1, 2014, may wind up or complete its winding up, as the case may be, pursuant to Article 6 and other applicable provisions of this Chapter.

(d)   A proceeding under G.S. 57D-4-06(a) in respect of an LLC formed before January 1, 2014, will not be barred if it is commenced no later than (i) two years after the distribution or (ii) the earlier of January 1, 2016, or three years after the distribution.

(e)   References in the articles of organization or operating agreement of an LLC made before January 1, 2014, to provisions of Chapter 57C of the General Statutes are to be deemed, to the extent applicable or the context does not clearly indicate otherwise, to be made to the corresponding provisions of this Chapter. (2013-157, s. 2.)

Vision Books Order Form

Fax Orders:	1-980-299-5965
Phone Orders:	1-704-898-0770
E-mail Orders:	www.visionbooks.org
Mail Orders:	Vision Books, LLC P.O. Box 42406 Charlotte, NC 28215

Shipp To:
Name_____
Address_____
City_____State_____Zip_____
Phone_____Fax_____
Email_____@_____

Bill To: We can bill a third party on your behalf.
Name_____
Address_____
City_____State_____Zip_____
Phone____(_____)_____Fax_____
Email_____@_____

Pamphlet Number ($15.00 Each)	Qty	Total Cost
_____	_____	_____
_____	_____	_____
_____	_____	_____
_____	_____	_____
_____	_____	_____
_____	_____	_____
_____	_____	_____
Full Volume Set 1-92	92 Pamphlets	1,380.00

Free Shipping Shipping & Handling on Full Volume Orders
Add $1.00 Shipping & Handling per pamphlet $_____

Total Cost $_____

Thank you for your support. Management!

DID YOU ENJOY THIS BOOK?

Vision Books, LLC would like to hear from you! If you or someone you know has been fasely imprisoned, we would like to hear your story. If the 'North Carolina Criminal Law and Procedure' has had an effect in your life or if you have suggestions, we would like to hear from you. Send your letters to:

Vision Books, LLC
Attn: Staff Writers
P.O. Box 42406
Charlotte, NC 28215
Email: staff@visionbooks.org

Order Additional Copies:

Fax Orders: 1-980-299-5965

Phone Orders: 1-704-898-0770

E-mail Orders: www.visionbooks.org

Mail Orders: Vision Books, LLC
                               P.O. Box 42406
                               Charlotte, NC 28215